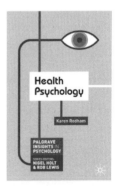

Research
Methods
and Statistics

Ian Walker

PALGRAVE
INSIGHTS IN
PSYCHOLOGY

SERIES EDITORS:
NIGEL HOLT
& ROB LEWIS

palgrave
macmillan

First published 2010 by
PALGRAVE MACMILLAN

Palgrave Macmillan in the UK is an imprint of Macmillan Publishers Limited, registered in England, company number 785998, of Houndmills, Basingstoke, Hampshire RG21 6XS.

Palgrave Macmillan in the US is a division of St Martin's Press LLC, 175 Fifth Avenue, New York, NY 10010.

Palgrave Macmillan is the global academic imprint of the above companies and has companies and representatives throughout the world.

Palgrave® and Macmillan® are registered trademarks in the United States, the United Kingdom, Europe and other countries.

ISBN: 978–0–230–24988–2

This book is printed on paper suitable for recycling and made from fully managed and sustained forest sources. Logging, pulping and manufacturing processes are expected to conform to the environmental regulations of the country of origin.

A catalogue record for this book is available from the British Library.

A catalog record for this book is available from the Library of Congress.

10 9 8 7 6 5 4 3 2 1
19 18 17 16 15 14 13 12 11 10

Printed and bound in Great Britain by
CPI Antony Rowe, Chippenham and Eastbourne

This book is dedicated to students who
ask questions

Contents

List of figures

Note from series editors

To read elegantly designed research for us as professional psychologists is rather like reading a beautifully written short story, or looking at a carefully drawn portrait. The best practitioners really are artists. Ian Walker produces just this kind of research. His work can be mainstream while remaining interesting and sometimes unusual. In every case it is carefully executed and analysed, and it adds to the body of science we all love so much. He most certainly is a reliable pair of hands where research methods are concerned and is regarded as such by those of us lucky enough to work with him. He is gaining a well-deserved reputation as a leading thinker in the area.

Ian's book sets out the principles of experimental design and statistical analysis in an approachable and enjoyable way. Walker was chosen to write this part of the *Insights* series because of his skill as a communicator and teacher, and because of his impossible-to-quench enthusiasm for this topic. Take the time to read this book. It will really change your view of methods as stuffy and dull, and help you to understand what so many of us see in it. The topic need not be frightening and whatever your background or motivation for reading this book, we are confident that you will find it an enlightening and indispensable tool that you will return to over and over again.

- *Those of you reading this book as preparation for your university studies* should do so confidently. Ian's teaching and duties revolve in part around research methods and he is all too aware of the problems students at all levels have in this area. This book gives you a heads-up and a very good grounding in the topic.

- *Those reading the book while at university* will find many of the topics familiar if you have pre-university experience in psychology. However, Ian's often unusual, but always focused and relevant perspective on some topics will make you smile and rethink some of the issues you may until now have found dull. This book we feel sure will help make clear all those things you never quite understood when you read about them before.

- *Those reading the book in preparation for pre-university courses, such as A-level,* will find Ian's take on research methods interesting, funny and extremely informative. This is not a dry or dull book, by any means. The Reading Guide at the end of the book tells you where different A-level specifications appear.

Remember, reading for interest is admirable, and encouraged. It is rare to be able to pick up a book that is engaging, informative and good fun, but we think that you will enjoy learning and learn to enjoy research methods with this book. Whatever your reason for reading this book, be it for interest or for any number of courses other than psychology such as marketing, sociology or nursing, it will provide stimulation and informed comment. We are delighted to include it in this series. We both laughed a lot, and learned a lot while reading this and we think you will too.

NIGEL HOLT AND ROB LEWIS
Series Editors

Preface

A psychologist must know how to carry out research, and how to understand what other people's findings tell us. This means learning about the methods used to carry out studies, and the statistics used to make sense of data. My aim with this book is to give you a really clear introduction to the various techniques that have been developed by researchers and statisticians. I've tried to cover the big ideas that a new psychologist needs to know, and have also tried to make this book the ideal primer for anybody who will go on to study research and statistics further. Either way, I do hope you'll find it useful.

I'd like to thank the *Insights in Psychology* editors Nigel Holt and Rob Lewis for their gentlemanly approach to this book; Jamie Joseph at Palgrave Macmillan for commissioning the *Insights* series; Andrew Bengry-Howell and Karen Rodham for their comments on the qualitative research chapters; Tim Gamble for spotting the section I forgot to write; Neil Osbourne and Amanda Laffan, who read over some parts of this book when they were in an earlier form; and the manuscript reviewers for their helpful comments. Particular thanks go to my wife, Sarah, who put up with long periods of not really seeing me while I did the writing – particularly as I wrote a big chunk of the book when we were in France on what was supposed to be a holiday.

Fellow geeks might like to know that this book was entirely written using free and open source software, primarily OpenOffice running on Linux. For statistical calculations and graphs I used a programming language called *R*.

IAN WALKER
drianwalker.com

Section One

Research Methods

Chapter 1

Introduction

Many people, when they start to study psychology, are surprised to find that research methods and statistics are a big part of the discipline. I mean, a *really* big part of the discipline. At the university where I work, psychology students spend 30% of their time over the first two years studying these subjects, and occasionally some of them feel that this wasn't what they signed up for. 'When do we get to the brains and the crazy people?' they ask. 'You know: the interesting stuff.' But there is a good reason why research methods and statistics are such a big part of psychology. It's not because psychologists love these subjects – trust me, very few do. No, research methods and statistics are a big part of psychology for one simple but important reason: people are not all the same, and we need a good set of tools for coping with that. If everybody were identical, you could study one person – any person at all – and learn everything you wanted to know about everybody in the world. But people are not all identical, and while this makes them much more interesting, it also makes them more difficult to study. Research methods and statistics are just *tools* which make studying people possible.

Here is your toolbox

I'd really like you to remember this idea that research methods and statistics are your tools. A builder working on a house is probably far more interested in the house than in their hammer, but they'll never build the house unless they know how to use the hammer. It's just the same in psychology: it doesn't matter if you find research methods and statistics interesting, and nobody really expects you to find them interesting. But you need to know how to use research methods and statistics if you want to learn new things about people, or if you want to understand what other people have discovered.

Now, it just happens that I find research methods and statistics fascinating in their own right. Perhaps that makes me like a builder who is more interested in the hammer than the house, but I hope I can share some of my enthusiasm for these subjects with you in this book. Like many people, I started studying psychology because I wanted better to understand the world around me. I thought subjects like personality and social psychology would help me make sense of the things that happen in my everyday life, and in some ways they did. But to my surprise, I found that the area of psychology that best helped me understand the world was statistics. Let me tell you a short story, which will give you one little example of how knowing basic statistics proved useful. This will also introduce you to some of the big ideas that underpin research, and will start you thinking in the right way to understand the rest of this book.

⊙ Spreading it around

Recently, a large multinational company – which I won't name, as they'll certainly have better lawyers than me – was running a television commercial for their brand of yellow butter-like spread. In this advert they claimed that 'more people preferred' their spread than a rival product. Now, there's nothing particularly exciting there: it's the kind of thing adverts say all the time. But what caught my eye was the little writing down at the bottom of the screen. This said 'Out of 200 people tested, 48% preferred our spread, 45% our rival's spread, 7% had no preference'.

Hmm, I thought. *More people preferred your product, did they?*

To show you why this got me interested, let's make it a bit easier to see the real numbers. The advert gave the percentage of people choosing each spread, but we know that there were 200 people overall and so it is easy to calculate the number of people who chose each option:

Chose the advertiser's spread	Chose the rival spread	No preference
96 people	90 people	14 people

'Fair enough,' you might be thinking. 'More people chose the advertiser's spread. People prefer it, just like the advertiser said.' But is that really true? Because when you are a psychologist, you get very good at spotting when people are just making choices at random. And to me, it looked as if that's what the people were doing here.

To help you understand what was going through my mind, you need to know a slightly strange fact about research: whenever we do a study, we always start out by assuming that there is nothing interesting going on, and that we're not going to discover anything. Now, I know that sounds odd. We want to know whether people prefer one spread to the other, so it feels as though we should look at whether people have a preference. But we don't do that: instead, for reasons I'll explain later, we go looking for *no preference*. Think of it as a sort of 'worst-case scenario'. We decide what we would expect to see if there is nothing interesting going on, and then compare this with how people really behave. So in this case, we decide what people would do if they couldn't tell the two spreads apart, and then we look at how people really responded. Were the people in the advert acting just like people who couldn't taste any difference?

So how would people behave if they did find the two spreads equally tasty? Personally, I reckon that if people couldn't tell the two spreads apart, they might just pick one at random.

Imagine *you* are taking part in this test. Someone stops you in the street and hands you two pieces of bread and butter, both of which taste pretty much the same. What would you say when the researcher asks you for your favourite? If you found the two spreads really similar, you might just say you can't spot any difference. Sure enough, 14 people in the advert did this. But when people take part in research, they usually don't want to disappoint the researchers. People like to be helpful and to give positive answers. So you're trying to be helpful, and want to give a clear answer, but you can't tell the two flavours apart. What do you do?

In this case, you would probably just pick one – any one. 'Er ... that one,' you might say, pointing to either of the spreads.

'This one?' asks the researcher. 'This one here?'

'Er ... sure, why not?' you say.

Here's the big question, then: how many people would choose each of the two spreads if they really were just picking one at random? Fourteen out of the 200 people said they had no preference, so this means there were 186 people who picked one of the two spreads as a favourite. If these 186 people were really picking a spread at random, in the way I've just described, how many people would we expect to choose each one? Please do try to think of an answer before you read on.

If 186 people are choosing a spread at random, we'd expect to see:

Number choosing the advertiser's
spread

Number choosing the rival
spread

What did you decide? Many people say that we'd expect to see the people split in half, with 93 choosing one spread and 93 choosing the other, and that's a good answer. *If people were choosing at random, we'd expect half of them to choose each spread.*

So it looks as though our worst-case scenario is wrong. If 186 people really had no preference, we would expect to see two groups of 93, but what we saw in the advert was a group of 96 and a group of 90. It looks as though people weren't just responding at random. Perhaps the advertiser was right when they said people preferred one spread over the other.

How random!

But the story isn't quite over yet, because there's one other thing we need to consider: the number of people who were tested. In this piece of research we got data from only 186 people, which is quite a small number for a scientific study. This matters, because of a little fact about randomness ...

When things happen at random, we expect them to average out in the long term. If I toss a coin lots of times, I expect it to land on heads half the time and on tails half the time. But – and this is the important thing – I can only expect an *exact* 50:50 split if I toss the coin many many times (actually an infinite number of times). If I only toss the coin a few times, it probably won't *quite* give a 50:50 split between heads and tails.

To show you what I mean, I'll genuinely toss a coin just twice. A normal coin lands on heads half the time and on tails half the time, so if I toss a coin twice, it should come down once on heads and once on tails. But I've just tossed my coin twice and got two heads in a row. What do you make of that? Does it seem weird to you that I got two heads in a row?

If you just thought 'No, I'm not surprised – that just happens sometimes' then you have totally understood the point I am making here.

The coin is random and balanced. If I toss it lots of times it will land on heads half the time and on tails half the time. But if I only toss it a few times, we aren't surprised if it lands on one side a bit more often than the other. If I toss a coin 50 times it *should* give me half heads and half tails.

But I've just tossed my coin 50 times and it came up with 27 heads and 23 tails. Are you surprised that it isn't quite an even split? No, you probably aren't. Twenty-seven heads to 23 tails isn't quite an even split, but it's not that far away either, and that's just something we expect to see when the numbers are low.

So what if you tossed a coin 186 times: would you be surprised to get 96 heads and 90 tails? Again, I think you probably would not be surprised. One hundred and eighty-six tosses *should* give 93 heads and 93 tails, but 96 and 90 isn't really that far away.

And so here's the question to which all of this has been leading: if 186 people were tasting two spreads and choosing one at random, would you be very surprised if 96 chose one spread and 90 chose the other? I think that after all these coin examples you might not be surprised. Just as 186 is a fairly small number of coin-tosses, it's also a fairly small number of people. And 96:90 isn't *that* far from an even split. So our 'worst-case scenario' is actually looking quite good again: if 186 people were just choosing a spread at random, we wouldn't be surprised to see a group of 96 and a group of 90.

And that is why the advert caught my eye. What the advertisers saw in their research was just what we might expect to see if people were making random choices. It wasn't quite a 50:50 split between the two spreads but, as you now know, it doesn't need to be: when the numbers are small, people who are choosing at random can fall into slightly uneven groups.

There is a statistical procedure called the **binomial test** (I'll introduce you to it later) which can tell us what the groups might look like if people were choosing at random. I used this test after seeing the advert and it confirmed my suspicion: if 186 people split into a group of 96 and a group of 90, this fits really well with the idea that they were making their choices at random. *The people in the advert were behaving like people who couldn't tell the spreads apart.* As such, there was no way the advertisers should have claimed that people 'prefer' their spread over their rival's product.

The upshot of all this is that I, along with several other gallant geek heroes, complained to the Advertising Standards Agency. They investigated the commercial and ruled against the company, banning them from showing the advert again because of its bad statistics. A nerdy victory for consumer protection! You can thank me later.

In that example I worked out something useful about the real world – or at least the real world of butter-like spreads and dubious advertising – from knowing just a little bit about statistics. If you followed my explanation of how it all worked, you will already have learnt some really important lessons about research and statistics, and how we think about these topics when we carry out investigations.

Thinking scientifically →
What would a genuine preference have looked like?

I said that if 186 people made a choice, and 96 went one way and 90 the other way, it looked like they were choosing at random. You might be wondering just how uneven the split would have to be before it *didn't* look like people were making random choices. I did one last analysis with the binomial test (which, remember, you'll meet properly later) and found that with 186 people, we would need to see *at least* a 107:79 split before we could be reasonably sure that people had a preference for one spread. This is, I think you'll agree, quite a long way from what we saw in the advert.

Why we don't study just one person and think we've learnt something

My grandfather smoked 60 cigarettes every day throughout his life and yet lived until he was 98, when he died from something completely unrelated. As smoking cigarettes did my grandfather no harm, does that mean it is safe for me to smoke?

I think we might all agree that I should not take up smoking cigarettes based only on my grandfather's experience, no matter how cool I would look. But let's take a moment to think about this, because there are many other situations in our everyday lives where we *are* tempted to make decisions based on just one person. I recently saw a television commercial in which a suspiciously pretty woman said she loved her new shampoo, and therefore I would love it too. But even if that woman really did love her shampoo, and wasn't just saying it for the money, does this prove that I will feel the same as her? Of course not: people are all different. For all we know she might be a weirdo who, unlike the rest of us, only needs clean hair to feel happy. And we'll never know if that's true or not unless we compare her to some other people.

We see a similar issue all the time in the media: journalists love to tell us 'one person's story' and ask us to learn from it. But can we really learn anything from 'one person's story'? What if their life was nothing like ours? In that case, why *should* we try to learn anything from them?

Learning anything from individual people is difficult because people vary so much. If we study one person, we've no way of knowing if they can teach us anything useful about other people. And even if, through sheer luck, we found the most average person in the world (who sounds just thrilling), we would still know nothing about the *variety* that exists between people.

In fact, it's even more serious than this: we don't just find variety *between* people, we also see variation *within* people. If I asked you how you were feeling today, and asked you again in six months, you'll almost certainly give me a different answer the second time.

So because people are all different, and because everybody changes over time, in psychology we hardly ever look at individuals, or single measurements. Instead, we take lots of measurements from lots of people and look at averages, or overall patterns. This approach helps us see beyond any individual quirks, or measuring errors, to find general information about the subject we are interested in.

Once we have seen a pattern among a set of numbers, we can then use statistical tests to decide whether or not this will *generalize* to new situations. If a doctor takes 100 patients with arthritis and finds that a new drug helps some of them, statistics can tell us how likely it is that the drug will work for other people with arthritis. If a teacher tests 200 schoolchildren to see whether a new learning technique helps them to study, we can calculate how likely it is that other children will respond in the same way.

◉ Chapter summary

Research design and statistics are tools of the trade in psychology. People are not all the same, and these tools help us see through people's differences to learn general information about people.

Chapter 2

The first three stages of designing a research project

Research design and statistics go together like salt and pepper, which is why this book has the title it does. The reason the two subjects are so closely linked is that whenever you're working on one of the two subjects, it's usually a good idea to think about the other at the same time. If you design a research study without thinking about the statistics you will later use, you might end up collecting data which aren't good enough for your analyses. For example, let's say I'm carrying out a survey and I want to ask people how old they are. I could simply ask each person:

'What is your age?'

but I could also ask the same question like this:

'Are you under seventy or over seventy?'

As you'll see later (in fact, as you can almost certainly see right now), even though both versions of the question are asking people about their age, the first version gets me much more detailed information than the second. This matters, because statistical tests work better when they have more detailed information. So when I'm deciding how to ask people their age, if I'm thinking about the statistics that I'll carry out later then I'll probably choose the first version of the question rather than the second.

And just as it's good to think about the statistics when you are planning a research study; when you are doing statistical analysis on a set of numbers it is good to think about where those numbers came from. For example, let's say I have a set of numbers telling me how tall a group of people are, and let's say I want to find the average height for the group. The average I calculate will only make sense if the heights were measured properly, so before I do my calculations I need to ask myself whether the heights really were measured well. If I found that the heights had been measured badly – perhaps by some buffoon who used a piece of elastic instead of a measuring tape – I would know that the average I was calculating couldn't be trusted.

However, although research methods and statistics go together so tightly in use, I believe it is often a good idea to *learn* about them separately. This stops you getting overloaded with new information and helps you focus on one thing at a time, to give each topic the attention it deserves. Once you have understood each subject, they will naturally fit together in your mind. In this book, then, we're going to start by thinking about how to design research studies before we go on, in Section 2, to think about what we will do with the data after the study is over.

Planning a research study involves making choices

One of the things I really want you to take away from this book is that usually there is not just one 'right' way of carrying out a research study. If five researchers are asked to look at the same question, they'll probably do it in five different ways, and that's completely fine. Research design is all about making choices and while sometimes it's possible to make the wrong choice and do things badly, like trying to measure people's heights with a piece of elastic, a lot of the time you'll find you have choices and there is not just one correct option: it's up to you to decide which you think works best.

As an example, let's say I ask you to plan a study which will measure how fast people can read. Clearly this would involve timing people as they read something, and one of the first questions you would ask is 'What will I get the participants to read?' This is a good example of a design decision that has no right answer. Sure, if you were looking at 5-year-old children then it's probably best not to have them read *Beowulf*, but that's just common sense. The main thing is that you and I, faced with designing this study, would almost certainly give our participants a different reading task, and that's fine.

What I am saying, then, is please don't get hung up on the idea that there's always only one right way of doing things. As often as not, the decisions you need to make are a matter of judgement, and you shouldn't go wrong as long as you are sensible. When a decision *is* really critical, and there is a danger of making a real wrong choice, I'll flag that up. But a lot of the time you have discretion and can use your judgement when deciding how your research will take place.

The first stages of planning a research study

We will now go through the first three stages of planning a research study, to show you how a research project gets moving as it goes from being a vague idea to a proper scientific study. I'm going particularly to try and give you a feel for the sorts of decisions we need to make along the way.

Step 1: find a research question

The starting point for almost every study is to have a **research question**. It might sound obvious that you need to have a question before you can go looking for answers, but you'd be surprised how often people forget this – seriously, I see students do this every year. Actually, to be a bit more accurate, people don't really *forget* they need to have a question before they start doing research, but they don't get the question properly clear in their minds before they go out and start collecting data. As a result they find it difficult to plan their research properly because they are never entirely sure what it is they are trying to achieve.

So the first step in every study is to decide what the research question will be. This helps you establish the **aim** of your study. If you start out with a clear question – written down in big letters, with a question mark at the end – you will always know exactly what you are trying to achieve and will find it much easier to stay on track as you plan your project.

Examples of research questions might include 'Do people get more clumsy when they are tired?' or 'Do people who swim in the sea get eaten by sharks more often than sensible people who stay on shore?' Notice how these are proper questions, with question marks at the end.

Once you have a clear research question like this, you'll find the next set of decisions becomes much easier. Look at the question 'Do people get more clumsy when they are tired?' If we were going to study this question then we can immediately see that (1) we're going to need to study some people, (2) we're going to need to look at different amounts of tiredness, and (3) we're going to need to measure clumsiness somehow. In fact, those three issues, which popped out of the research question almost by themselves, are pretty much all there is to the study. See how easy things become when you have a clear question? It would be so much easier to get started with this question than if you did what many people do and said, 'Er, yeah, I'm sort of interested in tiredness so I guess I'll do a study on that. Somehow ...'.

On the write lines

As we're going to work through the first stages of designing a study in this chapter, we need a research question that we can use as an example. As it happens, I'm trying to write this section of the book while sitting on a noisy train full of screaming children and I'm finding it quite difficult to concentrate. I wonder if it's the noise of the children that is making the writing difficult? It certainly feels like it. How could I find out scientifically?

Research projects very often begin just like this: a researcher notices something during their everyday life and decides to investigate it more formally. The first step in moving from a casual observation to a proper scientific study is to turn the observation into a clear and simple research question. So we might now ask this question:

'Is it harder to write when there is a lot of background noise?'

What you should notice here is that the research question I've chosen is more general than my original observation. I've gone from thinking about writing *this book* to thinking about writing *in general*, and I've gone from thinking about *noisy children* to thinking about background noise *in general*. I could have used a really focused research question like 'Is it harder to write the book *Research Methods and Statistics* when there are noisy children nearby on a train from Exeter to Salisbury?', but if I did that then my study would only tell me about one incredibly specific situation and that would be of no use to anybody except me. By making the research question more general – by thinking about all forms of writing, and by thinking about all forms of background noise – I hope to reach conclusions that will be useful in a whole range of circumstances, not just in places where I am writing this book near some young children and their antisocial parents.

> ### Thinking scientifically → **Reaching general conclusions**
> Whenever we do research, it's better to reach a conclusion that is general rather than specific. For example, if I understand how my editor Nigel behaves, I can predict what he will do in the future. But if I understand how *people* behave, I can predict the actions of Nigel *and everybody else I'll ever meet*, which is far more useful.

Step 2: formulate a hypothesis

Okay, so we've taken the first step. By moving from a specific observation to a more general topic, we've got a research question that should let us discover something useful and interesting. However, at this stage it's still not completely obvious how we should go about answering the question. We need to narrow things down a bit, and the next step of the research process helps us do this. The second thing we do, after we've got a research question, is generate a **hypothesis**. A hypothesis is not a question; it is a *prediction*. And here's something really important about how research works: *our job is to decide whether or not the hypothesis is true, and we do this by collecting evidence.*

Based on the research question we are using, a sensible hypothesis would be this:

'People will write better when there is no background noise'

Is that true or false? We don't know yet, but we'll be able to make up our minds once we've collected some evidence. Sure, there are still quite a few decisions to be made before we can get that evidence. For example, we need to decide what we mean by 'write better' and what exactly 'background noise' will involve, and we'll get to those things in a moment. The point is that we've now got something nice and specific to work with – a clear prediction we can test by collecting evidence. We've now moved from a casual observation made while sitting on a train to a specific hypothesis that, with evidence, will tell us something useful about human psychology. That's pretty neat.

Step 3: operationalize the measures that will be used in the study

So far we've decided on the research question we want to ask, and we have set up a hypothesis which we can test by collecting evidence. Now we need to decide what measurements we need to get that evidence. Or, in more technical terms, we need to **operationalize** our measures.

The hypothesis we are going to test is 'People will write better when there is no background noise'. With this hypothesis, there are two things that need to be operationalized: what do we mean by 'write better'? and what do we mean by 'background noise'? (There's actually a third thing that we need to make a decision about – who are the people we want to test? – but we'll get to that later. As we're psychologists, there are almost always people involved and so I've devoted the whole of the next chapter to deciding who you'll test.)

Both these things – how we will operationalize 'writing better' and how we will operationalize 'background noise' – are great examples of how there is often no 'right' way of doing research. So have a think about how *you* might operationalize those two things. How would you measure how well a person writes, and what would you use as background noise? Do try to think of some answers before you carry on reading.

Here are my answers, which might or might not be similar to yours. First, I reckoned that 'writing better' could refer to either the quantity of a person's writing or the quality. If I decided to measure the *quantity* of people's writing then the research study would just involve getting them to write for a few minutes, with and without background noise, and counting up how many words they produced. But when I thought about it further, I felt that this approach wasn't really in the spirit of the original observation that started the project rolling. I began this research project by finding it difficult to write this book while on the train. I'm sure you'll agree that with a book like this, the important thing is quality, not quantity – otherwise I could just copy and paste one paragraph over and over until I reached the 80,000 words the publishers asked for. So given the original inspiration for the study, my decision was to measure the *quality* of people's writing, not the quantity.

But how should I measure the quality of a person's writing? This is tremendously difficult, because the quality of a person's writing is quite **subjective**, and there is no 'proper' way to measure it. (Compare this with something **objective**, like a person's height, which we could easily decide how to measure.)

Given that the quality of a person's writing is a subjective measure, I decided to take the samples of writing to a group of experts – English literature professors, in this case – and have them rate the quality of the writing. This certainly wasn't the only way quality could be assessed, but it was the one I chose.

Thinking scientifically → Criticism and replication

I decided here to measure the quality of people's writing by using a group of expert judges. Maybe you thought this was a good idea, or maybe you spotted a problem with my decision. If you spotted a problem, or just thought of a better way of measuring writing quality, then you might decide to write a critique of my study. You might describe the problems with what I did and show why your method is better. This is a healthy thing, and a good scientist will never mind having their work criticized like this (as long as the criticism is polite and constructive! Sadly, in the real world, it sometimes isn't).

Scientists are interested in ideas, and they know that ideas are meant to be challenged and tested. If somebody makes a claim, other people might try to show it is wrong. If they fail to show that the claim is wrong, the claim was probably a good idea we can trust. But if, after an idea is criticized, it proves to be weak, it'll fall by the wayside and another idea will take its place. Either way, we have made progress in what we know. Knowledge advances when ideas are challenged and tested.

Finally, even if after reading my study you didn't feel I had made a mistake, you might still want to test my conclusions by **replicating** my research. This means you repeat my study to see if you find the same things I found. If you do, this is further evidence that my findings were sound; but if you find something different from me, then perhaps I was wrong, and we all need to look into the subject further.

Replication is another very important way in which scientists test one another's ideas. If a researcher carries out a study and comes up with a big new idea, few people will really trust it until it has been replicated, at least once more, by other researchers. You see what I mean about testing ideas?

A noise annoys

Having decided on a way to measure writing quality, we need to decide how we will operationalize 'background noise'. I thought of this study while being disturbed by small children, so we might want to find a group of children (the sort whose self-absorbed parents don't understand that screaming and shouting might bother people in public places) and have our participants try to do some writing twice – once with the children in the room and once without. That would certainly match the original observation, but I wonder if you can see a possible problem? As I'll discuss in more detail later, one of the most important things in an experiment is to **control** everything as much as possible – that is, to make sure that everybody who takes part in the experiment gets exactly the same experience. Young children are a bit unpredictable, and if we used real young children we've no way of knowing if they will disturb all our participants in exactly the same way.

One solution might be, instead of using real children, to use a recording of some children being noisy. This way, we can be sure that each of our participants is distracted in exactly the same way. If there are any differences in our participants' writing, we can immediately rule out the idea that they were differently distracted when we try to explain those differences.

The nature of science: Kuhn on how ideas develop, and Popper on how we can know what is and what isn't science

Given that philosophers deal all the time with ideas, it perhaps isn't very surprising that for centuries philosophers have thought about how ideas develop. And it's a good job they've done this, because along the way they've come up with some very useful insights into the nature of science and how we use ideas in the scientific process. I'd like briefly to introduce you to two important philosophers who have said a lot about this: Thomas Kuhn and Karl Popper.

Thomas Kuhn, and the nature of science

Thomas Kuhn was a twentieth-century American academic who, after studying the history of science, suggested that scientific ideas develop through sudden shifts in thinking, rather than through gradual progress. We don't, Kuhn argued, learn more and more and move steadily towards ever greater knowledge as time goes by. Instead, he suggested, science works through a series of grand upheavals. Ideas change suddenly and dramatically, and these big changes are separated by long periods where we make relatively little new progress.

In his book *The Structure of Scientific Revolutions*, Kuhn said that most of the time researchers are doing 'normal science'. Normal science involves taking existing ideas and applying them to new areas; it involves getting better at measuring things; and it involves refining laws to make them work better. But while in normal science people apply existing ideas in new ways, they do not think up new ideas; people get better at measuring things, but they don't discover whole new things to measure; and people refine laws to make them work better, but they don't discover brand new laws. In Kuhn's words, normal science is a 'mopping up operation', in which the current way of thinking is cleaned and tidied. But – and this is the critical thing – in normal science, the basic way that people think stays pretty much the same.

As well as these long periods of normal science, where there is not much true innovation, Kuhn argued that just now and again, within each field, there are periods of 'revolutionary science', when our whole way of thinking about a subject changes dramatically. Take disease, for example – a topic that is currently on my mind as I have a cold while I'm writing this section. Everybody gets ill from time to time, and in the past people had all sorts of theories about why this happens. Some people thought we got ill thanks to the influence of evil spirits, others thought that illness was the result of being exposed to bad air (*malaria* means 'bad air' in Italian), and still others blamed having too much blood in the body. When a person got ill, the treatment they received depended on whichever theory their physician believed. If you fell ill, and were unlucky enough to have a doctor who thought this was because you had too much blood in your body, you would soon find yourself being cut open and bled to make you better.

Then, in the nineteenth century, people like Louis Pasteur and Robert Koch proved that diseases were really caused by germs that are too small to see, and quite suddenly the whole approach to understanding and treating disease changed right across the Western world. So when we look at the study of disease we see that the second half of the nineteenth century was a period of 'revolutionary science', when our understanding of disease changed completely. Since the 1890s, however, we have been in a period of 'normal science': our basic understanding of what disease is hasn't changed, and research today is all about 'mopping up' the big ideas developed in the past. Today we are improving our ability to detect and treat germs, but we still view germs in much the same way as people did one hundred years ago. I can treat my cold symptoms better than my grandparents could, because normal science has developed better remedies, but our basic understanding of what causes a cold has not really changed since my grandparents' time.

That's not to say that there won't be a revolution for our understanding of disease sometime in the future. One day somebody might hit upon a new idea or discovery that completely changes the way we understand viruses and allows us to treat them easily. But until then we are in a period of normal science, gradually modifying what we already know rather than making massive changes to the way we think.

Kuhn used the word **paradigm** to describe all the established ideas about a subject. So the old idea that illness was caused by bad air was a paradigm – a way of thinking about disease that both tried to explain where the sickness came from and suggested treatments. Then, when people like Pasteur demonstrated that this way of thinking was wrong, medicine underwent a *paradigm shift* as the old way of thinking was abandoned and a new way of thinking appeared.

Paradigm shifts can be caused by big new discoveries, or by sudden leaps of imagination by genius thinkers. But paradigm shifts can also be caused when we find that there are so many facts that cannot be explained by the current way of thinking that this paradigm is clearly no longer good enough, and people are forced to abandon the current paradigm in favour of a new, alternative way of thinking.

Karl Popper, and his ideas about what is and is not science

Karl Popper lived throughout most of the twentieth century and, although Austrian by birth, he spent much of his adult life in England. Popper's ideas are subtle and at times complex, but there is one big idea for which he is best known, which is that we can easily tell which theories are scientific and which are not.

To try and illustrate this idea, here are two theories which I have just invented. According to Popper, only one of these is scientific:

1   My pet cat makes it rain every time he sneezes.
2   My pet cat sometimes makes it rain when he sneezes.

Clearly these are both pretty silly theories, but the point is that one of these is an idea scientists could examine – and so is a scientific theory – whereas the other could never be studied scientifically.

Popper said we can tell whether or not a theory is scientific by asking whether or not it could ever be disproved. A theory that can be disproved is scientific, and a theory that could never be disproved is not. Look at the first of my two theories. The idea that my cat makes it rain every time he sneezes *could* be disproved. If, just once, we saw my cat sneeze without it raining afterwards, this would disprove the theory. Because it is possible to disprove this theory, it is scientific – it is something we genuinely could investigate and discover the truth about.

But the second theory is problematic. It says that my cat 'sometimes' makes it rain when he sneezes. This suggests that sometimes when he sneezes it'll rain and other times it won't. So how could we ever investigate that claim? If we see my cat sneeze and it doesn't rain, this could be because the theory is wrong, and my cat's nose has no influence on the weather *or* it could be because this is just one of the times when it doesn't rain after he sneezes. When he sneezes and it rains, this fits the theory; and when he sneezes and it doesn't rain this also fits the theory. *Everything that could ever happen fits the theory.* According to Popper, then, this theory is not scientific. Sure, we can talk about this theory, and we can passionately believe in it if we want to, but it is not something we can ever investigate scientifically. As such, we will never know for certain if it is true.

To give just one example of where this applies to psychology, Popper famously criticized Sigmund Freud's theories about the human mind because these were impossible to disprove. A patient tells their therapist that they want to kill their boss. 'Ah,' says the psychoanalyst, 'that's because you have violent urges.' But when the same patient says they *don't* want to kill their boss the psychoanalyst says 'Ah, that's because you have violent urges *but you are repressing them.*' Because Freud developed the idea of repression – which says that sometimes we hide bad feelings, even from ourselves, and sometimes we don't – this means there is nothing at all the patient can say to convince the psychoanalyst that they do not have violent urges. To the psychoanalyst, a statement and its exact opposite both mean the same thing, and so there is no way to disprove the idea that the patient is violent. As such, Popper said, this simply isn't science, and we will never get definite answers.

◉ Chapter summary

The first stages of a research project involve deciding what your research question will be; using this to generate a hypothesis, or prediction; and then deciding exactly how you will measure and define the various things that interest you – a process we call operationalizing.

Chapter 3

Who will you test and what will this tell you? Understanding populations and samples

If I ever wanted to study my neighbours, it would be quite a simple task. There are only around 50 houses on my street, so if I wanted to learn something about the people who live there – if I wanted to know their average age, for example – I could quite easily go and discover this by asking them all.

In situations like this, where you are interested in a nice small group of people and can get data from them all, you will always get exactly the information you want, and you will only need statistics to describe what you have found (by giving averages, for example). If I want to know the average age of my neighbours and, after speaking to all of them, I learn that the average age is 42, I now *know* my neighbours' average age. I could firmly conclude my research, with no lingering doubt whatsoever, by saying the average age of my neighbours is 42. But often things are not so simple, our conclusions cannot be so firm and we have to use statistical tests to help us understand what we have seen.

In research and statistics, the group you are interested in – the group you want to reach a conclusion about – is called your **population**. You need to be a little careful with this term, because the word means something different than in everyday use. Usually when we use the word 'population', we mean the people who live in a particular place, such as the population of South Africa. But in research the word has a more specific meaning: it means 'the people you want to reach a conclusion about.' If a developmental psychologist is studying how 7- and 8-year-old children interact with their teachers, the population they are studying – the set of people they want to learn about – might be 'all the 7- and 8-year-old children in the country'. If a cognitive psychologist is studying how people remember events, their population might be 'all human beings'. So in a research project, the population is the group you want to reach a conclusion about. This could be a group of people, but it can just as easily be a group of businesses, diseases, animals or events. It is always a good idea to be absolutely sure what the population is when you carry out a study; always be sure you know exactly who or what you want to reach a conclusion about. Seriously: write it down and look at it frequently; it's easy to forget otherwise.

Summary

The population is the set of individuals you want to reach a conclusion about. These individuals are often people, but they could instead be animals, organizations, events or whatever.

👁 The pick of the population: samples

Think about some of the research ideas I just mentioned: a developmental psychologist who wants to know about young children, or a cognitive psychologist who wants to know about how memory works for all human beings. In each of these examples, the population is simply too large for anybody realistically to study it.

Imagine I said to you 'I have suddenly become weirdly interested in trees, and would love to know how tall they are, on average. Could you go out and find the average height of all the trees in the world please?' You would clearly be overwhelmed by the size of the task, but you'd need to find some way of dealing with it, because 'all the trees in the world' is the population I've asked you to study.

This sort of situation, where the population is too large to study, is really common – indeed, it is what we have to deal with in most research. So how do we cope with populations that are too large to study? How do we reach conclusions that apply to individuals we will never see? To answer this, think what you would do if I really did ask you to find the average height of all the world's trees. Knowing you can never measure all the trees, you would probably try to answer my question by measuring *some* of the trees. You might take a group of trees, measure them, and use this information to estimate – to *infer* – what you would see if you somehow could measure every tree in the world.

When you take part of a population and study it, this is called a **sample**, and the process of choosing the individuals you will study is called *sampling*. You study some of the whole population and, once you have learnt something about this sample, you can estimate what you would see if you were able to study the whole population. In other words, you **generalize** from the sample to the population.

Summary

When the population you are interested in is too large to study, you study a sample of it and use this to estimate what the population looks like.

◉ Choosing a good sample

In research, we nearly always study a sample of people and use them to guess what the population looks like. As such, it's really important that your sample behaves the same way as the population. We often say that the sample must be *representative* of the population. So if you remember only one thing about sampling it should be this: a perfect sample is *exactly the same as the population, only smaller*. If your sample is simply a smaller version of the whole population, you can be really confident that whatever you learn from your sample is also true of the population.

So a major skill in research is choosing good samples which look like the populations they are going to represent. The problem is, we hardly ever know what the population looks like until after we have got the sample. We need a way of choosing a sample that will look like the population, even though we don't know what that population looks like. This looks like a Catch-22 situation!

The way we deal with this is to use one of the standard techniques for selecting a sample, each of which has good and bad points. With some techniques we can be more confident that we are getting representative samples, but there is usually a price to be paid – these techniques might be more complex or difficult to use.

Random samples

Your sample should look the same as the population – just in a handy, manageable size. The thing you absolutely want to avoid is getting a sample which looks totally different to the population. Imagine I was advising the government on a new health programme which would be given to every part of the country. And imagine I tested the programme in just one very small and very wealthy town. This would be a sampling problem: whatever I saw in this sample might not generalize to the population. This sample could be unrepresentative, or *biased*.

A very common way of trying to avoid **sample bias** is to take **random samples**. If I tested my health intervention on a sample of people chosen randomly from everybody in the country, there is no real way this sample could end up biased. If I want a sample of trees, I could randomly choose individual trees from all the trees in the world and this should leave me with an unbiased sample. Each tree that exists has an equal chance of being included in the sample, and this works well to get samples which look like the population.

Random samples are a great thing to aim for, although in practice genuine random samples are usually impossible to obtain. If I'm interested in all the trees in the world, or all the people, I would need some sort of list of all those individuals before I could start picking them at random. Where would this list come from? On the other hand, if the population I wanted to learn about was 'Canadian businesses with more than 10,000 employees' a list might be much easier to find.

Another practical problem with random samples of people is that, even if I could get a true random list of 1000 people for a study, I can't force those people to take part in my research because that would be unethical. Because I can't force people to be in my study, the final sample I tested wouldn't be random. It might be biased towards people who are particularly helpful.

Opportunity samples

An **opportunity sample** is a sample of individuals chosen simply because they are convenient. Let's say I want to do some research on young children – a study of how their reading skills develop, for example. And let's say I decide I need to test a sample of 50 children: where do I find that sample? Using random sampling I would need randomly to pick 50 individuals from all the children in the country (or possibly all the children in the world, if I wanted to be able to generalize my findings to children in general). But hold on: I live about a hundred metres away from a school! As long as the teachers don't mind, I can just stroll up the street and test 50 kids with no trouble at all.

If I were to do this, I would be using an 'opportunity' sample: a sample chosen simply because I had the opportunity to use it. This is also known as a 'convenience' sample (because the kids who go to school a hundred metres from my house are convenient), a 'grab' sample (because I am grabbing some individuals who happen to be nearby), or an 'accidental' sample.

If I'm interested in trees, and do all my measurements in a local wood, I would be doing opportunity sampling; if I were studying company accounts, and chose a sample of companies my friends work for, this is again an opportunity sample.

It is very important with this sort of sample to be careful when generalizing from the sample to the population. If I study how well the children in my local school can read, I need to ask myself how well they represent children in general. If my local school was a very exclusive private school, or if I lived in a heavily deprived area, then I would probably be quite cautious about generalizing what I learnt from the local children. In these circumstances, perhaps the best I could do is to say that I have learnt something about children who go to schools like the one I studied, rather than say I have learnt something about all children.

Stratified samples

I am trying to stress the idea that a good sample is exactly the same as the population you want to learn about – just smaller. One approach to getting a representative sample is very deliberately to select individuals of the right type, rather than leave it to chance. This is the basis of **stratified sampling**, a technique used a great deal in opinion polls and political surveys.

If the population is half male and half female, the people in the sample are deliberately chosen to be half male and half female; if 20% of the population is aged between 40 and 60, the sample is chosen so that 20% of the people in it are aged between 40 and 60. The stratified sample (or **quota sample**, which is almost the same thing) is an interesting concept, then: it very carefully tries to make sure the sample is representative of the population, which, as we have seen, is what we want. The downside is that because your sample is broken down by age, gender, ethnicity, income and so on, it is easy to end up with just one person representing, say, every single middle-class Asian women aged between 35 and 45 in the south-west of the country. That person has real power: if she happens to be odd in some way, your understanding of middle-class Asian women between 35 and 45 will be flawed. Also, stratified sampling assumes that factors such as age, ethnicity and so on are important for whatever it is you are studying. If you are looking at, say, working memory, which is pretty much the same for everyone, is it really worth going to all this effort?

Cluster samples

Cluster samples use existing groups to make the job of sampling easier. Let's go back to the example of choosing a representative sample of trees. If you were to choose a random sample of all the trees in the world (assuming this were possible), this would probably lead to your travelling all over the planet, measuring just one tree in each location.

One way you could make life easier would be to find existing groups of trees – or 'forests' as they're known. This way, instead of randomly choosing trees from around the world, you randomly choose *forests* and measure several trees in each. If you needed to measure a thousand trees, you might randomly select ten forests and measure a hundred trees in each. This is a lot more convenient than visiting a thousand different locations.

The existing groups you use will be different depending on what you want to study, but it is often possible to find some sort of groups that you can use, no matter what area you work in. If you were studying hurricanes, a natural group of individuals might be 'the hurricanes which happen in one year'. You then just randomly choose several years to get your sample of hurricanes. If you were studying children, a naturally occurring group might be 'schools': you choose schools at random and measure all the children in each.

Of course, there is a price to be paid for the convenience of cluster sampling: the individuals you test won't be independent. All the children in one school know one another and are taught by the same teachers. As such, they will tend to be quite like one another, and this could bias the sample.

Summary

Various methods exist for choosing a sample of individuals for study. They all aim to give a sample that is representative of the wider population you want to reach a conclusion about.

👁 How large should a sample be?

Your aim is to get a good representative sample of the population, and using an appropriate sampling method is an important step towards this. But it is also important to think about the size of the sample. The larger the sample, the more likely it is to be representative of the population. In other words, the larger the sample, the more likely it is that whatever you see in the sample is what you would see if you were able to study the whole population. One way to look at this is simply to say that the larger the sample is, the closer it is to *being* the population.

I can perhaps show you this best with a demonstration. Today I taught a large class where 60% of the students were female, so I decided to carry out a sampling exercise. I started out by picking groups of five students at random from all the people in the room. The first sample of five students had three women (60%) and two men (40%). This was a perfectly representative sample of the whole group – excellent! But when I tried to take a sample again I found a very different picture. This time I got two women (40%) and three men (60%), a sample which looked very different from the class as a whole. The third and fourth attempts both provided a sample with five women (100%) and zero men (0%) – samples which looked nothing like the population.

I then repeated this exercise, but instead of taking groups of 5 people, I took samples of 10, 30 and 50 people, as well as samples of one. Putting all the numbers together, I got this table:

Sample size	First attempt	Second attempt	Third attempt	Fourth attempt	Average
1	0 F (0%) 1 M (100%)	0 F (0%) 1 M (100%)	1 F (100%) 0 M (0%)	0 F (0%) 1 M (100%)	**25% Female 75% Male**
5	3 F (60%) 2 M (40%)	2 F (40%) 3 M (60%)	5 F (100%) 0 M (0%)	5 F (100%) 0 M (0%)	**75% Female 25% Male**
10	7 F (70%) 3 M (30%)	5 F (50%) 5 M (50%)	4 F (40%) 6 M (60%)	4 F (40%) 6 M (60%)	**50% Female 50% Male**
30	18 F (60%) 12 M (40%)	23 F (77%) 7 M (23%)	18 F (60%) 12 M (40%)	19 F (63%) 11 M (37%)	**65% Female 35% Male**
50	33 F (66%) 17 M (34%)	29 F (58%) 21 M (42%)	30 F (60%) 20 M (40%)	29 F (58%) 21 M (42%)	**61% Female 39% Male**

Remember, the population of students that I was working with was 60% female and 40% male. The table shows pretty clearly how the larger a sample was, the more it tended to look like the population. Some of the small samples were terribly unrepresentative: two of my five-person samples contained no men at all, whereas if I had only looked at single people I would probably have concluded my group of students was mostly male! This all demonstrates the problem of using small samples: they often don't look like the population. And whenever a sample doesn't look like the population then we have, as we have seen, **sampling error**, or **sample bias**.

So if a small sample is a problem, what is a 'large enough' sample? The simple answer to this is 'as large as possible': it is always good to get as many data as you possibly can.

The more complex answer is that you can use a technique called **power analysis** to decide how many individuals you need to sample for any question you might want to answer. I'm not going to teach you all about power analysis here as it's too complicated: rather, just find some corner of your brain to store the idea that if you ever want to calculate a minimum sample size, it *is* possible, and you can look it up, or get advice from an expert, if you are ever in a position where you need to do this.

Summary

You want a sample to be a smaller version of the population. However, you don't want it too small, because very small samples will often be unrepresentative of the population. The larger a sample is, the more confident you can be that it looks like the population.

◉ Chapter summary

Whenever we do research, we are interested in learning about a population, which can be almost anything: children learning to read, hurricanes, trees, prisoners, financial transactions, car journeys. Because most interesting populations are too big to study, we have to take a sample of the population and hope that whatever we see in it will generalize: we hope that whatever we see in the sample is what we would have seen if we had been able to study the whole population. This is much more likely if we take care to ensure that the sample is as close to the population as possible: ideally, the sample will be exactly the same as the population, only a manageable size (without being too small).

Chapter 4

Major types of quantitative research

Introduction

There are many different ways of learning things about the world, but for scientific research we use just a few main methods. In this chapter I'm going to cover **quantitative research**, which involves measuring people. You can tell when you're doing quantitative research because you'll be getting numbers from the people you study – measures of height, intelligence, reaction times, or whatever. In the next chapter I'll look at some **qualitative research** techniques: interviews, focus groups and case studies, which tend to look at the words people use, rather than take numerical measurements.

Incidentally, many people find the words 'quantitative' and 'qualitative' quite difficult to tell apart, and if you struggle to get your tongue around these terms consistently, you're not alone! A lot of professional researchers, when talking informally, shorten the words to 'quant' and 'qual', which makes their chats a bit easier.

Something else that people often confuse is the difference between experimental and non-experimental research on the one hand, and the difference between quantitative and qualitative research on the other. Just to make this really clear, experimental research is *one type* of quantitative research, in which we manipulate something and measure its effects. For example, you might take a group of people and give half of them a new type of mental exercise, while giving the other half no exercise, and measure how much everybody's thinking changes. In this case you have **manipulated** something – you have deliberately given some people the exercise and some people no exercise – and you are asking whether this has any effect. As you are studying the effects of a manipulation that you made, this is an experiment, and I'll say lots more about this approach later in this chapter.

However, a lot of the research we do as psychologists does not involve us manipulating anything, and so is non-experimental research. Examples of non-experimental work include observation studies and correlational studies, which I'll discuss in a moment, as well as research using interviews and focus groups, which I'll cover in the next chapter.

Experiments are usually quantitative, and non-experimental research is often qualitative, which is why some people tend to get the two ideas mixed up. But this is not a hard-and-fast rule. Although experiments nearly always involve taking measurements, non-experimental work can just as easily be quantitative or qualitative. It's probably best to remember that experiments are *one type* of quantitative research.

In this chapter we will cover:
- Observation studies
- Correlation studies
- The experimental method (and longitudinal studies)

Observation studies

Observation studies are a non-experimental approach that can be very useful when you want to study people's (or animals') natural behaviour, getting an idea of how often, and when, they do things. For example, you might be interested in how people move around a shop when they are choosing what they will buy, and what people tend to do before they buy an item. Observing people could help you understand this subject, and this knowledge might be useful for better designing shop layouts. Of course, a limitation of this technique is that it can only tell us about visible behaviour: it cannot tell us much about what is going on in people's minds.

A key aim, when carrying out an observation study, is to make the observations as *systematic* as possible. This means you don't just stand there jotting down random notes on what you see. Instead, you make a plan in advance about what you will look for. If you were carrying out a study of shoppers' browsing behaviour, you might make a list of behaviours that you think could be relevant to predicting buying behaviour. Your list might include actions like:

- Picking up objects to examine them
- Discussing items with other people
- Checking prices

You could then observe shoppers and note how often people carry out these behaviours and how often they buy items. Planning this checklist in advance helps make sure you don't miss anything, and you might even use your plan to produce a handy sheet for recording your behaviours as you watch them, something like this perhaps:

Record	Gender	Age	Examines item	Discusses item	Checks price	Takes item to checkout
1	Female	30–40	✓		✓	✓
2	Female	20–30			✓	✓
3	Male	40–50				✓
4	Female	20–30	✓	✓		
...						

You could then use these data to answer questions like whether or not people tend to check the price of an item before taking it to the checkout, or whether men and women behave differently.

Another big advantage of planning your observations in advance is that this can help remove biases caused by the observer – something we call **investigator effects**. It's easy for the observer's preconceptions to affect what they see. For example, I might have no idea that people tend to check the prices of items before buying them. If I observed some shoppers, my records might suggest that price-checking never happens, purely because I didn't realize I should be looking for this behaviour. But by planning in advance, I could show my checklist to an expert – such as a shopkeeper – who might help me see what I have overlooked.

Another big advantage of making an observation plan in advance is that it allows you to check how good your observations were when the study is over. It is a good idea for two people independently to observe the same behaviour, using the same checklist. After the study, they look at how often they agreed on what they saw, and this measure of **inter-rater reliability** gives an idea of how good the observations were. If both observers agree on what they saw most of the time, we can be confident that these are good records of the behaviour being observed.

One issue surrounding observational studies is that in most cases, there is a strong risk that people will behave differently if they know they are being watched. For this reason, it is often preferable to carry out observation studies without telling the people involved. But this raises a serious ethical dilemma. As we'll see in Chapter 6, there are issues with studying people without their consent, meaning we often find ourselves in a bind when we want to use observational studies. We might have to choose between observing people without their permission (which could be considered unethical) or getting their permission but knowing that this might change the behaviour we want to study.

Of course, there are other circumstances where this is not an issue. It is quite possible to use observational techniques to study the amount of violence in television programmes, for example. You would want to do all the same pre-planning (deciding which actions you will count as violent), but you would no longer have to worry about getting permission to view the people being observed, or worry that their behaviour will change because you are watching them.

◉ Correlational studies

In a **correlational** study we take two measurements and look at whether there is a relationship between them – the clue is in the name: *co-*, which means 'together', and *relation*. For example, we might take a group of schoolchildren and measure two things: how much one-to-one attention each child gets from their teacher, and how successful each child is with their school work. We could then look at whether these two measures are related to each other. As you can see, this is another non-experimental approach, as we are taking measurements of things that already exist. We are not making any changes to the world; we are just looking at the world and getting an idea of the links that exist within it.

If we actually did a correlation study of children's performance and their teacher contact, there are really only three things that we could find. First, we might find that there is just no relationship between the amount of attention a child gets and how they perform at school: some children might perform well after lots of attention and others might perform just as well with no attention. Second, we might find that there is a **positive relationship**: the more attention a child gets, the better they perform at school. Finally, we might see a **negative relationship**: the more attention a child receives, the worse they perform at school. Whichever result we find, we would have learnt something new about how the two measures we have taken are related to each other.

I'm not going to say much more about using correlation just here, as I've devoted a whole chapter to the subject later in the book. The main thing I want to mention before moving on is a possible problem with this type of study. Researchers use correlation all the time because it is often very interesting to see whether two measures are related. However, just because we find that two measures are related, this doesn't tell us anything about *how* or *why* they are related. Let's say we found that children who get a lot of attention in the classroom tend to perform worse at school. In this case, I can think of at least two explanations for that relationship: perhaps the teachers chose to spend more time with the children who were having difficulties, or perhaps the teachers weren't very good, and the more time they spent with a child, the more confused the child became! The only thing we know for certain is that teachers spent more time with children who performed badly at school, but because the study is correlational we still don't know whether the teachers *responded* to children who were performing badly or whether they *caused* the children to perform badly. There is always this sort of doubt after carrying out a correlational study, so they are mostly used for exploring new areas of research. Once we've found an interesting relationship, we can then probe into it more deeply using other techniques that can help us understand why those relationships are there. And probably the most important of these techniques is ...

◉ The experimental method

A few months ago I was having some trouble with my motorcycle – its engine was running badly and it struggled to get started on cold mornings. So I changed the oil, the oil filter and the engine coolant; I cleaned the spark plugs and flushed out the radiator. Afterwards, the bike was running fine.

On the face of it, that might sound like a nice happy story: my motorbike wasn't working properly and after a few hours of oily toil it was working well. But for a scientist, that story is a tale of disaster and woe!

Although I fixed the bike, because I tackled the problem unscientifically I still don't know *how* I fixed it, or what the original problem was. I made five changes all at once – the oil, the filter, the coolant, the spark plugs and the radiator – and so I've no way of knowing which of those changes solved the problem. I got a working bike, but no knowledge which might help me in the future.

If I had tackled my problem scientifically, making just one adjustment at a time and observing its effects before moving on to the next adjustment, I would have been using the **experimental method** and would definitely have learnt some useful knowledge as a result. In an experiment, we **manipulate** something and look at the effects of the manipulation while **controlling** absolutely everything else. As long as everything else is kept the same, then if we see something happen after we take an action, we can be pretty sure that this happened because of our manipulation and not for some other reason. If the only thing I did to my bike was to clean the spark plugs, and after this it started running properly, I can be almost certain that the spark plugs were the problem.

Let's say you want to look at whether drinking warm milk makes people sleepy. If you addressed this question experimentally, you might take a group of people and give warm milk only to a random half of them. The experimental manipulation is that some people get milk and some don't, and this should be the only difference between the two groups: everything else should be controlled – all the people should be tested in the same room, they should all get tested at the same time of day, and so on. If the people who drank the warm milk fell asleep more often, you could be fairly certain that it was the milk that caused this. But if you didn't keep everything else constant, you couldn't reach such nice conclusions. If you tested all your people at different times of day then for all you know it was this, rather than the milk, that caused some to sleep.

Variables

An important concept in research is the idea of a **variable**. A variable is *anything which you measure or manipulate in a study*. So in this study, one of the variables is the drink – half the people got milk and half did not. The study's other variable is the number of people falling asleep.

A simple experiment like this will usually only have two variables – the one you manipulate and the one you measure. In this case, you manipulated the drink and measured sleeping. But if you tested people at different times of day then the study would have an **extraneous variable** – a variable, other than the the the one you wanted to manipulate, which might affect the results. If an extraneous variable ever does affect your results then we say it has **confounded** the results, and has become a **confounding variable**.

One type of confounding variable you should particularly look out for is where you – the person who is running the study – affect the data being collected. This is known as an **experimenter effect**, and is a variation on the **investigator effect** I mentioned when talking about observation studies. To take a really obvious example, if you are rude and unfriendly to your participants, then you can't expect to get great data from them. Perhaps even worse than being unpleasant to everybody would be if you treat some of the participants one way – perhaps quite neutrally – but are super-nice to the rest (the ones you find attractive, perhaps). This would mean that some of your participants have a different experience to others, and this could lead to their data looking quite different. You might have introduced a confound into your own data – an experimenter effect. It is important you always do everything you can to treat all participants exactly the same.

For similar reasons, wherever possible a study should use only one person to collect the data. If you are running a study and you divide the testing up between you and somebody else, it is inevitable that you will both treat your participants slightly differently, even if you're not aware of it, and this could again lead to differences appearing in the data. Let's say you and your co-investigator divide the research up by saying 'Tell you what: why don't I test a hundred people in this town and you test a hundred people in some other town?' If you found a difference between the two towns, this could be because the people really are different in these two places, or it could just be because the people in each town were tested by different experimenters. Critically, you would have no way of knowing for certain what caused the difference you saw.

Nurse – the IV!

The reason the experimental method is so important is that it is the main tool we have for learning how one thing causes another to happen. To take a slightly silly example, there is an old belief that when cows lie down, it will rain shortly afterwards. Seeing this correlation between the cows' behaviour and the rain would be interesting and useful (we could use it as a short-term weather forecasting tool), but we still would not understand the link: do the cows lie down because it is about to rain, or do the cows *cause* the rain by lying down? An experiment could let us investigate this correlation more closely: we could *manipulate* the cows, making them lie down or stand up as we pleased, and observe the results. If we kept everything else constant – the season, the general weather conditions – and found that every time we made the cows lie down, it started to rain, and if we found that every time we made the cows stand up it stopped raining, and if we saw this happen again and again, this would be good evidence that the cows controlled the rain (I *knew* they were up to something!).

Unfortunately, because the experimental method is such a common and important tool, there is quite a bit of specialized vocabulary that goes with it. You have already seen the terms 'manipulation' and 'control', and two other important terms are **independent variable** and **dependent variable**. The independent variable (IV) is the thing you manipulate. So in the last example, the independent variable was the position of the cows – lying down or standing up. Earlier on we saw an experiment in which the independent variable was whether or not people drank warm milk.

The dependent variable (DV) is the thing you measure – whether or not it rains, in this example. The best way to remember these terms is that in an experiment you usually have just two measures, and the one you are measuring *depends* on the one you are manipulating. In this case, we are looking at whether rain (DV) *depends* on what the cows are doing (IV).

Independent-samples versus repeated-measures designs

When planning an experiment, one of the first decisions you usually need to make is whether you will study one group of people or more than one group. Let's say you want to discover whether drinking coffee causes people to fall over. Because you want to know if coffee *causes* people to fall over, it's not enough to do a correlational study, as correlational studies can't tell you what causes something to happen. A correlational study might tell you that drinking coffee and falling over go together, such that people who drink a lot of coffee tend to fall over a lot. But is this because the coffee makes people fall, or is it because some people naturally fall over a lot and drink coffee to comfort themselves? No, if you want to know

whether coffee *causes* the falling over then you're going to need to manipulate what people drink and look at the effects of that manipulation.

If you really did this study, you would need very early on to make a
choice about whether to test one group of people or two. One option
would be to take a single group of people and observe them for a while,
counting up how often each person fell over. You would then carry out
your experimental manipulation, by giving them all an identical cup of
coffee, before counting up how often they all fell over afterwards. By
comparing the 'before coffee' scores with the 'after coffee' scores, you
would be able to see if people fell down more after the coffee (and because
the only thing to change was the coffee, you could be pretty sure that the
coffee caused the effect). This approach is called a **repeated-measures
design**, because you have measured each person more than once.

The other option would be to take two groups of people, give coffee to
only one of the groups, and count up how often people in the two groups
fell over. In this case, you would compare the 'with coffee' and 'without
coffee' scores to see if the coffee caused people to fall over. This approach
is called an **independent-samples design**, because you have compared
separate (independent) groups of people.

The group who didn't have any coffee acts as your **control group**. A
control group doesn't experience the manipulation, and so gives you a
baseline measure for your experiment – this group shows you how
people who have not drunk any coffee behave, and you can compare the
baseline data to the experimental data to see how different they are. If
there is a difference between the control group and the group that has
experienced the manipulation, you can be pretty sure the manipulation
caused that difference.

Thinking scientifically → **Placebo effects**

If you really did compare two groups of people to see whether drinking
coffee makes people fall over, you probably should not give one group
of a people coffee and the other group nothing. There are two reasons
for this. First, if you gave one group coffee and the other group nothing,
you have actually manipulated more than one thing at once: the drink
group have had (1) a drink and (2) some coffee, so you still wouldn't
know which of these differences – having had coffee, or just having had
anything to drink – caused the effect. You should have given the control
group a different drink, such as water. This way, both groups had a
drink, and the only difference was that one group got coffee.

But there is also another reason for giving the control group a non-coffee drink: the **placebo effect**. When people believe something will happen to them, their belief often makes it happen. This effect was first discovered in medicine, where it has long been known that if you give people a pill that does nothing, but tell them it is a painkiller, they will feel less pain. More generally, whenever people believe they are experiencing an experimental manipulation, they respond to it. Just thinking that they are drinking coffee might be enough to start your people falling over.

For this reason, you would want to give both groups drinks that looked and tasted similar, and you would want to tell both groups that their drinks *might* be coffee. The control group would give you the baseline measure, showing you how often people who *think* they have drunk coffee fall over. The experimental group would give you the genuine measure of how often people who *have* drunk coffee fall over.

Order effects and counterbalancing

Whenever you use a repeated-measures design, which involves testing each person more than once, you always have to think about possible **order effects**. Imagine I am running a study to look at whether car drivers are distracted by having conversations with their passengers. A volunteer turns up, I put them into a driving simulator and have them drive for eight hours without a passenger, then for eight hours with a passenger, while I count up how many driving mistakes they make on each run.

Can you see the problem? When I test my volunteer the second time (with a passenger) I have actually changed two things at once: they now have a passenger (which is the experimental manipulation) *and* they have just been driving for eight hours, which will have made them tired. If they make more mistakes during their second drive I do not know whether this is because they now have a passenger distracting them, or because they are more tired than they were in the first session of driving. It's another type of confound.

Order effects are a risk whenever we use a repeated-measures design. In the driving example, the **fatigue effect** from having driven for eight hours might make people perform worse in the second test. But in other circumstances, people might perform better in a second test, because of **practice effects**. Let's say I want to know whether wearing a tinfoil hat makes people better at solving logic puzzles. I give everybody ten puzzles to solve, then place tinfoil hats on their heads before they tackle ten more puzzles. If they do better with the second set of puzzles this could be because of the hats, or it could be because doing the first set of puzzles gave them practice at solving this type of puzzle. I would have no way of knowing which of these was the real explanation.

The main way to deal with possible order effects is to **counterbalance** your study. This means half your participants do the tasks in one order and half do the tasks in the opposite order. If I counterbalanced my tinfoil hat study, I would have half the participants solve ten puzzles with a hat then solve ten puzzles without a hat, while the other half of the participants solve ten puzzles without a hat and then solve ten puzzles with a hat. This way, for each person who wore a hat during the first set of puzzles, there was another person who wore no hat; and for each person who had no hat during the first set of puzzles, there was another person who had a hat. Everything completely balances out, and if you see an effect of tinfoil hats on problem-solving, it cannot be explained away as an order effect.

	Half of the people	The other half of the people
First ten puzzles	With hat	Without hat
Second ten puzzles	Without hat	With hat
Analysis	Everybody is analysed together	

Which is better – the independent-samples or the repeated-measures design?

There is no simple answer to this, and very often you can happily carry out an experiment using either approach. To return to the example I used earlier, where we wanted to know whether drinking coffee makes people fall over, you could just as easily test one group of people before and after they have some coffee (a repeated-measures design) or compare a group who have had coffee with a group who haven't (an independent-samples design). Both approaches are fine, and each has advantages.

The big advantage of the repeated-measures approach is that the people you are testing stay the same. If you compare two different groups of people and see a difference between them, it is always possible that this difference wasn't caused by the coffee, but by the people in one group just being naturally clumsier than the people in the other.

However, if you have a single group of people and test them twice, you are testing exactly the same people both times. If you see any difference after the coffee, this must have been caused by the drink – there is no way the difference can be explained away by some of the people in your experiment being more clumsy than others, as the people didn't change. Experiments are all about keeping things constant, and so keeping the people constant is often a very good idea – it totally removes a major alternative explanation for whatever you see.

A second advantage of repeated-measures designs is that you often need fewer people. If you have a group of 40 people and test them twice, before and after a manipulation, this is pretty much the same as testing two groups of 40 people (so 80 in total) in an independent-samples procedure. Testing fewer people is usually easier, faster and cheaper than testing more people, and this is another big plus.

However, there are also advantages to comparing different groups of people in an independent-measures design. If you used just one group in the coffee-drinking study, you wouldn't be able to separate out true effects of coffee from any placebo effect. You compared the same people before and after they drink coffee, and so wouldn't have any people who *thought* they had drunk coffee, but really did not. If you compared two separate groups, however, then you can look at this and separate the placebo effect from the real effect of coffee. (In fact, if I did this study for real I would probably also use a third group, who had nothing at all to drink – this would give me three measures: the effect of no drink at all [baseline 1], the effect of pretend coffee [baseline 2 – the placebo measure] and the effect of real coffee.)

So both approaches have strengths and weaknesses, and in each experiment you design you need to weigh these up and make what you think is the best decision. Often there is no 'right' answer, and you need to use your judgement. If you want to know whether practice makes people better at juggling, you could either look at a single group of people, before and after they practice, or you could compare a group who have had a lot of practice with a group who have not. If you want to know whether owning pets makes people happier, you could either test a single group of people before and after they get pets, or you could take a group who have pets and another group who don't have pets and compare their happiness levels.

Sometimes, however, you have no choice about the design. For example, if you are interested in sex differences, you simply have to use an independent-samples design and compare a group of men with a group of women. If you are interested in the effects of ten years of practice on some task or other, you've no choice but to compare people who have had ten years of practice with people who have not – there's no way you can wait around for ten years to perform a repeated-measures study! (Having said that, sometimes psychologists do wait around a long time to look at how a single group of people changes. This is called a **longitudinal study**, and is particularly important in developmental studies. By following a single group of people over a period of months or years, we can get really good data on how and when people change and what factors predict who will change and who will not.)

Matched-pairs designs: a special type of independent-samples study

Before we move on, I'd like briefly to mention the **matched-pairs design**, which is partway between an independent-samples design and a repeated-measures design and has some of the advantages of both. With a matched-pairs study you have two groups of people, but the people aren't completely unrelated like they are in an independent-samples design. Instead, each person in the first group is paired with a similar person in the second group. For example, let's say you were doing a study on how easily car drivers get distracted, and let's say you had a 20-year-old woman with two years' driving experience in the 'distraction' group. In this case, you'd make sure you also had a 20-year-old woman with two years' driving experience in the 'no distraction' group. You get all the advantages of having two separate groups but, in addition, because each person in the first group is closely matched to a person in the second, if you see any difference between the two groups you know this can't be a result of differences in age, driving experience, or any of the other things you matched.

The most extreme form of the matched-pairs design is the **twin study**, where each person in the first group is paired with somebody in the second group who is genetically identical and who has had a very similar upbringing. Let's say you gave one twin from each pair some sort of treatment, leaving the other as a control. If you saw a difference between the two groups at the end of this study, it is difficult for anybody to explain this away as being the result of having tested two different groups of people, because the groups are almost identical – the difference is much more likely to be the result of your experimental manipulation.

Different locations for experiments: laboratory, field and naturalistic experiments

Most scientific experiments are what we would call **laboratory experiments**. This doesn't necessarily mean they are carried out in a room full of test tubes, retort stands and white coats; it just means we carry them out in a consistent, controlled environment. For example, we might choose to study people's reaction times in a quiet, empty room rather than in the street, as the quiet room is more consistent and has fewer distractions.

However, a common criticism of laboratory studies is that they can lack **ecological validity**. Imagine we are carrying out a social psychological experiment to look at how people make friends. Because we always like to have lots of control in our experiments, we might carry out the procedure in a quiet room where we can be sure all the participants have exactly the same experience. This control and consistency is great, because it removes the risk that the results will be affected by extraneous variables. But the thing is, people don't usually meet one another in quiet laboratories. So will this study really tell us about how people make friends in the real world? Perhaps it would be better to carry out the experiment in the sorts of places people really meet one another – cafes, bars or whatever. If we did carry out our experiment in this sort of place, we would be conducting a **field experiment**. Field experiments involve doing research in the places where the results are most relevant, rather than in a laboratory.

The findings of field experiments tend to have more ecological validity because they don't come from artificial environments, but at the same time they might be less reliable because the experimenter had less control over each person's experience during the study, and there might be extraneous influences (if we carry out our friendship study in a cafe, perhaps people's experiences would be affected by the background music being played there without our realizing it). So there is always a trade-off when you perform an experiment. If you want more control, you work in a laboratory; if you want more ecological validity you work in the field. Usually, if you *really* want to understand a subject, you need to use both approaches. You might carry out a study in the field and then see if you can **replicate** the finding in the laboratory; or you might find something new in a laboratory study and then see if you can replicate the effect in the natural environment. Using multiple sources of evidence like this, to work towards a better understanding, is sometimes known as **triangulation**.

The final kind of experiment you need to know about is one where there is a naturally occurring manipulation, rather than a manipulation you control. Imagine there are two schools near where you live, and you learn that the children at one of the schools are all about to be put onto a special diet. The diet is happening anyway – it wasn't your idea – but you can still study its effects by comparing the children at the two schools. If you did, this would be a **naturalistic experiment**, where you use a natural manipulation, or at least a manipulation outside your control, as the independent variable.

Assigning people to conditions, and quasi-experiments

Something I hope that you've now understood is that, when we use experiments, we are trying very hard to get reliable results which cannot later be questioned. In particular, we want to avoid any possible confounds or **bias**. If our study was biased in some way, the results would be suspect. To take a slightly extreme example, let's say I was carrying out an experiment, inspired by public lotteries, to see whether suddenly becoming rich made people happier. I might do this by taking a group of people and making half of them rich overnight, to see whether those people became happier than the control group.

The right way of doing this, like with most experiments, would be to assign each participant randomly to either the 'suddenly rich' group or the control group. If I assign each person randomly to one of the two groups, there can be no bias – the two groups should end up looking pretty similar before the experiment, which means I can fairly compare them.

But let's say I forget to do random allocation, and instead I simply ask people which group they want to be in. I'm sure you can imagine what would happen – everybody would want to be in the 'suddenly rich' group! My control group, if it had anybody in it at all, would probably be made up of people who were already super-rich and didn't want a few extra millions. I'm sure you can see that if I didn't assign people randomly to the two conditions, I could easily end up with biased groups and I would probably learn very little from comparing the two. *If two groups start out looking different, you have learnt nothing if they end up looking different* – they might end up different because they started that way, rather than because of the experimental manipulation.

So assigning participants to conditions at random is a really useful way of avoiding bias, and strictly speaking an experiment is only a true experiment if you do assign people randomly. But sometimes you don't have this option. The study I mentioned in the last section, where some children were assigned to a diet group and some to a control group, did not use random allocation. Any experiment that doesn't use proper random allocation is officially known as a **quasi-experiment**.

Chapter summary

There are various types of quantitative research, and perhaps the most important is the experiment. In an experiment you manipulate a variable and look for any effects on another variable while keeping everything else constant. If you see changes in the variable you are observing whenever you make a manipulation, you can be pretty sure that the manipulation caused those changes.

Chapter 5

Qualitative research and questionnaires

In the city of Bath, where I work, hot-air ballooning is a popular pastime. But, although I often see balloons soaring over the city in the evenings, I know practically nothing about what ballooning involves. So what would I do if I were asked to study ballooning? How could I decide which variables I need to measure? And, perhaps more importantly, what would I do if I wanted to know *why* people enjoy riding hot-air balloons, or what ballooning might tell us about bigger issues, such as the state of our society?

The thing is, there are many subjects in psychology where it is difficult to take measurements – or where taking measurements is just the wrong way to go about answering questions. Perhaps, like with my study of ballooning, we want to look at a topic that hasn't been investigated in the past, which means we don't have a theory to test and don't know what needs to be measured. And what about the question of why people enjoy ballooning? How could I measure something as complex and personal as 'enjoyment'? Sure, I could manipulate balloon rides, perhaps seeing whether people who have smooth landings are more likely to take another ride than people who have bumpy landings. But would that really tell me about the *experience* of riding in a hot-air balloon, and why people do it? I don't think it would.

With areas like this it's often good to turn away from measurements and experiments and use a whole different approach: **qualitative research**. Qualitative research learns lessons from what people write and say. It is often more exploratory than the approach I have described so far, and tries to develop theories and uncover new understandings, rather than testing predictions.

Qualitative research is a big and complex area, and I can't hope to explain all its subtleties and subdivisions in one short chapter. But I'd like to mention a few aspects of the subject that really show the differences from **quantitative research** – the scientific approach described in the rest of this book. Take, for example, the issue of objectivity. Most quantitative researchers try to be as **objective** and scientific as possible, and go to great lengths to make sure that their findings are not affected by their own beliefs, ideas or expectations. As a result, they will usually try to be as 'hands-off' as possible when carrying out a study, to avoid influencing the results.

A qualitative researcher, on the other hand, will probably be much more involved with the people they are studying. They might spend hours interviewing people, or might even embed themselves in a community for years to study it from within, becoming friends with the very people they are investigating – hardly a recipe for remaining objective. In research like this, the findings will be 'filtered' through the researcher; they will be affected by that researcher's personality, beliefs and experiences. In short, if you and I both interview the same person, the interview would unfold differently and different ideas might emerge from it, purely because you and I are not the same.

Of course, people who use qualitative research know this, but they deal with the issue in various ways. Some see it as a concern, and try to be totally open about the research process: they include a section in each report to describe themselves and their outlook – something Carla Willig[1] calls *personal reflexivity*. Most disagree with the idea that it's possible to do research objectively, and some turn the issue around, arguing that being subjective is actually a strength of the qualitative method.

Another big contrast from quantitative methods is that the use of qualitative methods is often closely tied to the researcher's beliefs or philosophies. Like many researchers, I switch between quantitative and qualitative methods as necessary, depending on what I want to investigate (or use both at the same time, an approach known as **mixed methods**). But for some people the decision to work qualitatively goes deeper. For example, some feminists feel that the scientific approach to research disadvantages women – they argue that it asks questions that interest the researcher, rather than trying to learn what women want to

---

1   Willig, C. (2008). *Introducing Qualitative Research in Psychology*. Open University Press.

talk about – and so deliberately use qualitative methods in an attempt to let participants speak in their own voices. Other psychologists use qualitative methods because they believe that for many of the things we study in psychology, there isn't a single 'true' reality out there for us to measure, and so 'scientific' measurements cannot work (I'll say more about this in a moment).

The qualitative research process

Qualitative research tends to be an involved and flexible business. With quantitative work, such as an experiment, there is a clear series of stages: develop a research question, develop a hypothesis, design a study, collect data, analyse the data to see what they tell you and then write it all up. But with qualitative work the process is different. We still begin with a research question, but we probably wouldn't try to test a prediction in the same way as in an experiment – instead, we would want our understanding of the subject to emerge from the data that are collected. And in particular, after we collect some data, we might repeatedly go back and refine the question we want to investigate, then collect some more data, then again refine the question in light of those data, trying to get closer to a deep understanding of the subject.

Qualitative data and how they are collected

Qualitative research often works by collecting people's words, and using these as clues about the subject being studied. Of course, as with every aspect of qualitative research, there is more than one idea about what words tell us! Some people believe that our words are descriptive. For instance, if you ask me how I feel about fashion, and I tell you, then my words *describe* my feelings. But as I mentioned above, others believe that words essentially *make* reality, rather than describe it. They would say that there is no such thing as 'fashion', existing somewhere out there in the world for us to study. Instead, 'fashion' exists only because we talk about it – we 'construct' it through our words, and the way we all talk about the subject determines what it is. This means that 'fashion' will be different things for different people in different cultures at different times. The same would be true for many of the things we study in psychology, including mental illness and social relationships.

So words are a big part of qualitative research, whatever we take them to mean. But where do the words come from in a study? In principle, any words will do: we could certainly study news reports or webpages, for example, to look at changing ideas about a subject. But perhaps the most important sources of qualitative data are interviews and focus groups. Individuals, or small groups, might be asked to discuss a topic while the researcher records that discussion. These interviews might be carefully planned, or they might be more free-flowing and improvised, depending on what seems best for the subject you are studying – you can't really stick to a rigid interview schedule when questioning drug-takers in nightclub toilets, for example!

Because people's words are so important in qualitative analysis, researchers are often careful to transcribe people's speech as accurately as possible. Interview transcription is almost an art form, and a good transcript provides a rich source of data. Sometimes the analysis might be as simple as spotting themes that came up more than once, but with some approaches, such as a technique called *Conversation Analysis*, every pause and stutter is potentially important. For this reason, a good transcript tries to record all this information. Here is a short section of transcript from when I interviewed a group of bus drivers about their driving experience.

> **IW:** I suppose just quickly (..) er e we may as well just sort of go round for this one (.) erm (.) how long have you been driving and how long have you been driving *buses?*
>
> **'Dave':** well I've been I've been a car driver for uh twenty-nine years
>
> **IW:** uh-huh
>
> **'Dave':** err bus driver for about a year and a half (.) also ride a motorbike and I've (…) obviously done a lot of cycling as well
>
> **IW:** mm-hm

You can see how this transcript tries to code all the pauses, from short, almost imperceptible pauses (.) to longer breaks (…), as well as the way people's talk is full of false starts, changes in stress or tone, and various umm-ing noises. Some researchers would even try to code body movements, glances and all the other ways that communication could be taking place.

As well as interviews and focus groups, another important approach to qualitative research, which I should mention briefly, is **participant observation** or **ethnography**, where the researcher spends time immersed among a group of people they want to understand, collecting data on real behaviours and language. The researcher might be open about the fact they are observing people (but risk their behaviour changing as a result) or secretive (but raise ethical concerns by observing people without their consent). Either way, the researcher is trying to get some insight from inside a group or culture which they might not otherwise see.

Research with questionnaires

I have included questionnaires in this chapter for convenience, but you should know that questionnaires can easily be entirely quantitative, entirely qualitative, or somewhere in between. This is because each question on a questionnaire can collect one type of data or the other. To give you a feel for this, I'll quickly run through the main types of question that might be used. It should be pretty clear which questions give quantitative measurements and which provide more qualitative, language-based data.

A really important thing you should know about questionnaires is that almost any question can be asked in more than one way, and one of the big skills of questionnaire design is deciding how best to ask each question. For example, let's say I wanted to discover how old people are. I could simply ask 'How old are you?' and give a space for people to enter their response, or I could give people a list of categories, such as '15 to 20', '20 to 25' and so on, and ask them to choose one. Or, I could present people with a big empty box and say 'Tell me about yourself...', letting them write whatever they like. All of these are valid ways of asking somebody about their age, but each does a slightly different job. The last version, for example, where the question doesn't even mention age, might tell me whether each person sees their age as an important part of who they are. Somebody who writes 'I've just had my eighty-fifth birthday!' probably sees their age as more important than somebody who doesn't even mention it.

Categorical questions

Categorical questions ask people to choose one category from a list. For example, we might ask the following question to a group of workers:

What do you do at this organization? (please mark one answer)
- Construction work
- Office work
- Management
- Other (please specify)

This type of question gives you mainly quantitative data – you count up how often each category was chosen – and is useful because it can help avoid bad responses. For example, imagine you asked some workers 'What do you do at this organization?' and just left a space for people to write whatever they liked. In this case, you would find people who don't understand what sort of answer you want, and so write things like 'I turn up, do my work then go home of course'; and you would find people who write jokey answers like 'As little as possible LOL!' If you give people categories to choose, this shows them exactly what sort of information you are looking for.

However, with this type of question you need to think of the categories in advance, and that might be difficult if you're trying to study a subject you don't know well – unless you already know something about what you are studying you might not know which categories matter. And if you forget to include an important category, you might miss out on useful data. For this reason, it's always a good idea to include an 'other' category. When checking your data, count up how many people used the 'other' category. If it's only a few, this suggests you chose a good set of categories; but if lots of people checked 'other' then you obviously missed something out.

Likert scales

Named after Rensis Likert, who developed it, this type of question gives people a sliding scale for their response. For example:

How much do you like sandwiches?

Not at all   1   2   3   4   5   6   7   A great deal

I'm slightly obsessed with Likert scales, and could probably write a whole chapter on them. But to keep things simple, our main decision is how many points we will put on the scale, and the first big question is do we use an even or an odd number of points? If you use an even number, people *have* to lean towards one end of the scale or the other as there will be no midpoint; but if you use an odd number then people can say that they are undecided, or have no preference. And how many points do you use? To make a long story short, you probably shouldn't use more than about seven as otherwise it makes the question too complicated.

Likert scales give you quantitative, numerical data, which are quite easy to process. For example, you can say 'On average, people rated sandwiches at 5.7 on a seven-point scale' or '86% of people rated sandwiches at 5 or above'. (However, try to remember Likert scales when you read Chapter 12, and ask yourself which level of measurement they really work on.)

Open questions

Here people are allowed to respond to a question in their own words. For example, 'Tell us about the service you received today ...' followed by a blank space for the respondent to write whatever they like. Clearly these questions give you qualitative information, and as such you will process the data differently, reporting them as I'll describe in Chapter 15, with a focus on the words people use. You'll probably be more interested in how often certain topics are mentioned, and whether certain key words appear, rather than straightforward numerical measurements.

Summary

There are different types of question available for questionnaires. Importantly, it is usually possible to ask the same question in different ways, and a key skill is choosing the most appropriate form of each question.

Validity and reliability

Validity and reliability are important ideas that crop up all over research, but they're easiest to explain when thinking about questionnaires and so I've decided to introduce them here.

Imagine I've developed a questionnaire which measures how much people like hats. If somebody gets a high score on this scale then they like hats a lot and if somebody gets a low score they detest hats. There are a couple of important questions we could ask about my questionnaire: is it *valid* and is it *reliable*?

Validity tells us whether a scale measures what it claims to measure. I've said that my questionnaire measures how much people like hats. If my new research tool is valid, then it will indeed measure feelings about hats. But if it is invalid then it will be measuring something else, or nothing at all.

Most simply, a measure like this should have *face validity*. *On the face of it*, does it look like the questionnaire will work? If my questionnaire doesn't include the word 'hat' anywhere, and just asks lots of questions about frogs and teapots, then it doesn't have face validity: it simply doesn't look like a questionnaire about hats and so probably isn't one.

However, it's possible that my questionnaire is very clever, and measures people's feelings about hats without their realizing. So a lack of face validity doesn't necessarily prove that my questionnaire is invalid. How else could we tell if my questionnaire really measures feelings about hats? One way would be to see whether people who get a high score on my scale buy more hats over the next six months. They certainly should do, shouldn't they, if they really like hats more? If we can predict people's future behaviour from the questionnaire like this, then we say the questionnaire has *predictive validity*.

The final major measure of validity is *criterion validity*: can the questionnaire separate existing groups of people? So in this case, do people with big hat collections get higher scores on my scale than people with no hats? All these tests get at the same idea of whether the scale really measures what it claims to measure.

Reliability, on the other hand, looks at whether the questionnaire works consistently. First, is it consistent within itself, so that all the questions measure the same thing? This is called *internal reliability* – in a questionnaire that only measures feelings about hats, all the questions should be on this topic. A question that is about something else is inconsistent.

Second, is the questionnaire consistent over time? If I test a person twice, do they get a similar score both times? This consistency over time is known as *stability*. Things like personality don't change suddenly. So if I measure your personality today and measure it again tomorrow, I really should be getting a very similar measurement. If I don't, this suggests my measure isn't reliable.

Summary

Any sort of psychological measure, such as a personality questionnaire, should be valid (it should measure what it claims to measure) and it should be reliable (it should measure consistently). If not, we need to ask whether we really should be using that measure.

⦿ Chapter summary

Qualitative research describes a range of non-experimental approaches with which we can study complex and difficult subjects, such as people's feelings and attitudes. Another important research method is the questionnaire, which can be quantitative and/or qualitative.

Chapter 6

Research ethics

If you ever study social psychology, you will almost certainly encounter a whole range of classic studies from the 1940s to the 1970s which, today, would not be allowed. Back then it was pretty routine to lie to participants, to electrocute them, to set groups fighting against other groups and to scare people silly without their even knowing they were being studied. Today, though, we are much more aware of the implications of what we do when we carry out research with people, and take seriously the **ethics** of research. This is to protect our participants (who, after all, are giving their time to help our research, and so deserve respect in return) and also to protect ourselves – a researcher is much less likely to find themselves in legal hot water if they carry out their work according to ethical principles.

Perhaps the main principle that should underpin all our research is that people should come to no harm as a result of taking part in a psychological study, and that they should leave the study in just the same state as they went in. As such, you need to think carefully about what the procedure will involve, and change any plans that might reasonably lead to harm.

There are also a whole load of other ethical issues which need to be considered. As a way of introducing these I am going to present several short descriptions of studies, and for each I will highlight the main ethical issues that arise. This will, I believe, make it much easier for you to see the sorts of issues that we need to consider than if I just list issues one by one.

Scenario 1: A teacher hands out some questionnaires at the start of a lesson and says they will collect the completed questionnaires at the end

There are a couple of possible issues here. First, it is a basic principle of all research with people that participants should be able to give **informed**

consent for taking part. That is, they should know what the study is about and, knowing exactly what they are getting into, they should have a free choice over whether or not to take part.

Let's assume the teacher has told their students what the questionnaire is about, as they should have done. There's still the problem that these students perhaps don't have a free choice about whether or not to take part: the teacher is in a position of power over the students, and will know who did and who did not take part in the study. This puts the students under pressure to go along with the study, so they're not really free to decide.

There's also a second problem: imagine you are in this class and decide you'd rather not take part in the survey. It's going to be really obvious to the teacher, *and to everyone else in the room*, that you are not filling in the survey. This could lead to your being singled out, and this is not acceptable.

The ideal solution to both these issues would be for the teacher to say something like 'Here are some questionnaires. It's up to you whether or not you fill them in – take them away and do them in your own time. If you do take part, I'll leave a box in the corridor where you can drop off your questionnaires later.' This way, people have complete freedom to choose whether or not they take part in the study, and nobody can know who did and who did not take part.

Another issue here is that everybody taking part in a study should have the right to **confidentiality**. The teacher in this study would be under a duty to protect the identities of everybody who takes part, and the easiest and most effective way to do this would be simply not to ask people for their names on the questionnaire, or for any other information which would identify an individual. This would also remove the issue of the teacher perhaps – even subconsciously – punishing people who didn't take part.

As a practical point, making questionnaires anonymous is almost always a good idea anyway because people are more likely to take part in a survey when their responses are anonymous, and are more likely to tell the truth. However, this becomes a problem if you want to carry out a follow-up survey later – you need some way to match up each person's first questionnaire with their second, and this means you need to know who each questionnaire comes from.

We were faced with just this issue in a research project. Our solution was to make our survey anonymous, but then ask people to write a memorable word or phrase on the first questionnaire, and to remember this and also write it on the second. That way, we could match up the first and second questionnaire while still keeping the participants completely anonymous. It worked a treat.

Key ethical issues in this scenario

- *Informed consent:* participants should be able to decide whether or not they take part in research, knowing exactly what it will involve.
- *Avoiding distress or stigma:* people should not be made to feel bad either through taking part in a study, or through deciding they do not want to take part.
- *Confidentiality:* people who take part in a study should have their information kept private.
- *Anonymity:* keeping people anonymous is useful for protecting their privacy, and for encouraging open responses.

> **Scenario 2:** A sample of workers have their job motivation assessed before and after taking an amphetamine drug stimulant. They are told they are taking part in a survey of mood, and that the pill is caffeine

Here, again, we have the issue of informed consent. In this study the participants are being lied to, and this is ethically very problematic – they are taking part in the study without fully knowing what they are getting themselves into. It is tempting just to say 'never lie to participants', but the problem is that in some studies lying can be necessary, because if people knew the true purpose of the study they would behave differently and we would not get useful data from them. For example, let's say you were looking at whether people prefer looking at websites with lots of graphics or lots of text. If you explicitly told people, at the start of the study, 'We're looking at whether people prefer websites with lots of graphics or lots of text' then they will very deliberately focus on these things, and you probably wouldn't get a good, realistic measure of people's first impressions of websites. In this case, you might want to use a small amount of deception, saying that it is a study of how people feel about different websites, rather than mentioning that the real hypothesis is about text and graphics.

In that example, the deception is very minor and the subject matter is uncontroversial, and as long as people are told the full facts at the end of the study I can't imagine too many people having a problem with that study. But if you are looking at any sort of controversial subject, or considering deeper deception, think carefully. Although occasionally it is necessary to deceive participants in a study, it is best whenever possible not to do this. Always try to think of a different way of carrying out the study that doesn't involve deceit, and be sure to get a deception study signed off by an ethics committee or some other body that can oversee research. Don't go down the road of lying to participants on your own, as if a participant later objects to being lied to, you could find yourself in a heap of trouble.

In research that does involve deception, it is really important to end the study with a **debrief** – a document, or conversation, which tells the participants exactly what the study was really about, and which makes sure they leave the study unaffected by having taken part. A good debrief should tell people where they can go for support if they suffer any ill-effects from the study – which could be vital in the example given here. What if one of the participants was a former amphetamine addict? They've taken this drug again without knowing it and could suffer all sorts of terrible consequences as a result. The experimenter would be under a serious duty to make sure there were no negative repercussions. (In reality, I can't imagine this study ever being allowed.)

Key ethical issues in this scenario

- *Deception:* wherever possible, you should not lie to participants as this means they are not able to make fully informed consent.
- *Debrief:* at the end of a study, people should usually be presented with full information about the research, and should be able to ask questions. The aim is to get people back to the state they would have been in had they not taken part in the study.

> **Scenario 3:** A researcher sets up hidden cameras overlooking a street and takes photographs of groups of people. They then put photographs of these groups on a public website and survey people's attitudes to the photographs

There are some interesting questions here regarding privacy, and informed consent. It sounds as though the researcher is photographing the groups without their permission. Normally, this would be a problem, but in many countries (but not all!) people in public places, like a public street, are actually considered 'fair game' for being photographed from a legal perspective, and so perhaps taking the photographs isn't so bad. But putting them on a public website? Again, legally this might not be a problem, but ethically ...?

Personally, I wouldn't be happy with this study as it is described. If I were carrying this out I would perhaps take the groups' photographs and then immediately approach them, show them the images and ask whether they were happy for those pictures to be used in research. I would offer instantly to delete any images they did not want to be used.

On the other hand, if the images were only for my own research use – for example, if I was just going to use them to measure how close people stand to one another, and just report these distances without identifying the people – I would see fewer problems here.

Key ethical issues in this scenario

- *Informed consent:* participants should be able to decide whether or not they take part in research, knowing exactly what it will involve.
- *Privacy:* people who take part in a study should have their information kept private. This is closely related to the issue of confidentiality.

Scenario 4: Ten-year-old schoolchildren are given a questionnaire in class on their attitudes to abortion. All fill it in together during a break between lessons

There are some interesting questions about consent here. Who gives it? The children? Certainly, they should be consulted about whether or not they want to take part in the study, but in most countries, minors are seen as not legally capable of making fully informed decisions. The researchers would almost certainly need to get permission from the school's head, and probably also from the children's parents, as well as from the children.

There is also the issue here that the children are being surveyed on a sensitive topic. Does this study really need to go ahead? Assuming it is important enough to be justified, there really needs to be a lot of consideration given to the subject matter.

There is also an issue that the children are all being asked to fill in the questionnaire at the same time. This is a bit like the first scenario, where it is difficult for somebody to refuse to take part without drawing attention to themselves. A neat solution that can help here is to write something on the front of the survey like 'You don't have to take part in this project. If you don't want to do it, here's a short crossword puzzle [or a Sudoku, or whatever] you might want to solve while other people do the survey'. This means people who don't want to take part can still do some writing at the same time as everybody else, and no attention is drawn to them because they didn't take part.

Key ethical issues in this scenario

- *Informed consent:* participants should be able to decide whether or not they take part in research, knowing exactly what it will involve. In this case, the issue is more difficult because the participants are legally minors, and so consent should also be obtained from other responsible people. There are situations where even adult participants might not be able to give informed consent, such as when studying people with mental illnesses.
- *Avoiding distress or stigma:* people should not be made to feel bad either through taking part in a study, or through deciding they do not want to take part.

> **Scenario 5:** I conduct an anonymous online survey of workplace bullying. There are 20 questions, people are free to skip any questions they don't want to answer and they are told they can stop taking part at any stage

On the face of it, this might sound fine. It's an online survey, so people are under no pressure to take part; participants are kept anonymous, which is important; and they are being told they can ignore any questions they don't want to answer (which is often good practice for a survey).

Two major issues come to mind, however. First, as with all studies, people need to be told *in advance* what the study will be about so that they are informed before taking part. And second, I need to give some thought to what might happen to people as a result of taking part. For example, imagine the survey has a question like this:

'Have you ever been bullied at work – for example, have you ever been teased, hit, pushed or sworn at repeatedly?'

And imagine a person reads this and thinks 'Hold on … yes, my boss swears at me all the time. I'd never thought of that as bullying, but now I see that I *am* being bullied at work! Oh no!' Alternatively, there might be a question that asks people to describe an example of being bullied at work, and some people who answer this question get traumatized by remembering incidents they have experienced. In both cases, people are worse off because they have taken part in my study, and I have to make sure that my debrief, at the end of the study, tells them what they can do to deal with any issues that are raised. They need to end the study just as happy as they would be if they had never taken part, because if they don't, I've made their lives worse by asking them to be involved in my study. I might, therefore, refer people to sources of counselling or support.

In any study, and particularly one on a difficult topic like this, participants should know that they are free to leave the study at any time at all, and that there will be no consequences of their doing so. This means that if people are being paid to take part in a study, they still get paid if they decide to leave partway through because they don't feel comfortable.

Key ethical issues in this scenario

- *Informed consent:* participants should be able to decide whether or not they take part in research, knowing exactly what it will involve.
- *People may be harmed by taking part in the study:* in this case, taking part in the study may cause them to relive traumatic experiences. We deal with this through careful debriefs, and through helping people find support if they need it.

◉ Professional bodies

You can probably see that conducting ethical research can be a minefield, and there is a huge amount to think about – I've tried to cover the big issues above, but there are all sorts of other things that researchers need to think about, some of them surprisingly subtle.

To help in this process, there are various professional bodies around the world which issue guidelines for researchers. In the United Kingdom, psychologists usually work within guidelines from the British Psychological Society, which can be found on their website; in the USA, the American Psychological Association have their own (similar) guidelines. It is an excellent idea to read the documents these organizations provide.

◉ Chapter summary

Research is conducted within ethical guidelines that protect the participants and the researchers. Key points involve getting informed consent from people who take part in research, avoiding deception wherever possible, and doing everything you can to make sure people suffer no ill-effects from taking part in your studies.

Section summary

Welcome to the world of statistics, where we use numbers to help make sense of the world. The use of statistics falls into two main parts. The first (and smallest) part of the field is *descriptive statistics*, which is all about taking a set of numbers and summarizing them in a useful way. You will already be familiar with a lot of this; I am sure you have, at some point, used the words 'on average ...' or drawn a graph. If so, you have used descriptive statistics. There is no real mystery about descriptive statistics, and in the next two chapters I will take you through the main things you need to know.

The other, larger, branch of statistics is called *inferential statistics*. Let's say that, after summarizing your numbers, you see something interesting. For example, you might have two groups of people who have taken a test and, when you summarize their scores, you see that one group performed better than the other. Once you see an effect like this, you can use inferential statistics to decide whether the effect is worth getting excited about. Inferential statistics will tell you whether what you have seen in the people you studied will generalize to other people you haven't tested. This new drug seemed to help the fifty people I tested it on: will it also work for other people? This new teaching method seemed to help the hundred students I studied: is it likely to work for other students? Inferential statistics answer questions just like these.

What I am saying, then, is that using statistics is usually a two-step process: first you use descriptive statistics to summarize the numbers you have collected, then you use inferential statistics to decide whether other people in the future would look the same as the ones you tested.

I will have plenty to say about the second stage, inferential statistics, soon. But before any of that, you need to know how to summarize and describe the numbers you have, and that is the job of descriptive statistics. So in the next chapter we will look at describing numbers using statistics and in the chapter after that we will describe numbers using graphs.

Chapter 7

Using statistics to describe research findings

👁 Introduction

Once you have designed a study and carried it out, you will have **data**: measurements from the people you tested. For example, let's say you have timed how long it takes 50 people to solve a puzzle. This would give you 50 scores, one from each person. This is great, but not enough: you then have to decide what you will do with these numbers.

The first thing you need to do is summarize the data, so you and other people can see clearly what the data show. In this chapter we will look at some ways of summarizing data with numbers, and in the next chapter we'll look at ways of summarizing data with graphs.

In this chapter we will examine:
- What are measures of central tendency and measures of dispersion?
- The most important measures of central tendency (the mean, median and mode) and the most important measures of dispersion (the range and the standard deviation).

👁 Describing your numbers

The first thing we need to look at is *why* we use statistics to summarize research findings. To give you some idea of why statistics are so useful for summing up the data we collect in research, I took some people from two local colleges and asked everybody how old they were. Here are the ages I got:

College A	College B
18	0
19	10
20	20
21	30
22	40

Let's say I wanted to share this set of numbers with you. How could I best do that?

Perhaps the most obvious way would be for me simply to show you the ten numbers in the table. That way, you would have exactly the same information I have, and nothing could possibly be lost or hidden from you.

But would you really want me to share my numbers with you in this way? It would probably be fine if we were talking about just ten people, like here. But what if, instead of ten people's ages, I had the ages of ten thousand people? What if I was working on a national census, and had the ages of everybody in the country? Presenting millions of numbers to you would tell you nothing – in fact, it would leave you thoroughly confused and I would have failed to share my data effectively. So just giving people raw numbers is usually not very helpful.

What we need instead is a way of *refining* raw numbers before we pass them on. You might have heard of refining factories: they turn raw materials into useful products. Refining factories turn oil into plastics, or plants into sugar. Descriptive statistics do something very similar. They let us take raw numbers, like those above, and boil them down into useful summaries.

No matter how large a set of numbers is, we can usually sum it up nicely by calculating just two statistics – that is, by calculating two numbers. The first statistic we use for describing a set of numbers is a measure of **central tendency**, and the second statistic is a measure of **dispersion**. A measure of central tendency describes the midpoint in a set of numbers – the 'average', in other words. If I tell you that the average height of a group of people is 176 cm, I have given you a measure of central tendency. A measure of dispersion tells us how much the numbers are spread out around this average. Let's look at these two types of statistic in turn.

◉ Central tendency: finding the midpoint of some numbers

Think about any group of people to which you belong: the people you work with or study with, perhaps, or maybe your family. How do you compare with the other people in that group? Are you taller than most, or shorter? Are you younger than most, or older?

There's no way you can answer questions like this unless you know the *typical* height or *typical* age in the group. If you know what the typical age of the group is, you can easily see whether you are above or below this.

People often describe the 'typical' value in a set of numbers as the 'average'. But the word 'average' is one of those words people use in everyday talk without really thinking about exactly what it means, so let's just think about it for a moment. If you want to know whether you are tall or short compared to the other people in a group, what exactly is it you need to know? The answer is that you need to know how tall the people in the *middle* of the group are. Once you know how tall the people in the middle are, you can easily tell whether you are above or below this. If you are above the height of the people in the middle, then you must be taller than most people, and if you are below the height of the people in the middle then you must be shorter than most people.

So when we summarize a set of numbers we focus on the middle of those numbers. This is why, when we talk about 'averages' in statistics, the proper term is *measures of central tendency*: we want to know where the centre of some numbers is. If I have a group of people who are, on average, 176 cm tall, this means 176 cm is in the middle of those people's heights.

There are actually several different measures of central tendency that we use, and here we will look at the three most common. The first two – called the mean and the median – do a very similar job, and describe the midpoint in a set of numbers in the way I've just explained. The third measure of central tendency – the mode – does a slightly different job: it just looks at how often things happen and tells us the most common.

Summary

There is more than one way of measuring the 'average' of a set of numbers. Together these are called measures of central tendency, because they describe the midpoint of the numbers.

Measures of central tendency 1: the mean

The most well-known measure of central tendency is the **mean**, which is what most people are talking about when they use the word 'average'. The mean is just all your numbers added together, then divided by however many numbers there were. You have very likely come across this idea before.

To see how the mean works, let's take College A from the start of this chapter, where the people are aged 18, 19, 20, 21 and 22. If we want to know the mean age of this group – that is, if we want to know the 'average', or middle age – we simply add the five numbers together and divide by five (because there are five numbers). Give it a try:

	Age
Person 1	18
Person 2	19
Person 3	20
Person 4	21
Person 5	22
Add all the ages together:	____
Divide this number by 5: (because there are 5 people)	____ ← *This is the mean age*

You should have found a mean age of 20. As you can see, this mean age of 20 is right in the middle of the various people's ages and this is exactly what we want, as the mean is a measure of *central* tendency and so should tell us the midpoint in a set of scores.

The mean gets used all the time, and most people understand it – especially if you call it the average. However, you do have to watch out because the mean can sometimes give 'silly' answers. For example, thanks to the fact a few people have lost legs in accidents, the 'average' person has slightly fewer than two legs!

There is another problem with the mean, which is that it can easily get distorted if we have very high or very low numbers in a set of data. Let's calculate the mean age again, but this time we'll add one more person to our group:

	Age
Person 1	18
Person 2	19
Person 3	20
Person 4	21
Person 5	22
Person 6	110

Add the ages together: ____

Divide this number by 6:   ____   ← *This is the mean age*
(because there are 6 people)

What has happened to the mean age now? You should have found that adding this one older person to the group has shifted the mean age from 20 all the way to 35. This one person, whose age is higher than all the others, has totally distorted the group's average age. The 'average' is now no longer in the middle of the ages, as we want it to be. This is something you should always look out for when using the mean: extreme numbers can seriously distort the statistic. We call these extreme numbers **outliers**, because they lie a long way outside the rest of the numbers.

Measures of central tendency 2: the median

The **median** is another way of describing the midpoint in a set of numbers. Whereas you had to do some calculations to find the mean, the median describes the midpoint of some numbers in a very literal way: you line up your numbers, from the lowest to the highest, and the median number is just the one sitting right in the middle. Simple, no? Here are the ages of our five people again, arranged in order from the lowest to the highest:

18, 19, **20**, 21, 22

You can easily see that the number sitting in the middle position is 20. This means the median age of these people is 20. It's really that simple.

There is just one small extra detail you need to know about, which is how to find the median when you have an even number of people. As we have just seen, finding the median of five ages is simple because five people is an odd number. When we have an odd number of people and we line their scores up from the lowest to the highest, there will always be just a single score in the middle. But if there is an even number of scores, there will not be a single score in the middle. To show you what I mean, let's add another 22-year-old person to our list:

18, 19, **20**, **21**, 22, 22

Now we have an even number of people there isn't a single middle point. But the solution is really simple: we just take the mean of the two middle scores. In this case, the two scores right in the middle are 20 and 21. We add these together to get 20 + 21 = 41. We then divide this by two, because there were two scores: 41 ÷ 2 = 20.5. So the median age of these 6 people is 20.5.

The big advantage of the median is that, unlike the mean, it isn't really affected by outliers. We saw above how the mean age of our group was seriously distorted when a 110-year-old person was added. Let's see what happens when we calculate the median age of that group instead of the mean. Here are the ages again, arranged in order from the lowest to the highest:

18, 19, 20, 21, 22, 110

There is an even number of people here, so to get the median we need to take the mean of the two middle scores, which again gives us 20.5. So you can see that the median is completely unaffected by the unusually old person who has joined the group. It isn't distorted like the mean was. That's because the median only ever looks at the middle one or two scores, and ignores all the rest.

Measures of central tendency 3: the mode

The **mode** is probably the simplest of the three 'averages' we are considering here. It is just the most common value in a set of numbers. So, for example, if we have the numbers:

3, 6, 3, 8, 3

the mode is 3, because that number appears more often than any other. You can see that the mode measures the most 'typical' number in a very straightforward way.

Summary

There are three main measures of central tendency: the mean (add together all your numbers and divide the total by how many numbers you had), the median (the middle number when they are all in order) and the mode (the most common number).

⊙ If there are three measures of central tendency, which should I use?

Each of these three types of 'average' – each measure of central tendency – gives you a different way to describe a set of numbers. You're very likely wondering at this point why we need more than one way to summarize a set of numbers. The answer is that each of these three measures of central tendency does a different job, and one of the things you need to learn is when to use each of them.

The mean is pretty much our 'default' or 'standard' average. When you need to summarize a set of numbers, you will most likely use the mean. The main reason you would not use the mean is when you have outliers in your data. When your data have some extreme values, which would distort the mean, you will probably use the median instead because, as we saw, outliers don't affect it.

Why not use the median all the time, if it doesn't get distorted? The answer is that because the median only ever looks at the middle one or two numbers in your data, it ignores a whole load of detail. The mean is calculated using all the numbers you have collected, and so contains more information. That's why we usually use the mean to summarize a set of numbers instead of the median, and only use the median when we have to. For example, if I were calculating the median of these numbers:

1, 13, 19, 26, 42, 186, 4096

then I'd get the answer '26' because it sits in the middle. But I've completely ignored all the other numbers. One of my people got a score *way* higher than the others, and that might be really interesting, but I'm ignoring it when I calculate the median.

A useful thing to remember is that the mean and the median do pretty much the same job. They both describe the midpoint of a set of numbers, and whenever you want to describe the midpoint of some numbers you just need to decide if the mean or the median is most appropriate. The mode, on the other hand, does quite a different job from the mean and the median. It is usually used when the numbers you want to summarize come from counting up how often something happened. For example, let's say you are working at a museum, and you ask each visitor where they come from. This might get you some data like this:

Europe	56
North America	24
South America	14
Africa	9
Asia	31

What would you say if you had the information in this table and I asked you 'Where does the 'average' visitor to the museum come from?'

In this case, there is no point working out the mean or the median of these numbers. The mean of those numbers is 26.8 (feel free to check), but that number doesn't answer the question I asked. It doesn't tell you where the 'average' museum visitor comes from. In fact, that number 26.8 doesn't really mean anything at all.

In this case, it would make much more sense to use the mode, which is just the most common measurement. Here, more people come from Europe than from anywhere else. So the 'average' visitor is European if we use the mode, and this makes a lot of sense. We might then use this information to guide our advertising in the future: we know most of our visitors come from Europe so that's the best place to advertise. This gives you a very simple example of how a central tendency statistic might be used to make a decision about something in the real world.

Finally, before we leave averages, I can't resist telling you a quick story. Last year, only a single student had signed up for one of the courses I run. I met him during the first week. 'I'm sorry,' I told him, 'but no matter how hard you work this year, you're only going to get the average mark.' The poor guy's face was a picture for a moment, before he worked it out ...

Summary

The mean and the median do pretty much the same job: they both find the midpoint of a set of numbers. Unless your numbers have some extremely high or low values – outliers – you'll usually use the mean because it looks at all the numbers and so contains more information. The mode is used when you are counting up how often things happen and want to find the most common.

◉ Dispersion: how spread out are your numbers?

So measures of central tendency – averages – give us a way of describing the midpoint in a group of numbers. This is really useful, and working out a measure of central tendency is a major step in refining, or simplifying, a big set of numbers into a form people can understand. Instead of saying 'The numbers I collected were 18, 19, 20, 21, 22 ...' and confusing you, I can simply say 'The mean of the numbers I collected was 20' and you will have a good idea of what I found.

But a measure of central tendency on its own is not enough to describe a set of numbers. Look again at the two groups of people I mentioned at the start of this chapter:

College A	College B
18	0
19	10
20	20
21	30
22	40

The mean age for College A is 20, and the mean age for College B is also 20 (feel free to check). This shows you something important about descriptive statistics. If you tried to describe these two groups of people and only used a measure of central tendency, it would look as though the two groups are the same, when they clearly are not. Although the two groups have exactly the same midpoint, the ages in College B are much more varied than the ages in College A.

So if we want to describe a group of people, we need something else, as well as a measure of central tendency. We need a way of describing how much the numbers vary around their midpoint. We call this a measure of *dispersion*, because it tells us how dispersed (spread out) the scores are. When a measure of dispersion is large, the numbers are very spread out, and when a measure of dispersion is small, the numbers are all similar to one another.

There are several measures of dispersion, but here I only want to talk about two. All the other ways of measuring dispersion are just variations on the two I will describe here, so if you understand these then you'll find the rest very simple.

Summary

When you describe the midpoint in a set of numbers, using the mean or the median, you should also give a measure of dispersion, which tells people how much the numbers are spread out around this midpoint.

Measures of dispersion 1: the range

The range is the simplest measure of dispersion. It is a useful measure because everybody understands it. I could use the range to describe my two groups' ages much more clearly, by saying something like 'The people at College A have a mean age of 20 with a range of ages from 18 to 22; the people at College B have a mean age of 20 with a range of ages from 0 to 40'. This sentence describes the two groups quite well. It shows how, although the groups are the same age on average, there is a different spread of ages in each. With just two statistics – the midpoint and a measure of dispersion – I have summarized the two groups well.

But although the range is very easy to understand, it does have problems. In particular, it is very sensitive to outliers – extremely high or low numbers. A few paragraphs back, when I was talking about the mean, we added a 110-year-old person to our first group. This outlying person affected the mean, as we saw, and they would also affect the range. With this person in the group, the range of ages runs from 18 to 110, which doesn't really describe the group very well: five of the six people had really similar ages, and only one person stood out as being a lot older. But the range doesn't show us this. It only tells us that the ages ranged from 18 to 110, and that might easily exaggerate the amount of variation in the group.

Measures of dispersion 2: the standard deviation

Another way of measuring how spread out are some numbers is the **standard deviation**. This is the most common measure of dispersion, and you will encounter it all the time as you study and use statistics. The standard deviation is not the easiest statistic to understand as it does involve a few calculations, but I'm afraid you'll need to make the effort because it is so important.

Before I explain the calculations, here's a little tip. For a long time I used the standard deviation without properly understanding what it meant. Then, one day, I noticed the answer was in its name. Look at the two words separately before putting them together. Let's start with 'deviation'. We say a number 'deviates' when it is different from the mean. The people in College B had a mean age of 20. So somebody who is aged 30 deviates from this average, and somebody who is aged 40 deviates by even more.

If 'deviation' means 'being different from the average', what about the word 'standard'? In this case it just means 'typical' or 'average'. So the 'standard deviation' is the *typical* or *average* amount of deviation in a set of numbers; it is the typical amount by which each number is different from the mean. If you focus on that, you should be able to understand the standard deviation quite easily.

Using the techniques I'll explain in a moment, I've just analysed the people in College A – the ones aged from 18 to 22 – and found that the standard deviation of their five ages is 1.58. College B, on the other hand, has a standard deviation of 15.81. The standard deviation for College B is much higher, which tells us that the ages in College B vary much more. So think of it this way: in College A, the 'typical' or 'average' person has an age 1.58 years from the mean and in College B the 'typical' or 'average' person has an age 15.81 years from the mean. The ages in College B are much more varied than the ages in College A and these standard deviations reflect this.

Summary

When you see a set of numbers with a large standard deviation, you know those numbers are probably all quite different from one another. A small standard deviation, on the other hand, tells you the numbers are all quite similar.

Calculating the standard deviation

The standard deviation is a fairly easy thing to calculate. There are just two small complications in the process. The first of these is really very simple, and I'll explain it in a moment. The second complication is more difficult to understand: one of the calculations used for working out the standard deviation is not quite what you might expect, and the reasons for this are a little complicated. So for now I'm going to suggest you just trust me, do what I tell you and don't worry too much about why (but I've added a box with some more details in case you are curious).

I said earlier that the standard deviation is the 'typical' amount that each of the scores in a group differs from the mean. Let's see how this works with some real numbers. Let's take our long-suffering people from College A again:

	Age
Person 1	18
Person 2	19
Person 3	20
Person 4	21
Person 5	22

You have already calculated the mean of these five ages, so you know it is 20. Now we want to know how much all these ages deviate (differ) from this mean. Let's start with Person 3: how much does Person 3's age deviate from the mean age of 20? The answer is simple. We just subtract the mean age from Person 3's age:

$$20 - 20 = 0$$

So there is zero deviation (zero difference) between Person 3's age and the mean age for the group. What about person 5? They are 22 years old, so their age deviates from the group mean by 2:

$$22 - 20 = 2$$

We can already see that this person's age deviates from the group mean more than Person 3's age.

So it's pretty easy to see how much each individual person deviates from the group mean. We just subtract the mean age from each person's age and this tells us how far each person is from the mean. Once we've done this, and got the deviation for each person, we just need to work out what is the average of these deviations. This gives us the average, or 'standard', deviation.

Let's have a go at doing all this. I'll do the first lot of calculations for you, to show you how we get the five people's individual deviations:

	Age	**Deviation from the mean** (Age – 20)
Person 1	18	−2
Person 2	19	−1
Person 3	20	0
Person 4	21	1
Person 5	22	2
Mean age:	20	

Now we have each person's deviation, we just need to take the average of these: we add the deviations together and divide by the number of people. But wait! We've come to the first of the two little complications. If we just try to calculate the average of these deviations, something will go wrong. See if you can spot the problem with calculating the mean deviation before you read on, as it'll help you understand better than if I just tell you straight off.

Did you spot the problem? The issue is that if you add together those numbers, they will come to zero: the positive and negative deviations exactly cancel each other out. Let's take a moment to think about this. As we have seen, the mean's job is to describe the midpoint of some numbers. The mean is designed to sit smack-bang in the middle of the set of numbers it is describing. Because the mean is *always* right in the middle of the numbers from which it was calculated, there will always be as much deviation above it as there is below it. The deviations above and below the mean will always add up to zero, and cancel one another out.

So we need a way of stopping the positive and negative numbers cancelling each other out. Look back at the last table, and try to think how we might deal with the negative numbers.

Personally, I'd say the simplest way to stop the negative numbers cancelling out the positive numbers would just be to ignore all the minus signs. As you can see from the table, the five people's deviations are −2, −1, 0, 1 and 2. If we just ignored the minus signs then these numbers would be 2, 1, 0, 1 and 2, and we could happily calculate the mean of these deviations as there are no longer any negative values.

This approach would work just fine, but we don't do it that way. The reason we don't just ignore the minus signs is that the mathematicians who invented all our statistical tests don't like just to ignore things. Instead, they have a more elegant way of getting rid of minus signs.

What happens if you multiply two negative numbers together? The answer is that you get a positive number, because whenever you multiply two negative numbers together, you get a positive number as the result. This is a really useful thing to know, and is our solution to the negative deviations. What we do is *square* each of our deviations – that is, we multiply each of the numbers by itself. So, for example, we would square the number –2. This gives us $-2 \times -2 = 4$, and we can see that the minus sign has vanished. And the really clever bit is that if you then take the square root of this number, you get back to the number you started with, but with the negative sign removed. Let's quickly recap that:

1   Start with a negative number. For example, –3
2   Square the number (multiply it by itself) to get a positive number. $-3 \times -3 = 9$
3   Take the square root. This gets you back to your original number but with the minus sign removed. $\sqrt{9} = 3$

And the really neat thing about this is that it doesn't matter if you start with a negative number or a positive number: if you follow these three steps, you will always end up with a positive number.

So let's try all this with our five deviations. If you remember, the five people's ages deviated by –2, –1, 0, 1 and 2. You can do the calculations yourself this time. I've just done a couple to get you started. I've also given you the final total so you can check your answers:

	Age	Deviation from mean (age – 20)	Deviation squared (deviation × deviation)
Person 1	18	–2	4
Person 2	19	–1	___
Person 3	20	0	___
Person 4	21	1	1
Person 5	22	2	___
Mean age:	20		Total 10

So this gives us the total amount of deviation in our ages. We now need to divide it by the number of scores to get the average amount of deviation for each person. This is where we see the second little complication. Normally, when we calculate a mean, we divide the total by the number of scores. So for the data we've just seen, you might expect to divide the total by 5, as there are five scores. However, for quite complicated reasons we don't divide the total amount of deviation by the number of scores – we divide it by *one less* than the number of scores. Have a look at the 'degrees of freedom' box below if you want to know why we do this.

So let's recap where we've got to. We have calculated the total amount of deviation in our ages, and we saw this came to 10. We now need to divide this by one less than the number of people. There were 5 people, so we need to divide our total amount of deviation by 4. This gives us $10 \div 4 = 2.5$.

Now there's just one last step before we're finished. Our total (10) was calculated from *squared* deviations, which means this number we have calculated is also squared. So the very last step is to take the square root of this number. $\sqrt{2.5} = 1.58$ which means 1.58 is the standard deviation for the five ages. This is our measure of how much the ages vary, and as I explained above, you can think of it as the average of all the deviations.

Phew! That has been a lot of new information. So just to finish this standard deviation section, and to help you remember what I've explained, I'd like you to calculate the standard deviation for the people in College B. I've laid out the table – you just need to fill it in:

	Age	Deviation from mean (age – 20)	Deviation squared (deviation × deviation)
Person 1	0	___	___
Person 2	10	___	___
Person 3	20	___	___
Person 4	30	___	___
Person 5	40	___	___
Mean age:	20	Total	___
	Divide by the number of people, less 1		___
	Take the square root	___	← this is the standard deviation

Did you get it right? You should have got a standard deviation of 15.81. You can see that this is much higher than College A's standard deviation, and this makes a lot of sense as the ages in College B are clearly more varied than the ages in College A.

I think the standard deviation is probably one of the most complicated things you'll need to do in this book, so well done for getting through it. Let's just do a quick recap of the 'recipe' for calculating the standard deviation before we move on:

1 Work out the mean for the set of numbers you want to analyse
2 Subtract this from each individual score
3 Square these numbers
4 Add them together
5 Divide by one less than the number of scores you had in your set
6 Take the square root. This gives you the standard deviation
7 Bask in the warm glow of having done some excellent statistical analysis.

Summary

The standard deviation is really just the average deviation – that is, the average difference – between each score and the mean score. There are two complications. First, we need to square all the deviations and later square-root them, to get rid of the minus signs. Second, we don't get the average by dividing by the number of scores. Instead, we divide by one less than this.

A very short note: variance

If, when calculating the standard deviation, you ignore the last stage (where you take the square root) then the measure you have is called the **variance**. So the variance is just the standard deviation squared, and is another measure of how much a set of scores vary. Now you know, in case you see the term anywhere.

Thinking mathematically → **Degrees of freedom**

When I was working out the standard deviation of five scores I did something a little strange: I worked out the total amount of variation and then divided this by four, not five, to get the average amount of variation. I used a number which was one less than the number of scores I was processing. This concept is known as **degrees of freedom**: if I have five scores then I have four degrees of freedom, if I have 88 scores then I have 87 degrees of freedom, and we tend to do this sort of thing all the time in statistics. But why?

One way to think about this is that we are not allowed to get free information. If I measure five people then I have five numbers. But if I then calculate the mean of those numbers, I now have six numbers: the original five scores and their mean. I'm not allowed to have free information like this – I'm not allowed to make six numbers out of five. So, by subtracting one, and acting as though I only had four people when I calculated the standard deviation, I am balancing the books and keeping the overall amount of numbers at five.

Here's another way of saying the same thing. Let's say I have three numbers and I tell you that they add up to 20. In fact, here are three slots for holding the numbers:

———

———

———

Total   20

What number goes in the first slot? Well, actually it can be any number at all. Let's say, for the sake of argument, I write 4 in the first slot, but I could have written any number I wanted. The same goes for the second slot – this can also be any number at all – so let's just say I write 5. I had complete freedom to put any numbers I wanted into the first two slots. With the last slot, however, I have no freedom. Because the first number is now 4 and the second number is now 5, and because I know the three numbers have to add up to 20, there is only one number I can possibly put into the third slot: it *has* to be 11. So with three slots, I had two degrees of freedom – the freedom to choose what goes in two of the slots.

'Degrees of freedom' is a statistical way of saying how many numbers we are dealing with in an analysis, which takes into account how many numbers we collected *and* how many statistics we have taken from those numbers. It's not the easiest concept in the world, I'll admit.

👁 How confident are you about your descriptive statistics? The standard error of the mean

Yesterday I was teaching a group of 40 students and I asked everybody in the room how many brothers and sisters they had. Some people had more siblings than others – there were quite a lot of only children, and one person had five brothers and sisters – but I can tell you that for my students the mean number of siblings was 1.4, and the standard deviation (which tells me how much the students varied from one another) was 1.2.

As a scientist, I always want to get knowledge that is as general as possible. It's nice to know something about these particular 40 students, but it would be even nicer to know something about students *in general*. So what can I say about the larger population, of students in general, after looking at this sample? With the information I now have from studying my sample, the best guess I can make is that students, in general, also have an average of 1.4 siblings. This is a really important point about descriptive statistics: whenever we look at a sample of people and calculate a descriptive statistic, such as the mean number of siblings, this is an *estimate* about the population. In this case, the best estimate I can make, with the information I have, is that students in general have 1.4 siblings on average.

But how confident am I about that estimate? How confident am I that, if I somehow could question every single student, I would again find an average of 1.4 siblings?

There are two things that will affect my confidence here: I will be more confident about this estimate if the people in my sample all looked really similar, and I will be more confident about this estimate if my sample was large. If every student in my sample had exactly two siblings, then I'll be quite happy to say that students, on average, have two siblings. And I'll be more confident in my estimate if I've tested a large sample of students. If I've only tested three people, I can't really trust my findings – those three could easily be unusual somehow. But if I've tested ten thousand then it is really unlikely that my sample will somehow be biased.

Statistically, we can combine these two factors – the number of people we tested and the how consistent they were – into a single measure called the **standard error of the mean**. This is a really useful statistic which helps us judge how trustworthy a mean is. If we calculate a mean – like 1.4 siblings in this example – we can also calculate its standard error. If this standard error is low, the mean is probably a good estimate of how the wider population looks; but if this standard error is high, the mean we have calculated from the sample might not be a good estimate of how the population looks, and we should treat it with caution. The standard error of the mean, then, is a measure of *uncertainty*. If it's high, we're uncertain about the mean we have calculated; but if it's low, we're quite certain.

The standard error of the mean (SEM) is simply calculated with this formula:

$$SEM = \frac{standard\ deviation}{\sqrt{number\ of\ people}}$$

Like most statistics, this is a ratio, with one number divided by another. Because the standard deviation is on the top, the SEM will be higher when there is a high standard deviation, and because the number of people is on the bottom, the SEM will be lower when there are lots of people. In this case, where I had a standard deviation of 1.2 after testing 40 people, the result would be:

$$SEM = \frac{standard\ deviation}{\sqrt{number\ of\ people}} = \frac{1.2}{\sqrt{40}} = \frac{1.2}{6.32} = 0.19$$

My estimate, then, is that the mean number of siblings, for students in general, is 1.4, and the standard error of that mean is 0.19. This standard error is quite low, suggesting that my estimate of 1.4 siblings looks like a pretty reliable estimate of how many siblings students in general have. The standard error is fairly low because my students were not too varied, and it would be lower still if I tested more people. As the standard error is a measure of uncertainty, and as it is low in this case, I am not very uncertain about the mean I have calculated. If I somehow could test all the students in the country, it's very likely that I'd find they have an average number of siblings somewhere close to 1.4.

◉ Chapter summary

When we collect a set of numbers from somewhere, it is useful to summarize it. We often do this by describing the midpoint of those numbers, and by giving a measure of how much the numbers vary around this midpoint.

Chapter 8

Displaying data with graphs and tables

Introduction

I hate a cliché as much as the next rolling stone hates a bird in the bush, but there really is a lot of truth in the old saying that a picture tells a thousand words. Graphs are a wonderful tool for displaying your findings in a clear way. There are various different types of graph, and it is pretty much the case that each one does a different job. In other words, you usually don't have a choice which type of graph you will use – the decision is made for you by the type of data you need to display. In this chapter, I will walk you through the main types of graph you might need to use and give you information about when each is used.

A quick note: categorical versus continuous variables

As you might have noticed already, something we talk about a lot in research is the idea of a variable: anything which you measure or manipulate in a study. All variables fall into one of two different types: **continuous variables** and **categorical variables**. A continuous variable can have any value at all. For example, height is a continuous variable. As you grew during your childhood, at some point you will have gone from being 50.000 cm tall to 50.001 cm to 50.002 cm and so on. Height can take absolutely any number, and can change by tiny amounts. As such, we say it changes *continuously*.

Categorical variables are different. These, as their name suggests, describe a limited number of *categories*. For example, consider marital status: people are either single, engaged, married, separated, divorced or widowed. There are only these few categories, everybody falls into one category or another, and you can't make small changes like you could with height – you can't be partway between engaged and married, but you can be partway between 150 and 151 cm tall.

The difference between continuous and categorical variables is quite an important one. The two types of variable are used differently in graphs, as you will see below. And as you'll see later in this book, we have to use different statistical tests with the two types of variable. So get used to spotting, for each variable you see, whether it is continuous or categorical. With a little practice, it becomes second nature.

👁 A second quick note: the names of axes on graphs

One of the difficulties with graphs is that there is a specialized vocabulary for the axes. Almost all the graphs I'm going to talk about here involve two axes at right-angles to each other, and the axes go by various names:

Simple name	Coordinate name	Alternative name
horizontal axis	*x*-axis	abscissa
vertical axis	*y*-axis	ordinate

These names aren't really very easy to remember, but you just have to make the effort to memorize which is which because there's no short-cut that I know of. In this book I'll mostly use the terms *x*- and *y*-axis because these are probably the most common (see Figure 8.1).

👁 The bar graph

Used for: showing how often various categories have been seen, or showing average scores for various categories.

A bar graph always has a categorical variable along the *x*-axis and a continuous variable along the *y*-axis. You can use it to show how often you saw various members of a category, like in Figure 8.2, or you can use

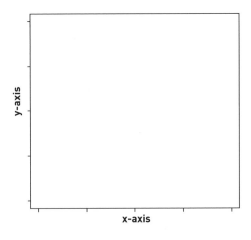

Figure 8.1 The names of graph axes

it to show the scores obtained by different categories of people, like in Figure 8.3.

Watch out for: the bars in a bar graph do not touch each other – this is one way you can tell a bar graph from a histogram.

Alternative versions: You can also flip a bar graph 90 degrees if you like, and have the categories along the *y*-axis and the scores along the *x*-axis. This isn't wrong, but it's much less common in scientific work.

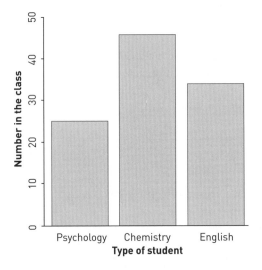

Figure 8.2 A bar graph showing how often we saw three categories of student

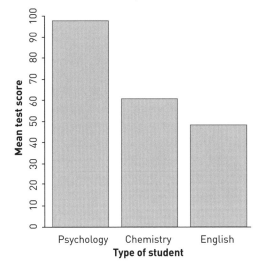

Figure 8.3 A bar graph showing the mean scores from three categories of student

The histogram

Used for: showing how individual scores are spread along a range.

The histogram has a continuous variable along each axis. The *x*-axis has a variable you measured, such as height, weight, test score or whatever. The *y*-axis shows how often you saw each score in the group you studied. The example in Figure 8.4 shows how often the people in a group obtained various scores on a test.

One of the main uses for a histogram is for us to see the **distribution** of scores in a group – that is, what range of scores the group got, how often each score was seen, and how the scores were spread out across the people you studied. In Figure 8.4 you can see that the distribution has two peaks in it. This tells us that the people who were tested tended to get either a low score or a high score. A histogram with two peaks like this tells us we have a **bimodal distribution**, where there are two modes – two scores which were seen most often.

Watch out for: each column in a histogram touches its neighbours. This is to show that the *x*-axis has a continuous range of scores, rather than separate categories like in a bar graph.

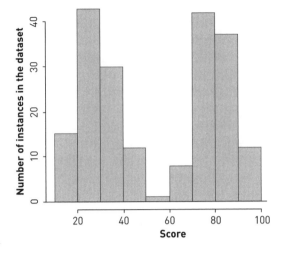

Figure 8.4 A histogram

👁 Line graphs

Used for: showing how numbers change across categories, or along a series.

A line graph can be drawn in two ways. The vertical y-axis always shows some sort of score, or a count of people, like in a bar graph. The difference between a bar graph and a line graph is that on a bar graph the x-axis shows completely separate categories whereas on a line graph there is a logical progression along the x-axis. For example, look at Figure 8.5, where the y-axis shows the time people take to complete a jigsaw puzzle and the x-axis shows how much practice they have had. The x-axis shows a series, from zero attempts to eight attempts, and because it follows a logical sequence, it is okay to use a line graph and join the points together.

👁 Scatterplots

Used for: showing how people score on two different measures at once (Figure 8.6).

All the graphs so far have had a score on the y-axis and some sort of grouping measure on the x-axis. The scatterplot is different as it has a continuous variable on each axis. Each person is represented by a single point on the graph, and each point shows what score that person got on two different measures.

Scatterplots are extremely useful in correlational work, for seeing the relationship between two different measures. We will see lots of examples of this in Chapter 14.

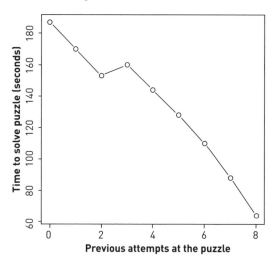

Figure 8.5 A line graph

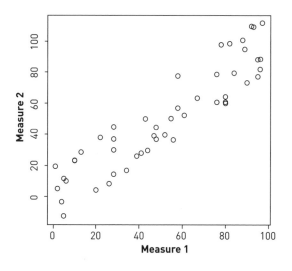

Figure 8.6 A scatterplot

◉ Pie charts

Used for: showing how a single thing breaks down into smaller parts.

A pie chart is the only graph we'll cover here that doesn't have axes. It shows how a single thing – such as a group of people, or a budget – is made up of smaller parts. For example, Figure 8.7 shows how a group of people who took part in an experiment is made up of different professions.

Watch out for: a pie chart must not be used to show scores. If you had three groups of people, it would be wrong to draw a pie chart with three segments, each representing a group's score.

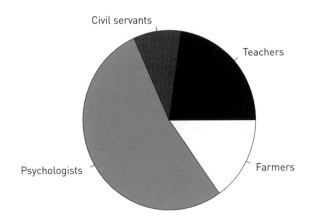

Figure 8.7 A pie chart showing how a group of people is made up of different professions

◉ Two-dimensional graphs or three-dimensional graphs?

For once, I've got a nice short answer for you: always use two-dimensional graphs. I know your computer will produce some gorgeous three-dimensional graphs, but you can't display a three dimensional object in two dimensions without it being distorted – just ask any map-maker. Leave three-dimensional graphs to businesspeople who find the distortions useful for hiding bad news. The only exception to this is when you are plotting three variables at once, like I have in Figure 8.8 – but that's quite a specialized task and you're unlikely ever to need to do it.

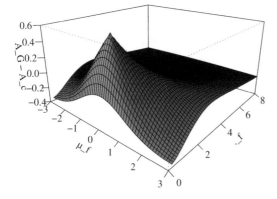

Figure 8.8 A graph showing three variables at once

👁 Displaying data with tables

Compared to graphs, there perhaps isn't a huge amount to say about tables, as many of the things you need to think about are a matter either of common sense, or of personal preference.

What do I mean by personal preference? Well, for example, I know a lot of people who say that a table should include no vertical lines. So while this is okay, because it only uses horizontal lines:

	Group1	Group 2
Time 1	23	39
Time 2	27	31

many people don't like to see this:

	Group 1	Group 2
Time 1	23	39
Time 2	27	31

But as I say, this is largely a matter of taste.

Something else to think about with tables is to make them consistent. Use the same number of decimal places throughout, and make sure all the headings are formatted in the same way. It just looks bad when a table isn't consistent – in fact it looks as though the person who drew the table didn't care about it very much.

And finally, perhaps the biggest question you should ask with any table is 'Do I even need this table in my document?' I often see tables like this:

	Group1	Group 2
Mean	23	39
Standard deviation	2.7	3.1

But is this table really necessary? If you only have four numbers to report, it would probably be a lot easier and neater just to put them in the text, like this:

> Group 1 got a mean score of 23 (standard deviation = 2.7) and Group 2 got a mean score of 39 (standard deviation = 3.1).

For me, the key rule when reporting data is not to report the same information more than once unless absolutely necessary. I recently marked a set of statistics coursework where many of the students presented exactly the same set of numbers in a graph *and* in a table *and* in the text! Sure, this is good for boosting the page count in your reports, but it's really just a waste of time. One of the skills of a researcher is knowing how best to present data, so when you have some numbers to report you should decide what works best for those data – a table, a graph, or merely some numbers in your text – and just use the one method.

👁 Don't forget the title

Both tables and graphs, in a report, need to have titles, and a good title should stand alone. That is, somebody should be able to chop the graph or table out of your report and it should, just from its title, make sense. So, for example, this title above a graph wouldn't be very helpful:

> Mean scores

The mean scores of what? And who did they come from? Far better is a title like this:

> Mean extroversion scores of bakers and butchers

A graph with that title would make complete sense even if it was completely on its own.

◉ Chapter summary

Graphs are a powerful tool for describing your data. However, each type of graph is intended for a different task, so be careful you don't use the wrong one for the data you are describing.

Chapter 9

Hypothesis testing, and the only two errors you can possibly make with statistics

👁 Introduction

Almost all the time in psychology, there are too many people for us to test. We might want to learn about how children develop, for example, but we would soon find that there are far too many children for us to study them all. Our only option is to study a sample – a convenient group of the people we are interested in. We hope that this sample will behave just like the full population, so we can 'scale up' from the sample to the population, and reach conclusions about lots of people after studying just a few.

As we move from looking at a sample of people to making conclusions about a whole population, we rely on statistics. Statistical tests help us weigh up the evidence and decide whether whatever we saw in the sample would also be true for the whole population.

In this chapter we will examine:
- Using the null hypothesis in research
- Using *p*-values to evaluate research findings
- The null hypothesis and the alternative hypothesis
- Type I and Type II errors
- The idea of 'statistical significance'

◉ Using a sample to make estimates about a population

Back in Chapter 3 I talked about how, when you want to study a population that is too large to test, you need to study a sample of it. You take a sample of people, look at them, and use whatever you find to guess what the rest of the population looks like. In other words, you look at the sample and *generalize* whatever you see to the wider population.

For example, let's say you take a sample of teachers and find that 62% of them have been on a training course during the past year. In this case, you would probably conclude that about 62% of *all* teachers have been on a training course in the past year. You would 'scale up' from the sample to the population.

Of course, something you must never forget is that you might end up being wrong after you generalize like this. When you announce '62% of teachers have been on a training course in the past year', this just might not be true. Yes, 62% of your sample went on a training course, but maybe all the other teachers, the ones you didn't actually test, look totally different. You've no way of knowing for certain, which is why we use inferential statistics. Inferential statistical tests help us make this judgement: they tell us how likely it is that we will be wrong if we scale up from a sample to its population.

In practice, the way that inferential statistics help us is really quite simple: they give us a single number called p, which stands for 'probability'. Practically every statistical test you use will give you a number, called p, which will have a value like .75 or .02 or whatever. This number is what you use when you decide whether or not your sample data will generalize to the population.

As you deal with statistics you might encounter dozens of statistical tests, each with an exotic and confusing name. So here's a tip, which will help you a great deal: all these tests do the same thing – they all produce this number called p, and it always means the same thing. Because all statistical tests produce p, once you understand what it means, you can understand what a whole lot of statistical tests are telling you – even ones you haven't see before.

In the rest of this chapter I have several new ideas to communicate to you, and they will only make complete sense at the end, when all the information comes together. So read the chapter right through with a relaxed mind, confident that it will all make sense eventually. When we get to the end I'll give you some examples from real research to help you make sure you've understood it all.

A simple idea is a good idea

If I told you there was a unicorn living under my bed, would you believe me?

I do hope you would not. If *you* told *me* you had a unicorn under your bed, I wouldn't believe you. It's nothing personal. It's just that I woke up this morning with the idea that unicorns don't exist. That's a nice, simple, plausible idea, so I'm going to need a very good reason to abandon it and start believing you have a unicorn. In fact, I'm only going to abandon my no-unicorn idea if I have some very good *evidence* that it's wrong.

What I am saying, in a round-about unicorny sort of way, is that whenever we carry out a statistical analysis, *we start with a nice simple idea, and stick with it unless we have good evidence it's wrong.*

We always start with the same nice, simple idea

We start every statistical analysis with the simplest idea possible: the idea that we have found nothing interesting. I know that probably sounds odd. If you are carrying out an experiment to see whether owning pets makes people happier, you might expect to start out with the idea that people who own pets will be happier than people who do not. But this is not what happens. Whenever you are doing statistical analysis, you start out with the idea that *nothing* will happen – in this case, you would look at whether owning a pet makes *no difference* to people's happiness.

Think of it this way: you start every analysis with the 'worst-case scenario'. You start out assuming that you've found nothing interesting and you stick with this idea unless you find good evidence that it's wrong. So in this case you start out by assuming that owning a pet has no effect on happiness, and you stick with that idea unless you find some good evidence it's wrong.

Why start out with the idea you've found nothing? Why not start out assuming that you have found something interesting, and stick with *that* unless you find it's wrong? There are actually two reasons. First, the assumption that you've found *nothing* is just a whole lot simpler than the assumption that you've found *something*, and that in itself is a pretty good reason to start out assuming you've found nothing. (Whenever you have two equally good ideas to choose from, it's usually best to choose the simplest. This principle is called **Occam's Razor** after the medieval monk William of Occam – it helps you 'shave away' ideas.)

Second, and perhaps more important, if you start by assuming that you've found nothing, you are less likely to reach a risky conclusion. Imagine you're testing a new drug to decide if it's safe. If you get this wrong, you might seriously harm people by allowing them to take a dangerous substance. As such, you don't start out assuming the drug is safe; you start out with the worst-case scenario and assume that the drug is dangerous. You only abandon the idea that the drug is dangerous if there's really good evidence that this is wrong, and this approach helps protect people. As I'll explain shortly, *whenever* you do research, there's a risk you'll make a mistake and reach the wrong conclusion. Starting out with the worst-case scenario means that if you do make a mistake, it's less likely to become a problem.

◉ The null hypothesis and the alternative hypothesis

All our analyses have the same starting-point, which says that nothing is going on. This starting-point is so important it has its own name: the **null hypothesis**. The null hypothesis is the simple idea that nothing is happening in the population – there is *no difference* between the groups you studied, or there is *no relationship* between the measures you have taken. Owning a pet has *no effect* on people's happiness and there are *no unicorns* under people's beds. You always start out assuming these really simple ideas are true and stick with them unless you find a good reason to abandon them.

Once you have a null hypothesis – that is, once you have imagined nothing interesting is happening – you can also think about what you will say if the null hypothesis turns out to look wrong. The gives you an **alternative hypothesis**, which is the idea that something *is* happening, and is your fall-back position: if you look at your data and find that the null hypothesis seems to be wrong, the alternative hypothesis will give you your conclusion instead. So, for example, we might work with these two hypotheses:

Null hypothesis: Owning a pet has no effect on people's happiness.
Alternative hypothesis: Owning a pet will make people happier.[2]

We start with the null hypothesis and stick with that unless we find good evidence it is wrong. But if we do find evidence suggesting that the null hypothesis is wrong, we will go with the alternative hypothesis instead. If we found that people who own pets are *much* happier than people who don't own pets ... well, this just wouldn't fit with the idea that pets make no difference. As such, we'd reject the null hypothesis and conclude that owning pets might indeed make people happy.

Mathematical revision → **Probability**

Every statistical test gives you, as its end product, a number called *p. p* is an abbreviation of 'probability'. If you are already happy with the idea of probability and how it is measured then feel free to chuckle knowingly and skip this box, because I'm going briefly to review the subject.

Probability simply tells us how likely it is something will happen. In a desperate bid not to talk about tossing coins again, I'm going to use a DVD which I have here on my desk. If I drop the DVD on the floor, it will fall either with its label up or its label down. If I drop it over and over, it will fall with its label up half the time and with its label down half the time.

We describe the probability something will happen with a number between one and zero. When something *always* happens – when it *will* happen – we say it has a probability of 1. So if I drop the DVD, there is a probability of 1 it will fall down, because here on Earth things *always* fall down when we drop them. When, on the other hand, something will *not* happen, we say it has a probability of 0. There is a probability of 0 your nose will turn into a lemon during the next ten seconds, for example.

Usually, we don't see such certainty; most of the time we see probabilities somewhere between zero and one. Dropping a DVD gives a probability exactly halfway between zero and one: the probability of the DVD landing label-side-up is .50. A probability of .50 means landing label-up will happen exactly half the time.

Similarly, if an event has a probability of .25, it will happen one time in four, or 25% of the time ($1 \div .25 = 4$, and $1 \div 4 = .25$). If there is a probability of .05 that I will fall over and be bitten by my dog the next time I walk downstairs, this is the same as saying there is a 5% chance, or a 1 in 20 chance ($1 \div .05 = 20$).

---

2   You might notice that what I'm now calling the alternative hypothesis is the hypothesis I mentioned back in Chapter 2. This is the prediction that naturally arises out of your research question.

Using statistics to test your null hypothesis

Let's say we take a group of men and a group of women and see how long everybody takes to complete a puzzle – perhaps a simple wordsearch or crossword puzzle. We find that the women, on average, take 94 seconds to finish the puzzle and the men, on average, take 100 seconds. As the women we tested were six seconds faster, it looks as though women are better at this task, doesn't it? Certainly this is what someone who doesn't understand statistics might think after looking at those numbers.

But what if men and women are actually the same at solving these puzzles? Even if this were true, it would be odd if we tested some men and some women and found they were *exactly* as fast, with a difference of 0.00000000 seconds, wouldn't it? The world's just too messy for us to see *exactly* zero difference. If we take a handful of men and a handful of women and test them, we're going to see some difference, even if it's only small. So, whenever we see an effect like this, we need to ask whether it is big enough to mean something. Is the six-second difference so large that we can only really explain it by saying men and women are different? This is where statistics come in.

As ever, we start with the null hypothesis, that men and women take the same amount of time to solve problems, and then we see how well the evidence fits with this. If we had seen a one-second difference between our men and our women, then the null hypothesis probably would still look okay; but if we had seen a 60-second difference then it probably would not.

But how does a 30-second difference fit with the idea that women and men are the same? Or a 12-second difference? Or the 6-second difference that we actually saw? For any given difference between the groups, we need some way of deciding what it tells us. And this is what statistical tests do. With almost any statistical test, once the calculations are over, you will have a single number called p, and *this tells you how well your results fit with the null hypothesis*. If your results are compatible with the null hypothesis then you'll stick with it; but if they are totally incompatible then you'll say the null hypothesis was probably wrong.

Summary

We start every statistical analysis with a 'null hypothesis'. This is the simple idea that nothing is happening in our population – there is no difference between the groups we're studying, or there is no relationship between the measures we've taken. We only abandon this idea with good reason, and a p-value helps us make the decision. If we do abandon it, we base our conclusions on an alternative hypothesis instead.

👁 Using p-values to evaluate a null hypothesis

Almost every statistical test produces a p-value as its end result. p is a probability, with a value somewhere between 0 and 1, and you can use it to decide whether or not your findings fit with the null hypothesis. What exactly is p the probability of? To show you this, let's return to our puzzle-solving example. We saw a six-second difference between some men and some women, and we need to decide if this fits with the null hypothesis: is a six-second difference the sort of thing we'd expect to see if men and women are really the same? Or is a six-second difference so large that we can only really explain it by saying that women are better at solving problems?

To make this decision, we run a statistical test on our scores and get the number called p. For example, we might find that $p = .77$. This is the probability that our findings fit with the null hypothesis. More precisely, *it is the probability of seeing an effect, at least as large as the one we saw, if the null hypothesis is true.* So in this example, p is the probability of seeing a difference, of six seconds or more, if the null hypothesis is true. It is the probability of seeing a difference, of six-seconds or more, if men and women are really the same at solving puzzles.

If we analysed the scores from our men and women and got the result $p = .77$, this means that there is a 77% chance of seeing a difference of six seconds or more in the people we tested if men and women are really the same at solving puzzles. In other words, if men and women are really the same at solving puzzles, $p = .77$ tells us that a six-second difference between the two groups we tested is *totally* something we would expect to see, and so we shouldn't find that difference very interesting. *The high* p-*value means that our data fit with the null hypothesis.* As such, we'd conclude that men and women are the same at solving puzzles. We aren't saying that the null hypothesis *is* true, but we are saying that, thanks to the high p-value, we don't have any good reason to reject it.

So that is the proper explanation of what p means: p is the probability of seeing a result, at least as large as the one you saw, if the null hypothesis is true. Do try to remember that, as it's the official definition of what a *p*-value means and you need to know it, and to use it when you write research reports.

The thing is, I know that for a lot of people, this explanation is difficult to grasp at first. Soon it will just 'click' (maybe it has already?), and you'll wonder why you ever found it difficult. But for now, until the official explanation makes sense, I'm going to give you one other way of thinking about *p*-values which I know most people find easier. Let's be clear: this explanation I'm about to give is totally wrong and naughty and will offend any professional statisticians; in fact, you've already committed a statistical crime just by reading this far. But what I am about to say really will make it easier for you to use *p*-values.

(Incidentally, using a 'wrong' idea to help you do something right is a totally valid approach. Think about sports. People are always taught to 'follow through' after striking a ball, as this helps the ball fly straighter. In reality, of course, this is nonsense: once you've hit a ball, and it's started moving, nothing you do will change its path. *But if you act as though it will*, and follow through along the path you want the ball to take, you'll hit it better in the first place.)

The wrong, but useful, way that I think about *p*

When I have a *p*-value, like *p* = .77, I like to think that *this is the probability I will be wrong if I say I've discovered something*. I'm being loose with my language here, and I know from bitter experience that any statisticians reading that last sentence have just sprayed coffee everywhere and are now throwing furniture around in anger.[3] But I'm saying it anyway. The idea of being wrong, and looking foolish, really focuses the mind. So when I think that *p* is the probability I will be wrong if I say I have discovered something, I find it much easier to weigh up the risks.

In this case, our *p*-value was .77. There is at least a 77% chance we would be wrong if we said that men and women are different at solving puzzles. That seems like quite a high chance of being wrong, doesn't it? It's probably best to stick with the null hypothesis and say men and women are the same.

As you study statistics and write about your work, you need to use the first, 'official' explanation which talks about the null hypothesis; but if this other explanation makes more sense to you, by all means use it when

---

3 Statisticians: do remember that *p* gives the Type I error probability, which might make my statement more acceptable.

you are talking to yourself – as we will see below, you will always come to the same conclusions. Just don't tell your statistics teacher!

Summary

p is the probability of seeing an effect, at least as large as the one you saw in your sample, if the null hypothesis is true. If it helps, you might also think of p this way: it is (sort of) the probability you will be wrong if you say you have discovered something.

◉ Using the p-value to reach conclusions – when is it low enough to say you've found something?

So far I have shown you how we use the p-value as evidence when we decide whether or not to stick with a null hypothesis. The question I have not yet answered is how you know when you have a 'good' p-value. When is a p-value low enough to reject the null hypothesis, and when is it high enough that you don't?

In our example, where we compared a group of men with a group of women, we found $p = .77$. This means there is a 77% chance of seeing a six-second difference between the men and women, or an even larger difference, if the null hypothesis is true. Or, in looser, naughty terms that we don't tell anybody about, there is at least a 77% chance we will be wrong if we conclude men and women are different.

What would you conclude if you did a statistical test and it gave you this result of $p = .77$? Would you conclude men and women are different, or would you stick with the null hypothesis and say there is no difference?

If there is a 77% chance of seeing a six-second difference or more if the null hypothesis is true – if there is a 77% chance I would be wrong if I say men and women are different – I know what I would do: I would definitely conclude men and women are the same; there is no way I'm going to reach a conclusion where there is an 77% chance I am wrong! No, when $p = .77$ it's the null hypothesis for me, baby.

But what if p were .40? Would you take a 40% risk? It certainly sounds as though the balance is in your favour. If there is a 40% chance of being wrong, there must be a 60% chance of being right. But $p = .40$ is still no good to us as researchers. Would you take a new medicine if your doctor said 'I'm 60% certain it won't kill you'? Of course you wouldn't! Forty per cent doubt is still far too much.

So what about a 10% chance of being wrong? What if you have tested some men and women, found a six-second difference, and your statistical test says $p = .10$? This tells you there is only a 10% chance of seeing a difference, of six seconds or more, if men and women are really the same – a 10% chance you'll be wrong if you say you've found a difference between men and women. Would you go with that? It's a harder decision: I think none of us would be happy with a 77% chance of being wrong, but 10% sounds much better.

In fact, there is no one 'right' answer here, because it depends what you are studying. If you are testing a new drug to decide whether or not it is safe, you need to be very sure about your conclusions. In this case you will only accept a small amount of doubt – perhaps a 1% chance of being wrong, or even less – and so will look for p-values of .01 or less. But if you are testing something less important you might tolerate a higher chance of being wrong – a higher chance of wrongly rejecting the null hypothesis.

For various reasons, most of the time we use a cut-off – or **alpha level** – of .05. You will see this value of .05 being used as a cut-off all over the place in psychology, and in other fields of research. In most studies, if p is less than .05, we say that the evidence doesn't seem to fit with the null hypothesis, and so we say that there probably is a real effect going on in the population. But if p is greater than .05 we stick with our null hypothesis and conclude that there probably is nothing happening in the population.

So let's say that our analysis of men and women, where we saw a six-second difference between the groups, had actually ended with $p = .03$. This is less than .05, and so we would conclude that men and women, overall, really do seem to solve problems at different speeds. If we found $p = .03$, then there is only a 3% chance of seeing this difference in our sample, or a larger difference, if men and women are really the same. This (more or less) means there is only a 3% chance we would be wrong if we said men and women are different. In this situation, where $p = .03$, we would almost certainly take the chance and reject our null hypothesis: we would have enough evidence to say the null hypothesis is implausible; we would conclude that men and women – in general – really are different when they complete our task.

Summary

All statistical tests give us a number called p. In most research, we stick with our null hypothesis unless we see a p-value less than .05. In this case, we say that we have good evidence against the null hypothesis and so we abandon it. Our conclusion would be the alternative idea that something probably is happening.

If you forget everything else from this chapter, then as long as you remember the next sentence you'll be able to bluff your way through most situations: If you do an analysis and the p-value is less than .05, you'll say you've probably found a real effect; if the p-value is .05 or more, you'll say you've probably not found a real effect.

Putting it all together: two quick examples

That's been a lot of words on p-values, as I had quite a bit to explain: the null hypothesis; the fact p is the probability of seeing an effect, at least as extreme as the one you saw, if the null hypothesis is true; and how to use this to reach a conclusion by comparing your p-value to a cut-off value called alpha. It *will* all make sense – have faith in that. And to help it all settle into your mind, let's quickly finish by looking at two examples of p-values in action, taken from real research. I'll talk you through how I interpret the p-values from these studies, and this should really help you understand how p is used.

A recent study from Turkey[4] looked at whether children with asthma got less sleep than those without asthma. The researchers found that children with severe asthma woke up more often than children with mild asthma, and when they analysed this effect they found a p-value of .01. There was just a 1% chance of seeing such a strong effect if the null hypothesis was true. The p-value was less than .05, so the authors concluded that there almost certainly is a real relationship between how severe a child's asthma is and how much their sleep is disturbed.

(One of the things that continually fascinates me about statistics is that we can measure our doubt. Before the twentieth century, people could only ever say 'I think X is true' or, if they were quite intolerant, 'X is

---

4   Yuksel, H. and others (2007). Evaluation of sleep quality and anxiety-depression parameters in asthmatic children and their mothers. *Respiratory Medicine, vol. 101*, pages 2550–4.

true, and I'll hit you on the head if you don't agree with me!' Now we have inferential statistics, we can measure exactly how certain we are about things: we can say 'It really looks as though children with severe asthma get less sleep then those with mild asthma, *and I have only 1% doubt when I say that*'. This ability to measure our doubt seems to me to be a major leap forward in human thinking.)

Finally, in one of my own studies[5] we used an eye-tracker – a computer which knew exactly where people were looking – to see what car drivers' eyes were doing when the drivers saw a bicyclist in a street. We found that the first thing drivers looked at was usually the bicyclist's face and, as a follow-up question, we wanted to see whether the driver's gender made a difference: did women look at the face more than men, for example? We analysed the data to see whether the male and female drivers behaved differently, and found that the women did indeed look at the face more often than the men. However, the difference between the two groups showed $p = .12$. This meant that, although we did see a difference between the men and the women in our sample, there was a 12% chance of seeing that difference – or even a larger difference – if the null hypothesis was true. In other words, there was at least a 12% chance of seeing a difference like that if men and women are really the same. As our p-value was greater than .05, we stuck with our null hypothesis and concluded that there was probably no real difference between men and women.

👁 The only two errors you can make in statistics

Usually, when we want to learn about a group of individuals, we find the group is far too large to study. As we have seen, particularly in Chapter 3, we deal with this by testing a sample of those individuals; we look at that sample and use what we find to judge the larger population. If we want to know whether firefighters can, on average, run faster than police officers, we measure a sample of both and use what we find to decide whether or not firefighters and police officers, in general, differ in their running ability.

Something you really need to remember is that whenever you look at a sample of people, there will *always* be some sort of effect there – there

---

5   Walker, I. and Brosnan, M. (2007). Drivers' gaze fixations during judgements about a bicyclist's intentions. *Transportation Research Part F, vol. 10*, pages 90–8.

will always be a difference between the groups you compared, or a relationship between the measures you took – even if it is only small. Earlier on, I said it would actually be quite weird if we compared two groups of people and saw *exactly* zero difference between them. That just doesn't tend to happen, even if the groups are supposed to be the same. So if you see a little bit of difference between some groups, this is totally normal. The question is whether the difference would still be there if you could somehow test the whole population. Did you see a difference in your sample because that's how the population looks, and your sample is behaving the same? Or did you see the difference in your sample just through coincidence? Would the difference disappear if you tested more people?

As you now know, when we do research we always start out with the idea that any effect we see in the sample will *not* generalize to the population. Every statistical test gives us a number called p and, using this to guide us, sometimes we stick with our null hypothesis and conclude there is nothing interesting happening in our population; other times we reject the null hypothesis and conclude the population will show the same effect the sample did.

Now here's something important you need to remember about p: in the real world, it will never be as low as zero. This means there is always some doubt at the end of an analysis: there is always some risk you are going to reject the null hypothesis, and say you have found an effect, when you should not have done. And, in the opposite direction, there is always some risk you are going to hang on to the null hypothesis when really it is false. In other words, there is always a risk that the null hypothesis is wrong, but you didn't find the evidence you need to say this. So, to summarize, the two risks you face when you analyse some data are *making false claims* (saying there is an effect when really there isn't) and *missing effects* (hanging on to the null hypothesis, and saying there is no effect, when really you should have let it go).

Risky ice cream

To show you what I mean about these two risks, let's say you want to know whether people prefer chocolate ice cream to vanilla ice cream. The population you are interested in is 'all the people who eat ice cream', which is clearly too large to study. So you study a sample of these people and try to generalize from this to the wider population.

Across all the people who eat ice cream, there are only two possibilities: either people prefer one flavour over the other, or they do not. You need to choose one of these two possibilities as your conclusion. To do this, you will start with the second possibility – the idea there is no preference – and stick with this unless you find a good reason to believe it's wrong.

Have a look at the table below which shows how, when you reach a conclusion in any study, there are two ways you can be correct – and two ways you could go wrong. Let's focus on how you could go wrong. First, you could say that people prefer one flavour of ice cream over the other when this is not true (a false claim, shown in the bottom-left cell of the table). Second, you could say there is no preference when really a preference exists (you fail to see the difference, shown in the top-right cell). We tend to make this second error when there is something going on in our sample – a preference for one ice cream over the other – but the difference is not big enough for us to be sure it is real.

	You say	
	There's an effect	There's no effect
There is really an effect	Correct	Error: Missed the effect!
There is really no effect	Error: False claim!	Correct

Here's another example of these two types of error. Let's say you are looking at whether or not a new type of vitamin supplement works to make children grow taller. You take a group of children, all living in the same conditions, and you give the supplement to just half of them. If the supplement works and you say it works, this is fine. And if it doesn't work and you say it doesn't work, this is also fine. Either way: well done! But you can go wrong in two ways: if you say the supplement works when really it does not, you have made a false claim; and if you say the supplement doesn't work when really it does, you have missed the effect. Either way: not so great.

Now here's the important thing: you can never escape the risk of making an error. In fact it's worse than this: if you try to avoid one type of error, the other becomes more likely. What a horrible situation to be in: imagine if everything you ever did to avoid getting ill made it more likely you would be hit by a car! But balancing risks like this is just something we have to deal with in research: if you try to avoid the risk of missing an effect you are more likely to make a false claim, and if you try to avoid the risk of making a false claim you are more likely to miss an effect.

Here's how that trade-off works. Let's say that in your vitamin study you are desperate to avoid a false claim – you really don't want to say that the vitamins work when really they don't. So you make a decision: you decide you will only say that the supplement works if the evidence is *amazingly* clear. For example, you will only say the supplement works if the children who took it grow at least five kilometres taller than the control children! By insisting on seeing such a massive effect, you definitely aren't going to make a false claim: there would have to be children banging their heads on aircraft before you say the vitamins work. But at the same time, you have set yourself up to miss a real effect. If the supplement made the children grow by four kilometres you would miss this, because the effect just wasn't big enough for you. This is an extreme example, but it shows how whenever you make the effort to avoid a false claim, by insisting on the effect being more obvious, you are more likely to miss a real effect. This trade-off is always there.

Going further → **Statistical power, the secret shame of behavioural science**

We have just seen that, when we decide whether or not to stick with a null hypothesis, we are balancing between two possible errors: making a false claim and missing an effect. The question, then, is how do we find the right balance between the two? The answer is that there is quite an easy way to find the balance, but traditionally psychologists, and other behavioural scientists, have not bothered! This is pretty much an historical accident, so let me briefly explain.

I have already said how, when we reach conclusions at the end of our research projects, we are guided by the *p*-values that our statistical tests give us. And I said that we usually use a cut-off of .05 to decide whether or not we should stick with the null hypothesis. Indeed, traditionally most research pretty much just involves collecting data, getting a *p*-value from an analysis and seeing if this is less than .05. If it is, we say we have found an effect; if it is not we stick with the null hypothesis and say we've not found an effect.

This cut-off, which we use to judge our *p*-values, is called **alpha.** It is the biggest risk of making a false claim that we are prepared to take. So when we use .05 as our cut-off value for judging *p*, we are saying we will accept up to a 5% chance of making a false claim but no more. We know there has to be *some* risk of making a false claim, and so we control that risk – we make sure we keep it below 5%.

But as well as alpha, it is possible also to calculate **beta**, which is the probability you will miss an effect. And traditionally in the behavioural sciences, because we have tended to listen to some statisticians more than others, we have been quite bad at thinking about beta. When we make decisions about the null hypothesis, what we should do is look at both alpha (the probability of making a false claim) and beta (the probability of missing an effect). But we have been so worried about the risk of making false claims we have tended only to look at this, and to ignore our chances of missing effects. The statistician Jacob Cohen showed how a typical psychological experiment, comparing two groups of 30 people on a task, might easily have a 50% chance of missing a real effect.

Thankfully, all this is now changing. In fact, you are learning about statistics at a really exciting time when the way we do things is shifting. Psychologists are becoming much more aware of **power analysis**, a technique which helps us balance the two types of risk more efficiently. When we use power analysis, we don't just worry about false claims, as we have traditionally done; we pay attention to the risk of missing an effect as well. In practice, this usually means we pay more attention to how many people we test, and test more people when we think we are looking at a subtle, hard-to-spot effect. If you compare two groups of people, and are expecting the difference between them to be small, you need to test more people so you can be sure you see it.

The exact details of how to use power analysis are beyond the scope of this book, but at least you are now aware of the technique. If you are able to learn about power analysis in the future, though, this will help you pay attention to the number of people you test and the size of the effects you will see, and this will help you avoid missing effects as well as avoid making false claims. A good starting point is to look online for some free software called G*Power, which can do all the necessary calculations for you, telling you how many people you need to test to see particular effects.

The names for the two types of error

The two types of error that I have described are officially called Type I and Type II errors (usually with Roman numerals). A **Type I error** is where you make a false claim and a **Type II error** is where you miss an effect. These names are, as you can see, terribly confusing and it is very hard to remember which is which. The names were chosen by Egon Pearson, the son of the statistician Karl Pearson. Pearson senior was a colourful character with a strange fondness for classifying things using confusing names (he once separated a set of statistical patterns into 12 types, which he called Type I to Type XII. Very helpful).

Egon inherited his father's love of statistics, which is good for us as he helped advance the discipline quite considerably. Sadly, however, he also inherited his father's love of confusing names, hence 'Type I' and 'Type II' errors. The best method I've ever seen for remembering which way round these go was once printed as a joke in *The Psychologist*:

> Error, type one: the results are a con;
> Error, type two: the results have slipped through.

Summary

There are two ways you can make a mistake when doing research: you can claim to have discovered something when really you haven't, or you can fail to spot a real effect because it wasn't obvious enough for you. You can never get both these risks down to zero! As you reduce the risk of one, the other becomes more likely. The usual p-value cut-off of .05 helps us manage the risk of making a false claim, and if we pay attention to statistical power we can also manage the risk of missing effects.

'Significance'

What would you think if I said 'I have carried out an analysis and my findings are very significant'? The chances are you would think I had made a discovery that will change the world. However, I would actually be saying something else. You see, it is common for people who use statistics to say their findings are 'significant' whenever they see a p-value less than .05. This causes quite a lot of confusion to ordinary folk. If I carried out a study of snails' eating habits and announced I had found a 'significant' difference between two very similar species of snail, most people would say 'Significant? That doesn't change the world one little bit! How can you describe it as significant?'

So the word 'significant' has two very different meanings. There is the everyday meaning of the word, where it more-or-less means 'important'. However, when a statistician says 'significant' they do not mean 'important': they simply mean they have seen a low p-value and so have rejected their null hypothesis. So – and this is the confusing thing – a statistical analysis can produce findings which are significant – but not significant. That is, the results of an analysis can be significant (p is less than .05) but not significant (nobody cares about them)!

Interestingly, the Royal Statistical Society's in-house magazine is called *Significance*, which shows that the double meaning of the word isn't lost on professional statisticians either.

👁 Going further: problems with p

One of the things many people struggle with when they first learn about statistics is this cut-off value of .05. If a statistical test comes back with an end result of $p = .001$, meaning there is only a 0.1% chance that the effect you saw in your sample would not be seen again, then everything is fine – you have almost certainly found an effect and can happily say so; similarly, if $p = .96$ it is easy to conclude there was nothing going on in your sample (there would be a 96% chance you would be wrong if you said there was). But what about when we see values close to the alpha cut-off? Does $p = .049999$ really mean there is a 'significant' result that you can tell people about, while $p = .050001$ does not? After all, the two values are hardly different. What would you conclude if you did an analysis and the result was just over the usual cut-off, at $p = .051$? Would you say you found something noteworthy or not?

The problem is that the .05 cut-off is just an arbitrary figure chosen by the statistical pioneer Ronald Fisher. Nobody can seriously defend the idea that a p-value of .049 means we have a useful finding but a p-value of .051 does not – I'm certainly not going to try and defend it. Don't think I'm criticizing Fisher: a cut-off was definitely needed for judging p-values and he gave us a good one. But it does mean we have difficult decisions to make whenever we find a p-value close to the cut-off point.

There is another reason p-values can be a problem: the same effect (the same difference between two groups, for example) will have a different p-value depending on how many people you tested. Let's say I go to a school and test a group of boys and a group of girls on a spelling quiz; the boys score an average of 23 points whereas the girls score an average of 20 points. This exact same difference – 3 points – would not be significant if the groups were small but would be significant if the groups were large: if the difference between two groups stays the same, p will change as the group size changes. Because the same difference has a lower p-value when the sample is large, we can often shrink our p-values, and make non-significant findings become 'significant', simply by collecting more data.

In many ways this is exactly what we want. We saw back in Chapter 3 that larger samples tend to represent their populations better than smaller samples. Statistical tests know this: they know larger samples tend to be better, and so are more 'forgiving' with large samples than with small – they give a lower p-value to the same finding.

However, this becomes a problem when we collect a lot of data in large studies. Because p-values get lower as we look at more people, if we collect enough data then almost any effect will become significant. I once carried out a survey of almost 5000 people. With this many people, almost every effect I looked at was statistically significant. If I were dishonest, I could exploit this: I could say 'Look! I've found dozens of statistically significant differences – am I not an amazing researcher?' when in fact most of the effects are tiny and just not worth getting excited about.

The problem is that statistical tests were only designed to handle up to a few hundred individuals; when we use them with larger groups they get overexcited and start seeing effects all over the place. Imagine if I asked you to watch the people in a public place and to alert me when you saw somebody wearing a red hat. If there were only 30 people present, it would be quite surprising and interesting if you saw one of them wearing a red hat. But if there were thousands and thousands of people, it would be odd if one of them *wasn't* wearing a red hat: in a crowd of 10,000 people *of course* one will be wearing a red hat, so I'm not going to be very interested when you tell me. Something similar to this happens with statistical tests: if I have tested thousands of individuals, *of course* there'll be a bit of a difference between the groups I'm comparing, but this doesn't necessarily mean it's worth getting excited about.

Summary

Judging whether what you saw in a sample will generalize to other people is usually done using p. However, we have difficult decisions to make when a p-value is very close to our alpha cut-off point. Also, p-values aren't really helpful with very large samples because when we test a lot of individuals, p is almost always very low, even when the effect we have seen is tiny.

◉ Chapter summary

With most statistics, we start with the idea that there will be no effect of whatever we are studying – this idea is called the null hypothesis. We calculate how likely it is that we'd see the results we collected if this null hypothesis were true. If there's not much chance of seeing our results if the null hypothesis were true, we conclude that it probably isn't true and that the thing we are studying probably does have an effect.

Chapter 10

Did you see what you expected to see? Understanding the chi-squared test

In this chapter I will introduce you to your first proper statistical procedure. The test we'll cover is called the chi-squared test. 'Chi' is a Greek letter. It is pronounced 'kai', and in Greek is written with a sort of squiggly letter x – χ – although usually when we talk about it we write it out in English: chi.

The chi-squared test does something really quite simple. We count up how often something happened, and the test tells us if we saw what we expected to see. For example, let's say I had 100 people in a room and, laying out four plates of sandwiches, I asked everybody to take a sandwich. What should I expect to happen? How many people would I expect to choose each plate?

As you now know, every study starts with a null hypothesis – we always start out assuming that there is nothing interesting going on. So in this case, we would assume that people don't prefer one plate to the others. If this is true, and people don't prefer one plate to the others, I would *expect* people to choose a plate at random, and so I would *expect* 25 people to take a sandwich from each plate. But what if 90 people took a sandwich from the same plate? This would be very different from what the null hypothesis predicted, and the chi-squared test would tell me this. This would tell me that people were not choosing plates at random; instead, they preferred one plate over the others.

I'm going to cover two different versions of the chi-squared test here, and let me say right away that this is a slightly unusual approach. The second version of the chi-squared test is the one that most people learn when they study psychology, and not all psychologists know about the first version I'll cover. This is a real shame! Not only is the first version of the chi-squared test incredibly useful (I find uses for it all the time), but it is also a lot easier to understand. So we'll start there, with the simpler version, and this will make it much easier for you to understand the second version of the chi-squared test when we get to it. If you're reading this book for a qualification then this second version – the two-way chi-squared test for association – is almost certainly the one you will need to know about, but trust me: it'll be much easier to understand if you read through the first version beforehand, and so it's worth taking those few extra minutes.

> **In this chapter we will examine:**
> - The goodness-of-fit chi-squared test
> - The two-way chi-squared test for studying associations

◉ Did you see what you expected to see? The goodness-of-fit chi-squared test

You might remember that back in Chapter 8, when discussing graphs, I mentioned the difference between continuous and categorical data. Continuous data are things like height and weight, where numbers can take almost any value, and can change by very small amounts. Categorical data are different: we have categorical data when people can only belong to a limited number of groups. So, for example, sex is a categorical measurement. There are only two sexes to which people can belong: they are either male or female. The plates of sandwiches also gave categorical data: people either took a sandwich from the first plate, the second plate, the third plate or the fourth, giving four groups, or *categories*, of people.

One of the great things about categorical data is that we can look at how many people fall into each group and decide if this is what we expected to see. Let me give you an example: I taught a group of 48 students yesterday and noticed there were 36 women and 12 men. In my class, then, I had two categories of student – women and men – and the numbers 36 and 12 simply show how many students were in each category.

When I learnt that my class had 48 people in it, I naturally expected an even split into 24 men and 24 women. Thirty-six women and 12 men is quite a long way from what I expected, which suggests there must be a reason why I had more women in my class than men. Perhaps the subject I was teaching appeals to women more than men, or perhaps my class competed with another class which men tend to find more interesting. Either way, just by looking at the numbers I was able to see whether the people were divided across the two categories as I would expect. Once I saw that the people were not divided as I expected them to be, this revealed a whole new question which I could explore further (*why* were there more women than men?).

Here's another example, which will let us go into a bit more detail. I met a university student a couple of years ago who complained that 'All my teachers are really old: most of the people teaching me are in their fifties.' Clearly, the teachers that she had didn't match what she was expecting, so let's think about what she should have expected.

It is more or less true that the people who teach in universities are aged between 25 and 65. Very few people join a university or college faculty before they are 25, as they usually need to study for two or three degrees first; most retire at about 65. If academics are aged 25 to 65, we can split them into four equal categories:

25 to 35
35 to 45
45 to 55
55 to 65

Now, I happen to know a college that conveniently has exactly 200 teachers. So at this college, how many teachers would you expect to see in each of these four age groups?

To answer this question, it's really useful to start out with an assumption. In this case, we might assume that teachers are spread evenly across all the possible ages, so there would be just as many in each of the four categories. This assumption is our null hypothesis, the idea that nothing interesting is happening in our data.

If this null hypothesis is right, and there is nothing going on at the college to bias the age groups, we would expect to see $200 \div 4 = 50$ teachers in each. We would expect around 50 teachers to be aged between 25 and 35, another 50 to be aged between 35 and 45, and so on.

On the other hand, the null hypothesis could be wrong, and perhaps there is something going on at this college which means the teachers aren't evenly spread across the four age groups. For example, perhaps the principal prefers to recruit younger teachers because they don't need to be paid as much. If something like this is happening, some of the age groups will have more people in them than others. This is our alternative hypothesis, and our job as researchers is to choose between this and the null hypothesis. So to recap:

- If the null hypothesis is correct, there will be more or less the same number of people in each age group.
- If the alternative hypothesis is correct, there will be more people in some age groups than in others.

We can choose between these two ideas using the chi-squared test. We start by working out how many people we would expect to see in each age group if the null hypothesis is correct. Once we know this, we count up how many people *actually* fall into each age group. For each of the age groups, we simply compare what we saw with what we expected to see. If there is a big difference between the numbers we saw and the numbers we expected, we know that there is something interesting going on, and that people are not evenly spread across the groups. But if we see exactly what the null hypothesis told us we would see, or something close to that, we know the null hypothesis is probably right, and that there is no difference between the four age groups.

In the college with 200 teachers we would expect to see this:

25 to 35	50 people
35 to 45	50 people
45 to 55	50 people
55 to 65	50 people

But the college I know actually looks like this:

25 to 35	90 people
35 to 45	25 people
45 to 55	45 people
55 to 65	40 people

Now that we know how the age groups really look, we can compare what we expected to see with the real data. All we need to do is calculate the difference between what we observed and what we expected for each age group. Let's do this now:

Age group	Observed	Expected	Observed – Expected
25 to 35	90 people	50 people	90 – 50 = 40
35 to 45	25 people	50 people	25 – 50 = –25
45 to 55	45 people	50 people	45 – 50 = –5
55 to 65	40 people	50 people	40 – 50 = –10

This is the first step to working out the chi-squared statistic. The full formula for the chi-squared statistic is this:

$$\chi^2 = \sum \frac{(Observed - Expected)^2}{Expected}$$

That's a slightly scary formula, so let's work out what it is saying, then go through it one bit at a time.

The formula can be read, more or less, in plain English. The first part is the Greek letter sigma, Σ, which means 'the sum of'. So we are going to sum, or add together, a group of numbers. What numbers are we going to add together? The rest of the formula, after Σ, tells us. The rest of the formula, to the right of Σ, says 'the observed value minus its expected value, then squared, then divided by its expected value'. Putting all this together, here are the steps that we need to carry out to calculate chi-squared according to the formula – you can see that using the equation is a lot like following a recipe:

1 For each group, get the Observed value (the number of teachers we actually saw) and subtract the Expected value (50, in this case)
2 For each group, square this number
3 For each group, divide the number you just calculated by the Expected value (50)
4 Sum (add together) the numbers you just calculated for all the groups.

This gives you chi-squared.

Let's follow these four steps for our teachers, to make the whole thing clearer. We already carried out step 1 when we calculated the Observed – Expected values for the four groups. Step 2 is to square these values to calculate (Observed – Expected)^2 for each age group:

Age group	Observed – Expected	(Observed – Expected)^2
25 to 35	90 – 50 = 40	$40^2 = 40 \times 40 = 1600$
35 to 45	25 – 50 = –25	$-25^2 = -25 \times -25 = 625$
45 to 55	45 – 50 = –5	$-5^2 = -5 \times -5 = 25$
55 to 65	40 – 50 = –10	$-10^2 = -10 \times -10 = 100$

We have now calculated the whole top part of the formula: the '(Observed – Expected)^2' part. Step 3 is to divide each of the four numbers we just calculated by the expected value. In this case, the expected value for each group is 50, because if there is nothing interesting going on then we'd expect to see 50 teachers in each age group. So let's do that:

Age group	(Observed – Expected)^2	(Observed – Expected)^2 / Expected
25 to 35	1600	1600 / 50 = 32
35 to 45	625	625 / 50 = 12.5
45 to 55	25	25 / 50 = 0.5
55 to 65	100	100 / 50 = 2

You can see that when there is a large difference between what we expected and what we actually saw, like in the first group of teachers, we have calculated a large number. When the number of people in a group was close to what we expected, like in the third group of teachers, we have calculated a small number. Now let's look at the chi-square formula again, just to make sure we're on the right lines:

$$\chi^2 = \sum \frac{(Observed - Expected)^2}{Expected}$$

Okay, we've done the (Observed – Expected)^2 part for each of the groups, and we've divided this by the Expected value for each group too. So we've calculated everything in the formula after the Σ symbol. The very last thing we need to do is follow step 4 and add together the numbers we just calculated, as the Σ symbol tells us. If we do this for our four groups of teachers, we get the result $\chi^2 = 32 + 12.5 + 0.5 + 2 = 47$.

And that's it! We've now calculated chi-squared. For our four groups of teachers, the chi-squared statistic is 47. Because of the way the formula works, this number will be large whenever there is a large difference between what we expected to see and what we really saw. So just how large is our value of 47? We find out by looking up the number in a chi-squared table. Most statistics books have these tables in the back, and you can also find chi-square calculators online. To help you out, I've calculated a small version of a chi-square table.

Degrees of freedom	Significance level		
	.10	.05	.01
1	2.70	3.84	6.63
2	4.61	5.99	9.21
3	6.25	7.81	11.34
4	7.78	9.49	13.28
5	9.24	11.07	15.09
6	10.64	12.59	16.81
7	12.02	14.07	18.48
8	13.36	15.51	20.09
9	14.68	16.92	21.67
10	15.99	18.31	23.21

The table probably looks quite daunting, so let me talk you through how we use it. We've calculated chi-squared for our four groups of teachers, and we know it is 47. We now need to compare this value we have calculated to the **critical value** in the table. In this case, the critical value will come from the row with 3 degrees of freedom. Why this row? Because *the degrees of freedom for this chi-squared test are the number of groups, minus 1*. As we have four groups here, the degrees of freedom are 3. (There was a box about degrees of freedom back in Chapter 7, if you can't remember what I'm talking about here.)

So we know that we need to get a number from row 3, but which column do we use? That depends how confident we want to be about our conclusions. If we get our critical value from the '.10' column, we will be checking whether or not p is less than .10; if we get our critical value from the '.05' column, we will be checking whether or not p is less than .05; and if we get our critical value from the '.01' column we will be checking whether or not p is less than .01. Remember: p is the probability of seeing the effect we saw, or an even more extreme effect, just by chance.

Most researchers focus on whether or not p is less than .05, so let's do that, and take our critical value from the '.05' column. We already know we're using the 3 degrees of freedom row for this analysis, which means the critical value for this analysis is 7.81. *If our chi-squared value is greater than the critical value, we know* $p < .05$, *and so we know we have found a significant effect.* In this case, our chi-squared value was 47. This is bigger than 7.81, so we have found something statistically significant. We can say, with a fair amount of confidence, that the 200 teachers at the college did not fall evenly across the age groups. As the analysis was significant, the null hypothesis seems to be wrong: there was probably something interesting happening which put more teachers into some groups than others. So we would reject this null hypothesis and conclude instead that the four groups did not have equal numbers of teachers – there was something going on to put more teachers in some groups than others.

Thinking mathematically →
Making formulae easier to understand

Some people can look at a formula, like the chi-squared formula, and instantly see what is going on. If you're one of these people then you're very lucky. I'm certainly not like that, and even though I regularly teach statistics like those we're covering here, and use them all the time in my research, it usually takes me some thought. So here's a quick tip that I find really useful for understanding formulae when I see them.

Most statistical formulae involve ratios, and so involve dividing something by something else. For example, in the chi-squared formula we divide '(Observed – Expected)^2' by 'Expected'. Whenever you see a formula that involves dividing something by something else, think of this:

$$statistic = \frac{When\ this\ bit\ is\ big\ the\ statistic\ is\ big}{When\ this\ bit\ is\ big\ the\ statistic\ is\ small}$$

In the chi-squared formula, the top bit of the equation involves 'Observed – Expected'. So when there is a big difference between what you saw and what you expected to see, the chi-squared statistic will be big. The bottom part of the chi-squared equation is 'Expected', so when you expect big values, your chi-squared statistic will be smaller. This last fact is useful, as it makes the test work the same way whether you are testing 200 people or 2000.

Have one more attempt at the goodness-of-fit test

The goodness-of-fit chi-squared test is the first statistical test that we've calculated in full in this book. Like a lot of statistical tests, it looks more daunting when it is explained in full, and the best way to understand the test properly is just to get stuck in and do it a few times. And remember that you don't need to memorize the test formula! If you ever need to use it in the future you can always just look up the exact steps involved. What you should focus on at this stage is making sure you understand what each of the steps is doing, and what the result means.

So if you want a bit more practice, to really help cement the goodness-of-fit chi-squared test in your mind, here are some more data you can analyse. My local coffee shop offers to make coffee from three types of bean: Columbian, Costa Rican and Sumatran. A question we might ask is whether these are all equally popular, or whether customers have a preference for some varieties over others. So I asked the shop's owner to count up how many people ordered each type of coffee one day. Here's what we found:

Columbian	112 orders
Costa Rican	88 orders
Sumatran	100 orders
(Total	300 orders)

Using the method we've just gone through, I'd like you to calculate the chi-squared value for these data. Then use the chi-squared table above to decide whether or not the customers at this coffee shop prefer one type of bean over the others. The null hypothesis will be that people have no preference, and so will choose the three coffees equally often. The alternative hypothesis will be that people have a preference, and do not choose the three coffees equally often. Answers in the next paragraph!

How did you get on? You should have found that $\chi^2 = 2.88$. You should also have found that the critical value, at the .05 level, is 5.99. Because our chi-squared value is less than the critical value, we do *not* have a significant result: although some types of coffee bean were chosen more often than others, the null hypothesis still looks like the best bet, and we would conclude that people have no preference. Yes, if we look at the data, people seemed to like Columbian coffee the most and to like Costa Rican coffee the least, but this difference just isn't big enough for us to reject the null hypothesis. This difference is small enough that it falls into a 'zone of doubt'. We would need to see a bigger difference than this before we could say with confidence that the customers had a real preference.

A very brief introduction to the binomial test

Way back at the start of this book, when I was blathering on about buttery spreads, I mentioned that I used a procedure called the **binomial test**. You can think of this as a special version of the goodness-of-fit chi-squared test which works with just two categories. You could use the binomial test to see if the number of men entering a building is different to the number of women, or whether the number of people who answer a question with 'yes' is different to the number of people who answer with 'no'. Although beneath the surface it uses different calculations to the chi-squared test, you can think of it as doing a very similar job.

Tables, *p*-values and computer software

In this book, as you will now have noticed, I am teaching you how to calculate statistics and then look up a critical value to decide whether or not the results are statistically significant. For example, in the test above we calculated the chi-square statistic and then looked up the critical value in a table. We had to decide in advance which *p*-value we were interested in. In the example I used the .05 cut-off, which means I wanted to know whether *p* was above or below .05. We knew that if the chi-squared number was greater than the critical value, then the *p*-value must be less than .05.

However, I just want to make you aware that things happen slightly differently when you carry out statistical procedures using computer software. If I carried out that chi-squared test using a statistical program, I wouldn't have to look at critical values. Instead, the software would give me the chi-squared statistic and an exact *p*-value. For instance, if I enter the coffee data into some statistical software I get this output:

```
χ-squared = 2.88, degrees of freedom = 2, p-value = 0.24
```

The end result is the same – I can see that *p* is over .05 and so I conclude that there is no preference for one type of coffee over another. However, by using a computer I can see the exact *p*-value and so have a little more information: I know that the result is not significant, and I can clearly see exactly how far away it is from the .05 cut-off. It's just two different approaches to doing the same thing. When learning statistics it's really good to see how the calculations are performed, as that way you properly understand the tests, but when you use statistics for real you might find you prefer the ease and the extra information that comes with using a computer. Throughout this book I'll describe both approaches so you can see how the two compare.

◉ Looking for associations: the two-way chi-squared test

As I mentioned earlier, quite a lot of psychologists never learn the goodness-of-fit chi-squared test. The main reason I covered it is because it makes it quite easy to see exactly what chi-squared does, which is to compare the numbers we saw with the numbers we expected to see. If you really focus on this idea – that we're comparing what we saw with what we expected to see – then you should always find the chi-squared test quite easy.

What we're going to do now is use the same sort of idea – comparing observed and expected numbers – to look at whether two different variables are associated with each other. As with most statistics, this is easiest to understand with an example, so let's look at these data:

	Scared of clowns?	
	Yes	No
Men	51	9
Women	36	14

In the goodness–of–fit chi-squared test we looked at just one variable, age group. Here, we are looking at two things at the same time: we are looking at gender *and* whether or not people are scared of clowns. Looking at these two variables together will tell us whether or not they are associated. For example, let's say we find men are more scared of clowns than women. In this case, there is an *association* between being male and being scared of clowns.

The only difference between this two-way chi-squared test and the goodness-of-fit test is that we work out the Expected values in a slightly different way. In the goodness-of-fit test we got the Expected values by dividing the total number of people by the total number of cells. Here, we cannot do that. To decide how many men we expect to be scared of clowns, we have to look at both the total number of men *and* the total number of people who are scared of clowns. In fact, the Expected number for each of the cells in the table is calculated with this simple formula:

$$Expected = \frac{row\ total \times column\ total}{grand\ total}$$

To use this, we need to calculate the various row and column totals. So here is the same table again with these numbers added.

	Scared of clowns?		
	Yes	**No**	Total
Men	51	9	60
Women	36	14	50
Total	87	23	110

There's nothing very complicated about that: I've just added 51 and 9 to get 60, added 51 and 36 to get 87, and so on. The grand total, down in the bottom-right corner, is just the overall number of people who were tested (51 + 9 + 36 + 14).

Now we have the row totals, the column totals and the grand total, we can work out the Expected number for each of the four cells in the table. For example, to work out how many men we expect to be scared of clowns:

$$Expected = \frac{row\ total \times column\ total}{grand\ total} = \frac{60 \times 87}{110} = \frac{5220}{110} = 47.45$$

It might seem a strange that we 'expect' a number of people that isn't a whole number – who is this 0.45 of a man?! – but don't worry about that. The important thing is that we now have the Expected value for the number of men who are scared of clowns, 47.45, and we can compare this with the Observed value, which was 51. We can see that the number of men who were scared of clowns in our data was actually quite close to what we should have expected.

Here are the Expected values for the other three cells in the table, which I've worked out in just the same way (feel free to check my calculations): the Expected number of men who are not scared of clowns is 12.54, the Expected number of women who are scared of clowns is 39.54, and the Expected number of women who are not scared of clowns is 10.45.

From this point, calculating chi-squared is exactly the same as for the goodness-of-fit test we saw earlier. Now we have the Expected values for each cell, we just use the same formula as before:

$$\chi^2 = \sum \frac{(Observed - Expected)^2}{Expected}$$

Let's break this formula down into simple steps again. The first part is to calculate $(Observed - Expected)^2$ for each category.

Category	Observed	Expected	Observed – Expected	(Observed – Expected)^2
Men, scared of clowns	51	47.45	3.55	12.60
Men, not scared of clowns	9	12.54	–3.54	12.53
Women, scared of clowns	36	39.54	–3.54	12.53
Women, not scared of clowns	14	10.45	3.55	12.60

Now we have the $(Observed - Expected)^2$ numbers for each category, we just need to divide these by the Expected value for each.

Category	(Observed – Expected)^2	(Observed – Expected)^2 / Expected
Men, scared of clowns	12.60	12.60 / 47.45 = 0.27
Men, not scared of clowns	12.53	12.53 / 12.54 = 1.00
Women, scared of clowns	12.53	12.53 / 39.54 = 0.32
Women, not scared of clowns	12.60	12.60 / 10.45 = 1.21

Finally we add these last numbers together to get the chi-squared value: $0.27 + 1.00 + 0.32 + 1.21 = 2.80$. We can look this value up on the chi-squared table above to see whether or not it is significant. The degrees of freedom for this chi-square test are (number of rows – 1) × (number of columns – 1). In this case, there are two rows and two columns, so the degrees of freedom are $(2 – 1) \times (2 – 1) = 1 \times 1 = 1$.

When we look at the chi-squared table I gave you earlier, we see that with one degree of freedom, and a significance level of .05, the critical value is 3.84. The chi-squared value we calculated was lower than this critical value, so p must be greater than .05 and the test is not significant. *There is no significant association between gender and being scared of clowns: men and women seem just as likely to be scared of clowns.* Yes, the data table makes it look as though men are slightly more afraid of clowns than women, but this effect just isn't clear enough for us to read anything into it. The statistics tell us that this difference is so small that we shouldn't give up the null hypothesis.

Have one more attempt at the chi-squared test for association

There's just no substitute for calculating statistics yourself if you really want to understand what's going on, so here is one more set of data. I'll steer you through the calculations needed to work out chi-squared, but you can do them yourself this time.

I took a group of students from my university, some from the psychology department, some from the physics department and some from the chemistry department. I then asked everybody whether they had any pets. Here are the results I found – note that, as with all chi-squared tests, each person falls into only one cell:

	Has pets	No pets
Psychologists	46	30
Physicists	9	26
Chemists	21	86

We want to see if there is any association between the subject a person studies and whether or not they own pets, so our null hypothesis would be 'There is no association between a student's subject and whether they own pets.' To test this, our first job is simply to calculate the row and column totals, and the grand total (the total number of people you have studied, in the bottom-right cell). So do that now:

	Has pets	No pets	**Total**
Psychologists	46	30	
Physicists	9	26	
Chemists	21	86	
Total			

The next step is to calculate the Expected value for each of the six cells. You already have the Observed values – these are the numbers I gave you in the table – and you can use the row and column totals to calculate the Expected values. Remember, the Expected value for each cell is calculated with:

$$Expected = \frac{row\ total \times column\ total}{grand\ total}$$

When you have calculated Expected values for each of the six cells, you have everything you need to calculate chi-squared according to the usual formula, so do this now:

$$\chi^2 = \sum \frac{(Observed - Expected)^2}{Expected}$$

Take your time and work out each stage of the recipe carefully:

1   For each of the six cells, calculate Observed – Expected
2   For each cell, square this value
3   For each cell, divide the result by the Expected number
4   Add together all the numbers you've calculated, to get chi-squared.

You should have got a result of 34.31 (or maybe something a *tiny* bit different if you rounded your numbers off differently to me). If you did get this result: well done!

Now you just need to look up this value on the chi-squared table to see if it is significant – that is, to see if it is larger than the critical value. We need to know the degrees of freedom for this test, and in this case the degrees of freedom are ...?

Did you say 2? Remember, the degrees of freedom for this chi-squared test are (number of rows – 1) × (number of columns – 1), so in this case we have $(3 – 1) × (2 – 1)$ which gives 2.

When we look in the chi-squared table, at the 2 degrees of freedom row and the .05 significance level column, we find a critical value of 5.99. Our chi-squared value was *may* bigger than this, so we certainly seem to have found a significant association between the students' subject and whether or not they owned pets. Because our chi-squared statistic was higher than the critical value, we know $p < .05$, and so we would reject the null hypothesis and say that the students were not all the same in their pet ownership: some types of student were more likely to own pets than others.

Now that we've worked all that out by hand, here are the results from when I analysed these data on a computer, to show you how the two approaches compare. The results I got were:

χ-squared = 34.27, df = 2, p-value = 0.000000036

You can certainly see an advantage of using a computer here. Whereas our hand calculation was able to tell us whether or not p was less than .05, the computer gave us more detail: we can see that the chances of seeing those data, if the null hypothesis is correct, are *incredibly* small – millionths of one per cent – and so I can say with a huge amount of confidence that there really is an association in those data: psychology students certainly do seem to own pets more than the other students.

◉ Chapter summary

The chi-squared test lets you look at how often things happened and decide whether there were any patterns – did some things happen more often than they should have, for example.

Chapter 11

One of the most useful things you'll ever learn: the normal distribution

I just did a strange thing: I just spent two hours flicking through a book over and over again, but never read a word.

The book was on top of a stack of books next to my desk – I had recently finished reading it and hadn't yet got round to putting it away. During a quiet moment I absently picked it up, turned to the back, and saw that it had 302 pages. I said to myself, 'I wonder how easy it would be to riffle quickly through the pages and stop right in the middle of the book, at page 151.' (Yes, I'm quite good at finding ways to avoid work ...)

So I flicked rapidly through the pages, trying to stop exactly halfway through the book, and landed on page 155. Not bad! Only a few pages away from where I was aiming.

But then I started to wonder how consistently I could do this, and so I had another go: I landed on page 135. This wasn't quite so good, so I had another attempt, landing on page 107. I was getting worse! The next two attempts were also poor, except on these two occasions I overshot my target, landing on pages 171 and 177. On my sixth attempt I managed to land on page 155 again.

(I would like to say I am not just inventing these numbers to make a point. I really did all this, and I would encourage you to have a go at this exercise yourself as it is really helpful to see the numbers appearing.)

So sometimes I overshot the page I was aiming for and sometimes I undershot. I started to wonder what would happen if I carried on doing this – would there be a pattern to how often I landed on pages before or after page 151? I put on some music and started to flick through the book over and over, noting the page number I hit on each attempt. Half the time I started from the front and landed on odd-numbered pages and half the time I started from the back and landed on even-numbered pages.

After a while, I had done this two hundred times, and had a list of all the pages on which I had landed. But a long list of page numbers didn't tell me anything useful by itself. I needed to summarize the page numbers somehow to make them easier to understand, and in this case I thought that a graph would be really useful. I started by putting the page numbers along the bottom of the graph. Then, just to make the graph easier to read, I took small groups of pages – 100 to 104, for example – and counted up how often I had landed on all those pages. This gave me the graph shown in Figure 11.1.

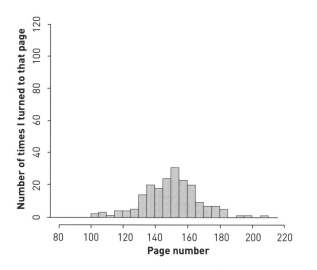

Figure 11.1 Distribution of page numbers after flicking through the book 200 times

The graph made things much clearer. Once I had plotted it I could see that overall I had landed on pages ranging from 103 to 206. It seemed that sometimes I got quite heavy-handed in my page flicking and went way past the point I was aiming for. But although I landed on a wide range of different pages, there was definitely some sort of pattern to where I landed: the closer a page was to the centre of the book, the more often I landed on that page. I landed on pages near 151 quite often, and the further a page was from this point, the less likely I was to land on that page. Interesting.

I decided to keep going. I repeated the exercise another 200 times, rapidly riffling through the pages and trying to stop in the dead centre of the book. Each time I recorded the number of the page on which I landed. When I had a total of 400 page numbers, I drew my graph again (Figure 11.2).

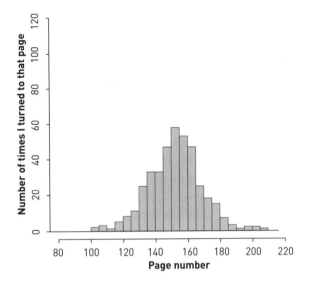

Figure 11.2 Distribution of page numbers after flicking through the book 400 times

It looked as though the pattern was holding. Sometimes I overshot the middle of the book and sometimes I undershot, but the closer a page was to the centre, the more likely I was to land on it. I only rarely landed on pages close to 100 or 200, but often landed on pages around 151. I repeated the task another two hundred times ...

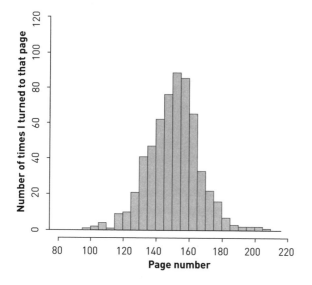

Figure 11.3 Distribution of page numbers after flicking through the book 600 times

... and the pattern continued to hold (Figure 11.3). Getting a bit bored by this stage, I repeated my flicking a final 200 times, giving me 800 page numbers in total. Figure 11.4 shows how my graph now looked.

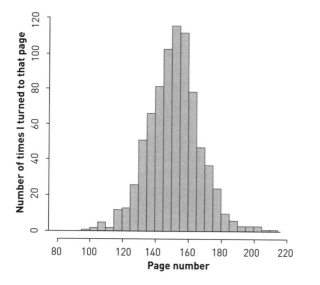

Figure 11.4 Distribution of page numbers after flicking through the book 800 times

So how had I performed overall? Clearly I had not landed in the centre of the book every time, but I landed close to the centre more often than I landed far from it. And the closer a page was to the centre, the more likely I was to land on it.

I decided to find the average of the 800 page numbers and was pleased to see that the mean page number was exactly 152. I had been aiming for page 151, and my attempts had been centred just one page away. As is clear from the graph, sometimes I overshot the middle of the book and sometimes I undershot, but across all my attempts the overshooting and the undershooting balanced out nicely.[6]

Looking at Figure 11.4, a couple of points were very clear:

- I landed near the middle of the book more than anywhere else. The further a page was from the middle, the less often I landed there.
- The graph was more or less symmetrical: each time I landed on a page before the middle of the book was balanced out by another time when I landed on a page after the middle.

This is all really interesting because the pattern in my graph, which shows the pages I landed on while flicking through the book, looks just like one of the most common patterns we see in statistics. (And I would like to stress again that these are genuine data.)

Before I discuss this statistical pattern, just take a moment to make sure you are completely happy with what I have told you about my morning of book-flicking. Here is a difficult question. If you answer this correctly, you will have learnt something really important about statistics.

I flicked through the book 800 times, and recorded the page number I landed on each time. This meant I had a list of 800 page numbers. I now close my eyes and pick one of those page numbers at random from my score sheet. I say, 'I'm not going to tell you which page number I chose, but I'll tell you this: it was either page 145 or page 182.' Looking at Figure 11.4, which of these two pages seems most likely?

The answer is page 145. You can see from the graph that I landed near page 145 far more often than I landed near page 182. In fact, I landed on page 145 twenty-five times but only landed on page 182 once. This means the number 145 is on my score sheet twenty-five times, but 182 is on

---

6   Writing this reminded me of a classic joke. A sociologist, a physicist and a statistician go hunting. Spotting a stag, the sociologist fires his rifle but the shot goes to the left. The physicist fires but the shot goes to the right. The statistician leaps in the air and shouts 'We got him!'

there just once. If I pluck a number at random from the score sheet, it is much more likely to be 145. This shows us something important: the **distribution** of page numbers, which is shown in the graph, can tell you how likely it is that something will happen.

◉ Normal distributions

I flicked through my book 800 times and looked at the way the pages were distributed. Had I not got bored, and had I instead continued to do this repeatedly, I would expect my graph to get smoother and smoother as I continued to flick through the book. Odd little coincidences – I once landed on page 155 three times in a row, for example – would start to get balanced out by other odd little coincidences. The graph would become more and more symmetrical.

Eventually, if I had the patience to flick through the book many thousands of times, I would almost certainly end up with a set of page numbers distributed as shown in Figure 11.5.

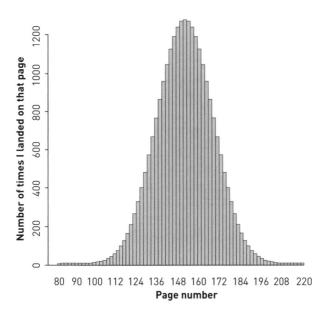

Figure 11.5 Typical distribution of page numbers after flicking through a book many times

This graph shows a pattern you might have heard of, as it is quite famous. Often known as the 'bell curve', because of its shape, it is more properly called a **normal distribution**, or a 'Gaussian' distribution after the German mathematician Karl Gauss who first described it.

Many of the things we measure follow this pattern – which is how it gets the name 'normal' – and so you will meet the normal distribution all the time. We use statistics to help us make sense of the world around us. The world is full of normal distributions, and so statistics are too.

When I say the world is full of normal distributions, I mean that if you measure all sorts of things – the time people spend commuting to work, the thickness of chimpanzees' hairs, the amount of pollen bees carry – you will often see curves like these. If the average time spent commuting to work is 25 minutes, and you pick a worker at random, that person will probably spend around 25 minutes commuting to work. The further you go from this average time – when you look at 2-minute commutes, or 90-minute commutes – the less likely you are to find people who travel for this length of time.

You might find a normal distribution, like the one in the graph, if you measured how worn out the carpet is along a corridor (it would be most worn right in the centre and less worn as you moved to the edges). You would see a normal distribution if you measured how fast people can run (most would run at around the average speed, and only a few would be particularly fast or slow). You might also see a normal distribution if you could measure the distance people drove their cars before they had a collision. Let's say, just as an example, the average driver travels 30,000 kilometres before they have a collision. If this were the case, most people should expect to have an experience close to this – most people will travel something like 30,000 kilometres before crashing. Of course, some would go further than this, and some would go a shorter distance, but for most people it would be somewhere not too far from 30,000 kilometres.

There would be a few people, however, down in the tails of the distribution, who would have a very different experience: there would be people who manage to drive millions of kilometres without anything bad happening to them, and a few poor wretches who crash after driving only a few metres. Understanding the normal distribution gives you a good grasp of what non-statisticians call 'luck'.

👁 Useful things to know about normal distributions

I think having looked at the graphs I've shown you, we would all agree the page numbers I landed on as I flicked through my book were more or less normally distributed. Had I carried on flicking through the book, the curve would have got more and more like a perfect bell curve. This is useful, because when you know you are looking at normally distributed numbers – and, when flicking through a book, it certainly seems we are – you instantly get a whole lot of extra information for free. Let me explain.

I said that after flicking through my book 800 times, trying to land on page 151, the average of all the page numbers was close to my target, at page 152. Do you remember, back in Chapter 7, I mentioned something called the standard deviation? I said if you have a group of numbers that vary from one another, the standard deviation shows the average amount by which the numbers are different from the mean.

With my book-flicking, we know the mean page number was 152. I've just calculated the standard deviation of all the page numbers I landed on and found it was 16. Now this is where it gets interesting: thanks to its shape, the normal distribution has some very useful properties which give us free information. One of the neat things about the normal distribution is this: when a set of numbers is normally distributed, as my page numbers were, almost exactly 68% of the numbers fall within one standard deviation of the mean.

In the page-flicking data, the mean page number, plus one standard deviation, is $152 + 16 = 168$. The mean page number minus one standard deviation is $152 - 16 = 136$. So here's the neat trick: I now instantly know that 68% of all the page numbers I landed on were between 136 and 168.

Why is it useful to know this? Here is just one answer: because flicking through my book gives normally distributed page numbers, I know – in advance! – that the next time I pick up my book and flick through the pages, there is a 68% chance I will land on a page between 136 and 168. In fact, let's try it …

Yes, I just flicked through the book one more time and got page 144, exactly as I predicted. It was more likely I would land somewhere between 136 and 168 than it was I would land outside this zone, and that's exactly what happened.

I will say more about this in a moment, but I think to focus your mind I need to move on from flicking through a book to a situation that involves a little more life and death.

Close encounters

In 2007 I published a road-safety experiment which got quite a lot of attention at the time.[7] I spent a few weeks riding around city streets on a bicycle, measuring how close vehicles came to me as they passed. In the study I was looking at how much space drivers left as they drove past the bicycle and what affected the amount of space they left, but let's ignore that and just look at the overall distribution of passing distances (Figure 11.6).

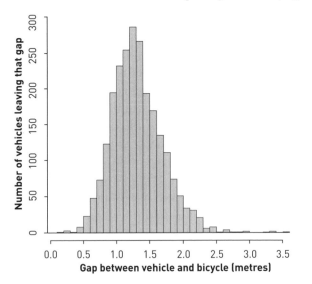

Figure 11.6 **Distribution of gaps left by drivers passing a bicyclist**

You can see the amount of space drivers left looks quite a lot like a normal distribution. The mean gap left by drivers was 1.31 metres, and sure enough you can see from the graph that a lot of drivers left a gap quite close to this – the graph is highest near the mean. As we move away from the mean, and look at very small and very large gaps, there are fewer and fewer drivers who left such gaps. (What you don't see on this graph

7   Walker, I. (2007). Drivers overtaking bicyclists: Objective data on the effects of riding position, helmet use, vehicle type and apparent gender. *Accident Analysis and Prevention, vol. 39*, pages 417–25.

are a couple of drivers who left gaps of less than zero metres – that is, drivers who hit me!)

This is another illustration of how very often, if you collect enough data in the real world, they start to look like a normal curve. It happens all the time. Now, in this case the curve isn't *quite* perfect, as there is a slightly longer tail on the right-hand side than the left-hand side, but let's just ignore that for the moment as I don't want to overcomplicate things.

The mean gap left by drivers as they passed my bicycle was 1.31 metres, and the standard deviation of the gaps was 0.38 metres. You now know that in every normal distribution, 68% of the measurements fall within one standard deviation of the mean. This means 68% of the gaps left by drivers were between 0.93 metres and 1.69 metres. This also means there is a 68% chance that the next driver to pass me will leave a gap somewhere between 0.93 metres and 1.69 metres.

The way I can work these things out, just from knowing the mean and the standard deviation, is pretty useful. But my knowledge of the normal distribution lets me go even further. Because I know about the shape of the normal distribution, I can also say things like, 'Five per cent of drivers passed within 0.69 metres of the bicycle' or 'Luckily, only 1% of drivers left gaps smaller than 0.42 metres!'

What's more, we can do all this stuff backwards. Let's say you are out riding a bicycle tomorrow and a car passes, leaving a gap of 0.75 metres. 'What are the chances of that happening?' you think to yourself. Well, I can tell you: exactly 92.92% of drivers would have left you more space than that, and 7.08% would have got closer.[8]

And that's the really important thing you need to take away from this chapter: thanks to the normal distribution, we can move back and forth between measurements out there in the world – measurements of over-taking gaps, in this case – and percentages and probabilities. You can pick a percentage and turn it into a real measurement ('How close did the nearest 10% of drivers get?'). Or you can do this backwards and turn a measurement into a percentage ('What percentage of drivers left more than 1.5 metres?') In particular, the thing I did a moment ago, where I identified the smallest 5% of the measurements, is incredibly useful for research thanks to the .05 cut-off we use in hypothesis testing.

So how did I calculate all those numbers? I used some free statistical software called *R*, but you can also quickly and easily do these sorts of

---

8   Assuming you were on similar roads to the ones I was on, and so on …

calculations with almost any statistics textbook. Most textbooks – including this one! – have a table in the back which lets you pick a point on the normal curve and see how much of the distribution lies either side of that point. So, for example, you could pick the point that is one standard deviation above the mean. When you look at the table in Appendix A, you'll see that 84.1% of scores are below this point (which means $100 - 84.1 = 15.9\%$ of scores are above this point). I've high-lighted this point in the table so you can check for yourself.

◉ Going further: making an ass out of u and me

When I introduced normal distributions, using the page-flicking data, I talked about the distribution being symmetrical – half the pages I landed on were before the middle of the book and half were after the middle. However, I also mentioned, when talking about my overtaking study, that the gaps drivers left when passing my bicycle did not quite form a normal distribution. If you glance back at Figure 11.6, you can see that the data tended to have a longer tail on the right-hand side than the left-hand side. The graph looked more or less like a normal distribution, but one that had been squashed over to one side a bit. If I were really to exaggerate this squashing, I might draw a distribution like the one in Figure 11.7.

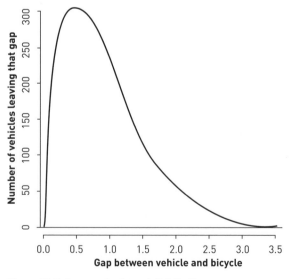

Figure 11.7 A severely skewed distribution

I mention this because it helps me make a useful point. As we saw above, when you know that some numbers are normally distributed, you instantly get all sorts of free information. For example, you instantly know that about 68% of those numbers lie within one standard deviation of the mean. Many of the statistical tests you will learn about make use of this free information. Because, when numbers are normally distributed, we get all this free knowledge, a lot of statistical tests *assume* the numbers you are analysing follow a normal distribution. Because these tests assume your data are normally distributed, if you try to analyse data that do not fit this pattern – if your data look like Figure 11.7, for example – your tests will get confused and may give you unreliable results.

A normal distribution is not the only assumption your tests will make. Most statistical tests make several assumptions, and it is your job to be sure you don't break those assumptions because if you do, the results of your tests will not be trustworthy.

I'm going to talk a lot more about these assumptions in Chapter 13, so I won't go into details right now about which tests make which assumptions. For now, what I will do is quickly show you why statistical tests make assumptions at all.

Tall or short?

Here is a question: I know a person who stands 160 cm (5 feet 4 inches) tall. My question is, are they a tall person? What would you say?

Did you say they were tall? Because I would look down on that person, and I'm not unusually lofty. Perhaps you said they were short? I *hope* what you said is 'I can't tell' or 'It depends', because I really didn't give you enough information to answer the question properly.

So try this instead: is this 160-cm (5 foot 4) person tall, *assuming they are two years old?*

Suddenly the question is a lot easier, isn't it? Now I've allowed you to make an assumption, you can give a definite answer to the question in a way you could not before ('Yes! They're a freakish giant-baby!'). Being able to make an assumption means you have more information available to guide your decision.

And this is exactly what happens with statistical tests. When you start doing analyses, you will often take sets of numbers – overtaking gaps, worker satisfaction scores, disease measurements, or whatever – and try to answer questions about them. This becomes *a whole lot easier* when the procedures you use can make some assumptions. Just as you found it easier to make a judgement about whether this person was tall when I allowed you to assume something about their age, statistical tests find it easier to make judgements about your numbers when they can assume things about those numbers.

Summary

Many statistical tests make assumptions about the numbers being analysed. If those assumptions are not met, the results of the analysis may be suspect.

A very short point about descriptive statistics

Back in Chapter 7, I described how, when we want to summarize a set of numbers, we can use more than one type of average, or 'measure of central tendency' as we say if we want to sound more official. I showed back then how the mean can be distorted by outliers – extreme numbers which don't fit the general pattern. But the mean can also be distorted by non-normal distributions.

When a set of numbers is normally distributed, one of the nice things to happen is that all three measures of central tendency – the mean, median and mode – are exactly the same. So if a set of numbers is normally distributed and the mean is 26, you know instantly that the middle number (the median) is also 26, and that 26 must have occurred in the data set more often than any other score (the mode). (This is a really useful fact that is worth remembering.)

When a distribution is not normal, however, the mean, median and mode will not all be the same. In particular, when data are bunched up at one end of the distribution, like in Figure 11.7, the mean again becomes misleading and it is far better to use the median. In some disciplines we encounter these bunched-up (or **skewed**) distributions quite often (cognitive psychology comes to mind here, where measurements of reaction times are usually skewed in a pattern just like Figure 11.7). As a result, you will frequently see people using the median as a measure of central tendency rather than the mean when they have this sort of distribution.

👁 Chapter summary

Many measurements are normally distributed: you see scores near the average more often than scores a long way from the average. When a set of numbers is normally distributed, you can work out the probability of any number being seen. You can also work out the percentage of numbers higher or lower than a particular value.

Chapter 12

When is a number not a number? Understanding levels of measurement

In statistics we use numbers to answer questions, so let's take a moment to think about numbers. Most of us start to learn about numbers early in our lives. By about the age of ten, they are almost like old friends, familiar and reliable. So what I am about to tell you might seem shocking, because I am going to suggest those old friends have deceived you for years. They are masters of disguise, and have been parading around in various different forms without your ever being aware of it.

To show you what I mean, let's take any number. Eight, for example. Think, for a moment, of some places you might see this number in your everyday life. Here are a few places I can see the number 8 as I look around my study right now:

- It is on my calendar, as it is 8 August as I write this section.
- One of my bookshelves has 8 books on it.
- I have a photograph of a street, which I took when I lived in Germany, and this shows a tram with the number 8 on the front.
- My web browser is open on a page with a book review. The book has been rated 8 out of 10 by the reviewer.

So I can see the number 8 in four places. The interesting thing is that in each of these, the number 8 is doing a totally different job and – and this is the key point – in each of those places the number 8 contains a different amount of information. That's right: the number 8 contains a different amount of information on my calendar than it does on the book review (it actually contains *more* information on the calendar).

This is probably a new idea to you, and in fact your mind might be boggling right about now, so I will go into more detail in a moment. First I want to tell you the most important point, which you really need to remember: because some numbers hold more information than others, you can't always just take two numbers and add them together; sometimes one, or both, of the numbers will not hold enough information for you to do this. So it is always really important, whenever you are dealing with numbers, to be sure how much information they hold.

The amount of information a number has is called its *level of measurement* – a number can be doing different amounts, or levels, of measurement. Sometimes a number will be doing a lot of measurement, and therefore will contain a lot of information; sometimes it will be doing no measurement at all. I will explain all this now by taking you through the various levels of measurement that exist from the numbers with the least information to the numbers with the most.

Summary

Any number can do different amounts, or levels, of measurement. When numbers are only doing small amounts of measurement, or no measurement at all, you might not be able to use them in statistical calculations.

⊙ When numbers are not numbers: the nominal level of measurement

Sometimes a number, like 8, is not measuring or counting anything at all. In this case, we call the numbers 'nominal'. As you might guess if you know any French or Latin, 'nominal' numbers are numbers that are acting as *names*.

To show you what I mean by numbers acting as names, and why knowing about this matters, imagine you come to see me to take part in an experiment I am running. You are shown into a room with 9 other people and I produce a bag containing 10 counters, numbered 1 to 10. You, along with each of the other people, reach into the bag and choose one of the counters without seeing the number on it. I then announce that everybody will receive a sum of money, and the higher your number is, the more money you will get; the person with number 1 gets nothing at all. Is this system fair?

Of course it isn't fair! How can the person with the number 10 deserve more money than any of the other people? They haven't done any extra work; they haven't done more of anything. In this example, then, *the numbers can't be put into order*. This is because they are just names, or labels. I have randomly labelled you all from 1 to 10. It makes no sense to then arrange you in numerical order and give some of you higher rewards than others.

At the beginning of this chapter I mentioned having a photograph of a German street with a number 8 tram in it. Here, the number 8 on the front of a tram is simply the name of the tram's route. It is just a short-hand way of writing 'This is the tram that runs from the central railway station to the eastern edge of the city and back again'. The number 8 does not mean the tram is in any way better, or faster, or more crowded than tram number 7: it is simply a name, or label, for the route.

One more place you see this sort of 'number naming' all the time is on sports fields. In many sports, the players' shirts have numbers on the back. But, crucially, these numbers act only as names – as quick and easy labels for individual players, or playing positions. As far as I know, there is no sport where the person wearing shirt number 6 is a better player than the person in shirt number 5. We simply cannot put the numbers into a meaningful order, as they are just names.

Why do we so often use numbers as names? The reason is that when we are talking about public transport routes, players in sports teams, people taking part in an experiment or whatever, it is useful to have some sort of simple, unique symbol to represent each individual. Numbers, because we all know them so well, are just a very convenient set of unique symbols.

The really important thing to remember is that when numbers are acting as names like this, you can do no calculations *at all* on those numbers. You cannot add them together, you cannot calculate their average and, as we have seen, you cannot even put them into order.

I am stressing this point a little because trying to carry out calculations on nominal numbers is a common mistake, one which I see students make quite often. For example, they label all the men who take part in a study as '1' and all the women as '2', and then try to do calculations on these numbers. It just doesn't work, as these are only labels.

Summary

When numbers are just acting as names or labels, you can do no calculations on them whatsoever. You cannot even put them into order and say, for example, 20 is above 19.

◉ When numbers are almost numbers: the ordinal level of measurement

When numbers are measuring at the 'ordinal' level they can be put into order – this makes them very different from nominal numbers, which, as we have seen, are simply names and cannot be arranged in a sequence. Let me jump straight in and give you an example of ordinal numbers you will almost certainly have seen:

> How good was the book you just read?
> Dire (1) – Poor (2) – Okay (3) – Good (4) – Excellent (5)

We probably all agree 'excellent' is higher than 'good', that 'good' is higher than 'okay', and so on. These numbers, then, behave differently to nominal numbers: a rating of 5 *is* higher than a rating of 4, and so it makes sense to put these numbers into order – which is why they are called 'ordinal'. Because ordinal numbers hold information about the order of things, and can be arranged from the lowest to the highest, they contain more information than nominal numbers.

However, going into order is about all these numbers can do. They still don't contain a lot of information, and can often mislead us by hiding differences. To show you what I mean, here are the results from an international bicycling race, which I chose more or less at random from a list of recent sports events:

Name	Position	Time behind previous rider
Marianne Vos	1	winner
Marta Bastianelli	2	1 second behind
Judith Arndt	3	1 second behind
Alexandra Wrubleski	4	7 seconds behind
Amber Neben	5	4 seconds behind

Look at the second column, which gives the finishing positions. These numbers can certainly be put into order: the rider in position 1 came before the rider in position 2, the rider in position 2 came before the rider in position 3, and so on. These finishing positions are ordinal numbers.

But knowing somebody's finishing position doesn't actually tell us very much about how they performed. Take the rider in third place, Judith Arndt. Her position – 3 – tells us she was slower than rider 2, but not by how much. It tells us she was faster than rider 4, but not by how much. It tells us absolutely nothing but the order in which she finished. If you look at the times in the last column you can see that Arndt actually finished much closer to the rider in front than she did to the rider behind, but the finishing positions – 2, 3, 4 – don't tell us this: they hide the gaps between the riders and make it look as though they were all evenly spaced. This is the first big issue with ordinal numbers: they tell us *only* the order of things: they can't tell us how far apart those things really are.

The second big issue with ordinal numbers is that they don't always mean the same thing in every situation. Let's say those bicyclists all took part in another race the next week, over the same course, and Judith Arndt came third again. All you know is that she came in third place once more: you don't know if she rode faster or slower than in the first race. What if she, and all the other riders, rode a lot faster? In that case, third place in one race is faster than third place in the other, but you've no way of seeing this just from the ordinal finishing positions.

Another everyday example of ordinal numbers, which illustrates this issue nicely, is the star ratings given to hotels. A five-star hotel has better facilities than a four-star hotel; a four-star hotel has better facilities than a three-star hotel; and so on. Because these numbers are ordinal, the hotels can be put into order from the best type to the worst. But, importantly, this does not mean every four-star hotel has exactly the same facilities. Just as the third-place contestant in one competition might be faster than the third-place contestant in another competition, some four-star hotels will be better than others. So, with ordinal numbers, a number like '3' doesn't always mean exactly the same thing, and this is quite a big limitation. Three centimetres always means exactly the same length, but three stars doesn't always mean exactly the same hotel facilities.

So ordinal numbers go into order, but do not tell us anything more than this. Most importantly, we still cannot add these numbers together or calculate their mean (although we can now calculate the median). This is a big limitation with ordinal numbers, and again is something you need to be careful of. I will say a little more about this shortly, but first, let's look at real numbers.

Summary

Ordinal numbers can be put into order. Five belongs above four, for example. However, we can learn little else from these numbers.

When numbers really are numbers: the interval and ratio levels of measurement

Interval and ratio numbers are 'proper' numbers. They contain a lot of information and we can do anything we like with them. We can add them together, calculate averages, and so on.

These 'real' numbers are different to ordinal numbers. Like ordinal numbers, 'real' numbers can be put into order. But with 'real' numbers, the distance between any two numbers tells us something.

Here are a few miscellaneous facts from the history of science. In the year 1600, the word 'electricity' was invented. In 1700, the mathematician Daniel Bernoulli was born. In 1800, Alessandro Volta invented the first electric battery. The facts I've chosen aren't relevant to what I'm about to say (although Bernoulli did do really important work in statistics); I just wanted to draw your attention to the years: 1600, 1700 and 1800.

The distance between the year 1600 and the year 1700 is 100 years. The distance between 1700 and 1800 is also 100 years. The distance – or *interval* – is exactly the same in both cases: 100 years. 100 years is the same length of time no matter where we start from, and so we would describe calendar years as an interval measurement. This is different from ordinal numbers, like the racers' positions, where a difference of one place did not always represent the same time difference.

What's the difference between interval and ratio numbers?

Interval and ratio numbers are exactly the same thing except for one subtle difference: ratio numbers have a genuine zero point.

When I say 'genuine' zero, I mean that zero means there is *none of the thing being measured*. The amount of money you have is a ratio measure, because when you have zero money, you have *no money*. When there are zero grams of cheese on a sandwich, there is *no cheese*. When you have zero pets, you have *no pets*. Most things you deal with day to day are ratio measures.

So a genuine zero point is very simple. But what about a 'false' zero point? I introduced interval numbers using calendar years – 1600, 1700 and 1800. Think for a moment about what 'year zero' would mean. Critically, it would *not* indicate the beginning of all time. Whichever calendar system you use, there were years before the year zero. Calendar years do not have a genuine zero, and so they are an interval measure and not a ratio measure.

The most common interval measure is temperature. In both the Celsius and Fahrenheit systems, zero degrees does *not* mean there is no temperature at all. Rather, zero degrees is just an arbitrary point, partway along the scale of all possible temperatures, and there are lots of temperatures below zero.[9]

This difference between real and false zeroes might sound quite trivial, so let me show you why knowing your zeroes is useful. When the thing you are measuring has a genuine zero, you can talk about ratios – that is, you can say things like this:

- You own one bicycle and I own two. I have *twice as many* bicycles as you. Or, equally, you own *half as many* bicycles as me.
- You drink one cup of coffee and I drink four. I have drunk *four times as much* coffee as you. You have drunk *one-quarter* of what I drank.
- Yesterday I worked for 6 hours and today I worked for 9 hours. Today I worked for *50% longer* than yesterday.

This sort of language is only possible when there is a genuine zero, which is the reason numbers with a genuine zero are called 'ratio' measures. You cannot talk like this with interval numbers. I once remember hearing a weather forecaster say 'It seems the good weather has ended very suddenly. Yesterday it was 20 degrees Celsius but today it's going to be just half that temperature.' The forecaster was totally wrong here! Because temperature in Celsius has no proper zero, and so isn't a ratio measure, you cannot say one temperature is half as high as another.

---

9   Here's how arbitrary the Celsius scale is: Anders Celsius originally set 0°C as the boiling point of water and 100°C as the freezing point, with the whole scale working upside-down to the way we use it today. The zero clearly has no real basis – it's just something people have invented. On the other hand, you might be familiar with the Kelvin scale, which is quite different: here zero is the lowest temperature that can possibly exist in the universe, and so is a real, meaningful zero point.

If this doesn't make sense right away, and you feel 20 degrees should be twice as warm as 10 degrees, then consider this: what if tomorrow the temperature were zero degrees? What temperature would be twice as warm as that? What temperature would be half as warm? What temperature would be 25% colder? Without a genuine zero, you simply cannot use ratio words like this.

Summary

You can do almost anything with interval and ratio numbers; you can do very few calculations on ordinal and nominal numbers. Whenever you see a number, get into the habit of asking yourself what level of measurement it is working at.

◉ Going further: controversy over levels of measurement

Have you noticed how online bookshops ask us to rate books from 1 to 5? And have you noticed how they give each book an average rating? I'm not sure they should do that ...

You see, the different levels of measurement I have explained here come from work in the 1940s by a researcher called S. S. Stevens. As with most things, not everybody agrees with Stevens's claim that we can split all numbers into four levels of measurement. Some argue there is a fifth level of measurement, perhaps between ordinal and interval (or perhaps between nominal and ordinal: it depends who you ask). In particular there is a lot of debate on what we should be allowed to do with ordinal numbers.

Ordinal numbers, which I described here as being 'almost' numbers, are very often used in psychology. Researchers frequently use rating scales to assess people's feelings or opinions. The difficulty comes when we have to think about what to do with the numbers. To show you what I mean, let's say you and I both read the same book then answer this question:

How good was the book?
Dire (1) – Poor (2) – Okay (3) – Good (4) – Excellent (5)

Let's say we both rate the book as '4': does this mean you and I have enjoyed it *exactly* the same amount? Almost certainly not: I can easily imagine us both giving the same rating but really, one of us likes the book more than the other. In fact, the problem is even deeper than this. Because this scale only works if we both completely agree what words like 'good' and 'okay' mean, I can even imagine you enjoying the book more than me but giving it a lower rating. For example, you might enjoy a book well enough but give it a low rating because you thought it was not original enough. So ratings like these aren't completely consistent: when we see a number like 4 it doesn't always mean the same thing. Imagine if we both measured our height and got exactly the same result, but I was really taller than you! How could we do anything with height measurements if they behaved like this? But that's the situation we're talking about with rating scales.

This is just one reason why there is a lot of debate about ordinal numbers. The biggest issue is whether ordinal numbers can be averaged together: if we take a group of people and ask them to make a rating on a questionnaire, can we really talk about the 'average' rating for that group? When online shops ask people to rate items on a scale of 1 to 5, can they really give the items an 'average' rating? Probably not. All these ratings are ordinal numbers, and your rating of '4' might mean something different to mine, so how can we treat them as the same?

The odd thing is, researchers, even those who know about this issue, take averages of ordinal numbers all the time (as do online shops that ask customers to rate goods). Indeed, researchers do all sorts of calculations on ordinal numbers which probably shouldn't be done. This is another great secret of statistics in behavioural sciences: almost all of us do analyses on ordinal numbers, like adding them together and averaging them, even though we know we shouldn't.

One thing we definitely *can* do with ordinal numbers is count up how often we see them. You can even do this with nominal numbers like those on trams or buses: you can certainly count how often you saw tram number 8 and tram number 9 in a day, for example. So one thing you can do with ordinal numbers is study them using tests like the chi-squared test. You could count up how many number 8, number 9 and number 10 buses pass you in the street and use the chi-squared test to decide if one type of bus comes more frequently than the others.

Summary

Because ordinal numbers do not measure consistently – the number 4 doesn't always mean the same thing – we should not really add together or average ordinal numbers. But in practice almost everybody does.

◉ Chapter summary

Some numbers contain more information than others. The amount of information a number holds can affect what statistics you can use with it.

Chapter 13

How to tell whether two sets of numbers are different from each other

Something we need to do all the time in psychology is take two sets of numbers and ask whether they are, on average, different from each other. For example, you might get two groups of people, measure how fast everybody is at reading, and look at whether the two groups, overall, read at different speeds. Or you might test a single group of people on their reading skill twice – before and after you train them in speed-reading. You would want to know whether the second set of scores is different from the first, as this would tell you whether the training had any effect. So comparing two sets of scores is an incredibly common task, and the tests we use for this are ones you will see again and again.

The slight complication here is that we have more than one test available for comparing two sets of numbers, and one of the key skills for a researcher is knowing when to use each. Some of the tests are better than others, but we can only use them when all the circumstances are right. As such, we need to know these better tests, and also alternatives for when the circumstances mean we can't use them. Don't worry – you almost certainly won't have to memorize all the different tests and when they are used. The main thing is that you understand that there is more than one test, and know how to look up the right test when you need to use it.

The tests that we're going to cover in this chapter do involve some calculations, and I have chosen to separate these out, and put all the details in Appendix B. This is partly so that the tests are easier to find when you need to refer to them in the future, and partly to make learning about them simpler. Read this chapter first, to learn what the tests are all about and what they mean. Then, once you've understood what the tests are for and how to understand what they tell you, read through Appendix B to see the details.

In this chapter we will examine:
- The sign test for comparing two sets of scores
- The difference between parametric and non-parametric statistical tests
- The importance of assumptions in statistical testing
- The *t*-test
- Non-parametric alternatives to the *t*-test: the Mann-Whitney test and the Wilcoxon test

A simple test for comparing two sets of scores: the sign test

Let's say we take a group of people and, because we are in a whimsical mood, we decide to measure how many seconds each person can stand on one leg before falling over. Then we give all the people a big cup of really strong coffee and test them again 20 minutes later. We know the caffeine in the coffee should make people a bit more jittery, so we would expect them to be worse at standing on one leg after the drink.

Here are some data from people standing on one leg, before and after coffee:

Person	Before coffee (secs)	After coffee (secs)
1	63	58
2	40	41
3	12	21
4	27	22
5	34	43
6	34	36
7	25	26
8	14	9
9	83	78
10	70	60
MEAN	39.7	39.4
STANDARD DEVIATION	23.57	21.17

You can immediately see that the two means are quite similar, so it looks as though the coffee didn't make much difference to how long these people could stand on one leg, but let's think about how we might analyse the numbers in the table to check this.

First, as ever, we start with a null hypothesis, the idea that nothing interesting is going on. In this study, the null hypothesis would be that coffee has no effect on balance – people balance just as well whether they have drunk coffee or not. The question is: how would the data look if this were true?

If coffee really has no effect on people's balance, we don't necessarily expect everybody's score to stay exactly the same after the coffee. The world is too messy and noisy for *exactly* no change. But, if coffee has no effect on people's balance, *there should be just as many people who got a higher score after drinking coffee as people who got a lower score.*

So now we have a nice simple way to test the data in the table. We simply count up how many people got better at standing on one leg after the coffee and how many got worse. If the number of people getting better is pretty much the same as the number of people getting worse, this suggests that the null hypothesis is correct – the coffee doesn't make a difference. But if most people get better, or most people get worse, then we have seen a pattern in the data. If most people change in the same way after drinking coffee, this is evidence that the null hypothesis might be wrong. In that case, we would reject the null hypothesis and conclude that coffee probably *does* have an effect on people's balance.

So now that we've sorted out the logic of the analysis, let's look at the data table again to see this in action.

Person	Before coffee (secs)	After coffee(secs)	Difference	Sign
1	63	58	−5	−
2	40	41	+1	+
3	12	21	+9	+
4	27	22	−5	−
5	34	43	+9	+
6	34	36	+2	+
7	25	26	+1	+
8	14	9	−5	−
9	83	78	−5	−
10	70	60	−10	−

You can see that there are five + signs and five – signs. There are just as many people whose scores went down after the coffee as there were people whose scores went up. That wouldn't happen if the coffee had any effect, so it's pretty clear the coffee didn't have an effect in this test – the evidence suggests that the null hypothesis was right. It's really quite simple, isn't it?

Significance testing with the sign test

With the example I've given here, it is very obvious that the coffee made no difference, overall, to people's ability to stand on one leg: exactly half the people got better after the coffee and exactly half got worse. But what if things had not been so equal? What if, out of 10 people, 2 got better and 8 got worse? In that case, would we say that the coffee made no difference? Or, if we saw 8 people out of 10 get worse at standing on one leg, would we say coffee had an effect? We need some sort of statistic to help us make this decision, and as we saw back in Chapter 9, the key thing we need is a p-value. This is the probability of seeing an effect, as least as large as the one we saw, if the null hypothesis is correct. So in this case, the p-value will tell us how likely it is for 8 or more people to get worse after drinking coffee, if coffee really has no effect.

To get a p-value for the sign test, we use the **binomial test**. I mentioned the binomial test back in Chapter 10, where I said it was a bit like the chi-squared test and can tell you if two categories are equally common. For example, a binomial test can tell you whether the number of men entering a building is reliably different to the number of women, whether the number of jellybeans in your pocket is different to the number of peanuts, or whether the number of heads is different to the number of tails when you toss a coin lots of times. In just the same way, we can use the binomial test to work out whether any particular mixture of + and – signs fits the null hypothesis or not: just as it can tell us whether the number of heads is different from the number of tails, it can tell us whether the number of + signs in a set of data is different from the number of – signs.

The calculations for the binomial test are a little too tricky for this book, but that's not a problem: the Web is full of sites that will do all the sums for you. Just search for 'binomial test calculator' and you should have no trouble finding one. All you need to do is tell it how many + signs you saw (many calculators refer to this as the number of 'successes') and the total number of people you tested, and it will give you a p-value for those results. If the p-value you get is less than the usual .05 cut-off, your results probably don't fit with the null hypothesis – in other words, if p is low then there is probably a real difference between your two sets of numbers.

Let's say you carried out the coffee experiment and saw that 3 people out of 10 got better at standing on one leg after drinking coffee and 7 got worse (so you have 3 + signs and 7 – signs). If you find a binomial test calculator and enter 3 'successes' from 10 tests, you should get a result of $p = .172$. You can use this number as a check to make sure you are using the calculator properly: whichever binomial calculator you find, try entering '3' out of '10'. If you get a result of $p = .172$, you know you are using it right.

(In this case, the result of $p = .172$ is quite high – it is higher than the usual cut-off of .05 – and so we would conclude that coffee probably doesn't affect people's balance. You saw 7 out of 10 people get worse at balancing, but the analysis tells you that if you take 10 people and ask them to stand on one leg twice, there is a .172 probability – a 17.2% chance – that you would see 7 or more people get worse the second time even if nothing is affecting them. So our finding that 7 out of 10 people got worse *suggests* that coffee makes a difference, but it's not very strong evidence. If you tossed a coin 10 times and got 7 tails, that wouldn't be very surprising. In the same way, it's quite possible that 7 out of 10 people would get a lower score even if the coffee had no effect: 7 out of 10 people fits the null hypothesis pretty well.)

Once you are happy you are using your binomial calculator correctly, you can then use it for any other sign test you want to run. For example, let's say you tested 80 people in a repeated-measures study. You measure everybody's intelligence, then make them watch eight hours of daytime television before testing their intelligence again. Your null hypothesis would be something like 'Watching daytime television has no effect on people's intelligence', and you'd have an alternative hypothesis like 'Watching daytime television affects people's intelligence.'

Now let's say that out of your 80 people, 25 got a higher intelligence score after the daytime television (there were 25 plus signs), 49 people got a lower score (there were 49 minus signs) and 6 people didn't change. In the sign test we ignore people who don't change, so this means you just need to think about the 25 plus signs and 49 minus signs: a total of 74 people.

If you put the numbers 25 and 74 into a binomial calculator (25 'successes' out of 74 trials), you should find a result of $p = .003$. This p-value is less than the usual cut-off of .05, and so you have a statistically significant result: people really do seem to get less intelligent after eight hours of daytime television! There is only a .003 probability – a 0.3% chance – of seeing 49 or more minus signs from 74 people if the null hypothesis is true. Because this is so unlikely, the null hypothesis probably isn't true – people probably did get less intelligent after eight hours of daytime television.

Thinking scientifically → **Cautious words**

Have you noticed that I am continually using words like 'probably' and 'seems' when I'm writing about the results from data analysis? This is because we can never be totally certain of anything. We could say that it *looks* as though people got less intelligent after watching daytime television, but we can never be 100% sure, and a good scientist always uses words that express this lingering doubt – even if it's only to cover their own backsides in case they later prove to be wrong!

Summary of the sign test

The sign test takes two lots of scores, looks at how many scores got higher and how many got lower, and compares this to what you would expect to see if the null hypothesis is correct. If what you saw looks quite different to this – that is, if most of the scores changed in the same direction – then the null hypothesis probably isn't correct, and there probably is a difference between the two sets of scores.

Now the bad news: after all that effort you've just spent understanding the sign test, you will most likely find you never need to use it. Sorry! The reason I explained the test in some detail is because it allowed me to introduce several important ideas about how we compare two sets of scores, and it allowed me to give a clear demonstration of how we use a p-value to reach a conclusion in such a test. So everything we've just covered will still be useful to you – perhaps just not the sign test itself.[10]

---

10   Actually, as Michael Crawley pointed out, one place you might find the sign test useful is where you can see differences but can't really measure them properly. He gives the example of judging a diving contest, where judges watch people dive twice, deciding if they are better or worse the second time round. A sign test could tell you whether divers tended to improve on their second dive, even though it is impossible properly to 'measure' the quality of a dive. [Crawley, M.J., 2005. *Statistics: An introduction using R.* Wiley.]

The reason for this is that the sign test isn't very sophisticated – it's quite a blunt tool, to use my toolbox analogy again. All it does is take two scores at a time and say whether one is higher than the other – it totally ignores the size of the difference. It treats these two people as the same, for example, when clearly they aren't:

Person	Score 1	Score 2	Change	Sign
1	10	20	+10	+
2	10	2,000,000	+1,999,990	+

Because there are other tests that look at how large the differences between scores are, and that don't just look at two scores at a time, we generally prefer to use those. The most detailed and powerful tests are known as 'parametric tests', and we will look at these in more detail shortly. First, however, I want to say a little bit more about how our statistical tests all work, to help you better understand exactly what's going on.

⊚ Two points about how statistical tests work

We will soon look at several more tests for comparing two sets of scores, to build upon what you learnt with the sign test. But first, I want to talk about a couple of points which will help you understand the tests that are coming up. I'd like to revisit the idea of null hypothesis testing, to give you more detail about that subject in the light of the new material you've learnt; and I want to introduce you to the idea of one- and two-tailed statistical tests.

Another way of looking at null hypothesis testing

You have learnt several new ideas since we first covered null hypothesis testing in Chapter 9, so before I go on with more statistical tests, I think it's time to look at the subject again, to give you a little more detail about how it works now that you have covered such important topics as the normal distribution. Don't panic at this stage! Everything I told you in Chapter 9 was correct; I'm just explaining it in a different way here, to give you more information about the underlying statistics.

As an example of a study with a null hypothesis, let's say I am interested in whether students from the north of the country are cleverer than students from the south. I don't have the time or the money to test every student in the country, so I test a sample of students from the north and a sample of students from the south and look at how they perform on an intelligence test. My starting point – my null hypothesis – would be that the two groups are equally intelligent, and I will stick with this unless I find good evidence that it is wrong. If I do find evidence against the null hypothesis, I'll reject it and go with the alternative hypothesis instead. In this case, the alternative hypothesis would be that students from the north are different to students from the south.

Obviously if the two groups get *totally* different scores, then this is good evidence the null hypothesis is wrong. If everybody in the northern group gets a score of 99% on the test and everybody in the southern group gets a score of 1%, this would be excellent evidence that the null hypothesis is wrong and that northern and southern students are different. In this case we could happily reject the null hypothesis and conclude that the two groups are not equally intelligent.

But what if the difference between the two groups was smaller? What if one group got an average score of 75.0% and the other group got an average score of 75.1%? Would this tiny difference be good evidence against the null hypothesis? Almost certainly not. With a difference this small we'd almost certainly stick with the null hypothesis and conclude that the two groups look the same.

So how big would the difference need to be before we said it *was* evidence against the null hypothesis? A massive difference is good evidence against the null hypothesis and a tiny difference is not – but what is the dividing line?

Back in Chapter 9 I said that we find this dividing line by looking at the number p. Every statistical tests gives you a p-value, and when this is less than your alpha cut-off criterion (usually .05) you have enough evidence to reject the null hypothesis. What I want to do now is give you more detail about exactly what p and alpha mean. This is quite an important concept for statistics, so I'm going to spell it out as clearly as I can. But don't worry if this doesn't all make sense right away. The most important thing is that you are able to look at p and use this to reject or retain your null hypothesis: if p is less than your cut-off (usually .05) you reject the null hypothesis – that's basically all there is to it, and so you can usually use p even if you don't really understand where it comes from. But in the long term you will find statistics much easier if you understand exactly what p and alpha mean, so do try to understand the rest of this section even if you have to read it a couple of times.

Me and a clone of my own

Imagine for a moment that I have two groups of people who are *exactly* the same. Think of them as all being identical twins, where each person in the first group has a genetically identical match in the second group. Or, even better, imagine I've taken a group of people and duplicated them all with my Clone-o-Mat machine, so that the second group is absolutely the same as the first, with the same genetics, the same life experiences, and everything.

Now let's say *you* are in the first group. This means there is an exact copy of you in the second group, who acts just like you and has precisely the same abilities and experiences as you. I ask you and your duplicate to stack wooden bricks on top of one another to create the tallest tower that you can produce before it falls over. Your 'score' on this task will be how many bricks you had in the tower before it collapsed.

Are you and your clone going to get exactly the same score when I test you? The answer is 'possibly not'. Even though you are identical in every way, this is no guarantee that you will perform exactly the same if you both do the task just once. Perhaps, while you build a nice tall tower, using lots of bricks before it falls down, your clone accidentally nudges the table and so gets a lower score (or perhaps the experimenter nudges it). Or perhaps there's a small earth tremor while it's your turn to build a tower, and this knocks your bricks down early while your clone suffers no such disturbance.

Sure, if you and an identical copy of you do this task lots and lots of times, all this good and bad luck should balance out. If you and your clone did this task thousands of times, your average scores should be the same. But if you do the task *just once*, there's no guarantee that you'll get the same score. If you both do the task just once, there's a good chance you and your clone will get different scores. The same goes for all the other people in your group and their clones in the other group.

So, to summarize what I've said so far, *even if two groups are genuinely identical, this is no guarantee they will perform exactly the same when you test them just once.* That is a hugely important point, and if there was some way of making those words flash in neon lights then I'd make them do so. Even if men and women are equally good at juggling, this doesn't necessarily mean you would see zero difference if you tested a group of men and a group of women. Even if students from the north are just as intelligent as students from the south, this doesn't necessarily mean you will see exactly zero difference when you test some students. People have 'bad luck', or off-days; tables get knocked and earth tremors happen. All these sorts of things affect the scores we collect (we say they introduce **noise** into the scores). This noise can produce differences between the groups we test which don't really mean anything. These differences probably wouldn't be there if we tested more people (which is one of the reasons we always try to **replicate** our findings).

Group differences and the normal distribution

Even if two groups are really the same, this doesn't mean they have to perform exactly the same when you test them. But here's a question: if you get two groups of people who are genuinely the same, like a group of people and a group of their clones, and you give everybody in these two groups some sort of test, are you more likely to see a large difference between the groups or a small difference?

The answer is a small difference. If you and your clone are carrying out a task, it's more likely you will get similar scores than it is you will get wildly different scores. After all, you're identical. You *should* perform the same. So even though you're both going to be affected by a thousand random factors outside anybody's control, you're more likely to perform at a similar level than you are to perform at a totally different level.

Statisticians have shown us that if we test two groups that are genuinely identical, the probability of seeing any given difference follows a normal distribution. I've plotted this in Figure 13.1, and it's worth having a really good look at this graph to make sure you understand what it's saying. The horizontal x-axis shows all the various differences that we could possibly see between two groups of people. A difference of zero (in the middle of the x-axis) means the two groups got the same score. A negative difference means group 1 got a higher score than group 2, and a positive difference means group 2 got a higher score than group 1. The curve shows how likely it is that we'll see various differences when two groups are really meant to be the same.

Look right at the centre of the x-axis, where there is zero difference between the two groups. The curve is at its highest here. This means that if we test two groups that are really just the same, there is a high probability of seeing zero difference between them. That makes a lot of sense, I'd say.

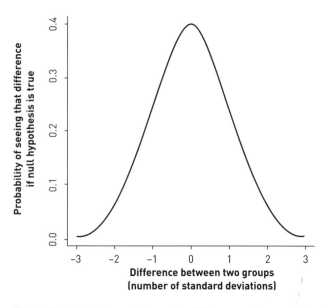

Figure 13.1 How often we see various differences when comparing two groups of people who really are the same

But now move along the *x*-axis just a tiny amount – to where there is a difference of +0.1. The curve here is nearly as high as it was for a difference of zero. The chances of seeing a tiny difference when you test two identical groups are nearly as high as the chances of seeing zero difference. And if you keep moving along the *x*-axis you'll see that the bigger the difference, the less likely it is that you'll see it. *When two groups of people are really identical, you've a good chance of seeing zero difference when you test them, but you might easily see a difference that isn't zero. The bigger the difference, the lower the chances of your seeing it.*

Just now and again, though, you may see a big difference between two groups that are really the same, purely by chance. This is when you find yourself down in the tails of that distribution, and it's important to understand that this can happen. *Just occasionally, two groups that are really the same will look very different when you test them.*

Using all this to understand p and alpha

So far we have seen that when two groups are genuinely identical, we don't necessarily expect them to get exactly the same score when we test them. And then we saw that the chances of seeing any particular difference depend on how far it is from zero: there's a fair probability of seeing zero difference, and the smaller a difference is, the more likely we are to see it when we examine two groups that really are the same.

Now it's time to see how all this applies to the null hypothesis. As you now know, we start every analysis with the null hypothesis – the idea there is nothing going on – and stick with it unless we have good evidence it is wrong. And, as you saw in Chapter 9, our usual criterion for making this decision is whether or not $p < .05$.

So here's how p-values, and the .05 cut-off, relate to the normal distribution. When we use a .05 cut-off point to make our decisions in research, what we are actually doing is taking the curve in Figure 13.1 and finding the most extreme 5% of it – the bit where the groups are most different. I've shown this in Figure 13.2, where I've taken the original graph and shaded in the top 5% of the space underneath the curve. If I test two groups of people and find a difference quite close to zero, then I can easily imagine this difference appearing just by chance. But if I test two groups of people and see a difference so large that it falls into this shaded region – in this case, if group 2 got a score that was at least 1.64 standard deviations higher than group 1's score – then this is a 'big'

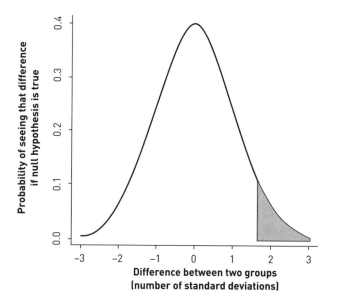

Figure 13.2 A distribution of possible differences with the top 5% highlighted

difference. If the difference between the two groups is so big that it falls into this top 5% region, I can't really imagine that the two groups really are the same. So ... they're probably not really the same. If the difference between two groups is so large that it falls into this shaded zone, then I probably don't have two identical groups after all; I probably have two different groups. In other words, *if the difference between two groups is so large that it falls into the most extreme 5% of the graph,* this *is the evidence we need to say that the null hypothesis is wrong* – this *is the evidence we need to say that the two groups are probably different.*

Summary

If you test two groups and the difference between them is small, you can say that the two groups are probably the same, and that the difference you saw doesn't really mean anything. But if the difference is so large that it falls into the most extreme 5% of the normal distribution, you'd reject the null hypothesis and say that the two groups you've tested are probably not really the same. You've tried to imagine them being the same, as the null hypothesis suggested, but your analysis has told you that it's unlikely for two groups, which look so different, really to be the same. And you have no more than 5% doubt when you say that, because you've used 5% of the graph to make the decision. I do hope you can see how this is all just a slightly more technical way of saying the things I said in Chapter 9.

One-tailed tests and two-tailed tests

Earlier on, when I introduced the sign test, I used the example of getting people to stand on one leg for as long as possible before and after drinking coffee. I don't know whether you noticed, but the hypothesis I set up there had a specific direction to it. I didn't just say that drinking coffee would make a difference to how long people could stand on one leg – I specifically predicted that drinking coffee would make people *worse*.

When you make a prediction about what you will see in a study, you must always choose whether to make a general prediction or a specific prediction. If you simply predict that you will see some sort of effect, we call this a **two-tailed hypothesis**, because the effect could go either way. But if you specifically predict the direction of the effect, we call this a **one-tailed hypothesis**, because you're predicting that the effect will go in one specific direction. Here are a few examples to show you the difference:

Two-tailed version	One-tailed version
Drinking coffee will affect how long people can stand on one leg	Drinking coffee will make people *worse* at standing on one leg
Revising for an exam will affect people's scores	Revising for an exam will give people *better* scores
Owning pets will affect people's happiness	Owning pets will make people *happier*
Poorer cities will have different levels of crime than richer cities	Poorer cities will have *more* crime than richer cities

The only thing you need to notice is that in every case, the one-tailed hypothesis is more specific: a two-tailed hypothesis predicts that something will happen; a one-tailed hypothesis predicts that something will happen *and* says exactly what that is. So, to stick with the standing-on-one-leg example, the two-tailed version of the hypothesis would allow for the possibility that drinking coffee would make people better at standing on one leg; the one-tailed version would not. The one-tailed hypothesis, that coffee makes people *worse*, completely rules out, right at the start of the study, any idea that coffee might make people better.

You might wonder why we need two different ways of setting up a hypothesis. Why don't we always make more general, two-tailed predictions? Why rule out any possibility of coffee making people better at standing on one leg? Why not just predict 'some effect' without worrying about the direction, if this means we are less likely to miss an effect?

The answer is that when you make a specific prediction, although you take the risk of missing an effect if your results go in the opposite direction to what you predicted, it is easier to find significant results as long as your results do go in the right direction. It is easiest to understand this if you look at graphs.

The terms 'one-tailed' and 'two-tailed' come from the tails of the normal distribution. Look back at Figure 13.2. In this diagram, I have shaded in 5% of the area under the curve. Any difference that is large enough to fall into the shaded region is big enough that it doesn't fit very well with the null hypothesis (in other words, any difference that falls into the shaded region is a statistically significant difference). The 5% of the graph that I shaded in on Figure 13.2 is all on one side, or *in one tail*, of the curve. This means that I will only say my groups are different if the difference between the two groups is large and *positive*. If group 2 got a much higher score than group 1 then the difference will fall into the shaded zone and I'll say I've found a difference between the two groups. But what if group 1 gets a much higher score than group 2? In this case, the difference would be negative, and it is impossible for it to fall into the shaded zone. If I have a one-tailed hypothesis, and the effect goes the other way to what I expected, then I will miss that effect (technically, I will commit a Type II error).

Now look at Figure 13.3. Again, only 5% of the graph is shaded in, but this time I've split that 5% into two parts, so that 2.5% of the graph is shaded on the left-hand tail and 2.5% is shaded on the right-hand tail. In this two-tailed graph, if group 2 gets a much higher score than group 1 then it'll fall into a shaded zone and I'll reject my null hypothesis *and* if group 1 gets a much higher score than group 2 then it'll also fall into a shaded zone and I'll reject my null hypothesis. Because I'm now looking at both tails of the curve, I won't miss an effect just because it's gone the opposite way to what I expected.

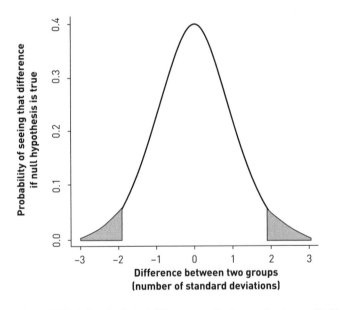

Figure 13.3 A distribution of differences with the most extreme 5% highlighted, and split between the two tails of the graph

If you compare Figure 13.2 and Figure 13.3, you should be able to get the answer to why people don't always make vaguer, two-tailed, predictions. In both diagrams, the same amount of the graph is shaded in: 5%.

But because, in the second diagram, this 5% has to be split into two parts, with half of it in each tail, any difference between two groups has to be bigger before it will fall into a shaded region. Look carefully: in Figure 13.2 the shaded region begins at $x = 1.64$, but in Figure 13.3 the shaded regions begin at $x = 1.96$ and $x = -1.96$. A difference needs to be more extreme before it falls into a shaded area when there is a two-tailed hypothesis. This means that when you use a two-tailed hypothesis, you won't miss an effect because it went the opposite way to what you expected, but it also means that you need to see a bigger difference before you have a significant finding.

Choosing whether you will use a one- or a two-tailed hypothesis therefore involves a risk trade-off. If you choose a one-tailed hypothesis you're more likely to find a significant effect, but you'll miss any effect that doesn't go in the direction you expected. If you choose a two-tailed hypothesis you won't miss an effect this way, but an effect needs to be larger before it becomes significant.

Summary

When you carry out research, you can choose between making a more specific one-tailed hypothesis, or a more general two-tailed hypothesis. The decision involves trading off risks. If you make a more general two-tailed hypothesis, you won't miss an effect just because it went the opposite direction to what you expected, but an effect needs to be larger before it is significant. The reason for this is that you have split your 5% rejection region over two tails of the distribution instead of one.

The difference between parametric and non-parametric tests

Back in Chapter 11, I gave an example of a person who was 160 cm tall, and I asked you if they were 'tall' or not. I suggested that it was much easier to make this judgement when you were allowed to make an assumption. In that case, it was much easier to decide whether this person was tall when I allowed you to assume something about their age. That is, your task was easier when I gave you a *parameter*, or limit, to guide your decision.

All statistical tests basically fall into one of two types: **parametric tests**, which make assumptions (they work within certain parameters, hence the name), and **non-parametric tests**, which don't make any assumptions (they work without parameters). In general, for any task you might want to do, such as comparing two groups of scores, there is a parametric test and a non-parametric test available to you. The two tests will do the same basic job – for example, they will both compare two sets of scores to see if they are different on average – but the parametric test will be more **powerful**. So when it comes to comparing two groups of people you can choose between a parametric test (known as the *t*-test) and a non-parametric test (the Mann-Whitney test). Both do the same task, but the *t*-test is more powerful.

When I say 'powerful', I simply mean this: if there really is a difference between two groups, a powerful test is more likely to see it. Think of the difference between a microscope and a magnifying glass. If you're looking at something that's fairly large and easy to see, like a human hair, then you'll see it with either device as you don't need very much power. But if you're looking at something that's harder to see, like individual cells, you've got no chance of seeing it with the magnifying glass – you need something more powerful: the microscope.

It's just the same with statistical tests. If you're looking at a really massive difference, like if you're looking at whether adults tend to be taller than babies, then this difference is so big and so easy to see that any statistical test will find it – even a simple non-parametric test like the sign test. But if you're looking at a smaller difference, which is hard to see, you might miss it if you use a non-parametric test. You need a more powerful statistical test like the *t*-test if you're going to go looking for little differences.

To put this into the proper technical terms, a powerful test is less likely to make a Type II error, which means it is less likely to miss an effect. I'm sure that by now you're desperate for me just to spell out what is the bottom line, so here it is: *parametric tests are better than non-parametric tests.*

If parametric tests are better, why would I ever use a non-parametric test?

Parametric tests are more powerful because they are able to make assumptions – just like how it was easier for you to decide whether a 160-centimetre-tall person was 'tall' when I let you make an assumption about their age. As long as all the test's assumptions are met, then you'll probably want to use the more powerful parametric test. But if the assumptions aren't met then you can't use a parametric test: it might give you false answers – it might tell you two groups are different when really they are not, for example. So that's why we have the less-powerful, non-parametric tests – they're backups, for when the assumptions of parametric tests aren't met and we find we need to use something else.

What it all boils down to, then, is knowing what assumptions parametric tests make. Whenever you need to carry out a statistical test, you just decide if these assumptions have been met. If they have, you can use a more powerful parametric test; if they have not, you have to use a less powerful non-parametric test.

Thinking scientifically → **Power versus flexibility**

Another way you could view this issue, which is just as valid as what I've just said, is to say that non-parametric tests are better than parametric tests because they are more flexible and have fewer restrictions on when they can be used. Their lower power is just the price we have to pay for this flexibility. I know a lot of statisticians do think this way, so it's good for you to know about this idea. However, in psychology we do tend to prefer power to flexibility, and so tend to favour parametric tests whenever we can use them.

The main assumptions of parametric tests

Depending on who you speak to, there are either three, four or five assumptions that parametric tests make, and if we're being really strict these assumptions can change a bit depending on what sort of test you are doing. But to keep things manageable, here are the three big ones, which you really should know about if you're trying to compare two groups of scores to see whether or not they are different.

1 The data follow a normal distribution

We saw back in Chapter 11 that when a set of numbers is normally distributed, we instantly get loads of free information. For example, we instantly know that almost exactly 68% of the people have a score that is within one standard deviation of the mean score (it's actually 68.27% of the people, if you're a fan of precision). This free information is one of the things that make parametric tests more powerful, so your data have to follow a normal distribution before you can use a parametric test. If they do not, you should use a non-parametric test.

2 The data are at the interval or ratio level of measurements

In Chapter 12, I said that numbers that are at the interval or ratio level – that is, proper numbers, like those you deal with every day – have more information in them than other numbers. As these numbers have more information, again it's not surprising that more powerful parametric tests insist that you only use numbers of this type. You can't do parametric tests if you have ordinal numbers such as finishing positions in a race. You couldn't use a parametric *t*-test to see whether left-handers tend to finish a race in higher positions than right-handers, for example.

3 'Homogeneity of variance' – both sets of numbers should be spread out in the same way

When you have more than one set of data – for example, when you are comparing two groups of people – parametric tests assume that for each group, the scores are spread out in a similar way. This simply means that if you look at a measure of dispersion for the groups, such as the standard deviation, this should be more or less the same for each.

Have a look at Figure 13.4. At the top, you can see two groups of people who are fine for a parametric test – the two groups' scores have a similar range (the two curves look the same; one is just further along the scale than the other, as one group had a higher mean than the other). At the bottom, however, we have two groups of people with very different amounts of variance – one of the groups is *much* more spread out than the other. This would be a problem for a parametric test. With these two groups, we just aren't comparing like with like, and so we wouldn't be able to use a parametric test.

The proper term for this criterion is **homogeneity of variance**, which is quite a mouthful, but you should try to memorize it. 'Homogeneity' is just a big word for 'sameness'; 'variance' just means 'variation.' So 'homogeneity of variance' just means 'sameness of variation': the groups' scores should vary by more or less the same amount.[11]

---

11   It's worth noting that many statisticians now say that we shouldn't worry about this assumption any more. See, for example, Zimmerman, D.W. (2004). A note on preliminary tests of equality of variances. *British Journal of Mathematical and Statistical Psychology, vol. 57,* pages 173–81. I've covered the assumption here as it's still taught on a lot of courses. If you are studying on a course that teaches you to check homogeneity then you should probably ignore this footnote for now …

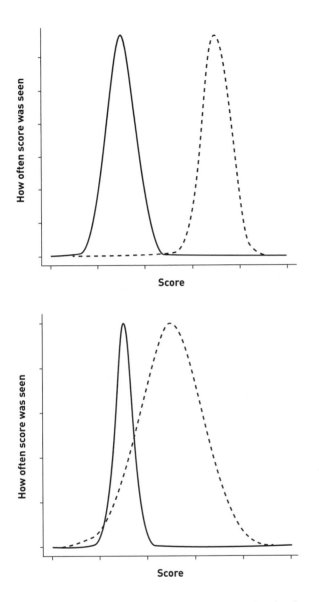

Figure 13.4 Two distributions that show homogeneity of variance and two distributions that do not

◉ Student's *t*-test

The rest of this chapter will cover tests for comparing two groups of scores. We've already seen the sign test, which is really quite a simple non-parametric test. Now we'll move on to a really important statistical procedure, Student's *t*-test.

Student's *t*-test has an interesting history. Despite its name, the person who invented it was not really called Student, he was called William Gosset. Gosset worked for the Guinness brewing company in Ireland which, at the beginning of the twentieth century, started taking a scientific approach to making beer – a process that until then had always involved guesswork and relying on the intuition of experienced brewers. Guinness wanted to move away from guesswork and intuition towards a more reliable and consistent way of making beer and, finding that they needed a way of comparing small samples of grain, they asked Gosset to see what he could come up with. The result was the *t*-test – a useful way of comparing two sets of numbers to see whether or not they are different, even when the sets of numbers are quite small.

The reason Gosset had to give himself a false name when he published the test was that Guinness didn't want their rivals to discover they were using statistics to improve their brewing, and so forbade him from publishing under his own name. The wonderful link between statistics and beer is one I celebrate as often as possible in the pub.

Anyway, here's how the *t*-test works. You have two sets of scores and you want to know whether they are, on average, different from each other. For example, let's say you gave an intelligence test to a group of students from the north of the country and a group from the south of the country. You're going to want to know whether or not the two types of student are, on average, different in their intelligence.

Let's say that on this intelligence test the students from the north have a range of scores – some get high scores and some get low scores – but on average they have a score of 46 points. And let's say that the students from the south also have a range of scores but that on average they have a score of 37. Overall, of the students we have tested, those from the north have got a slightly higher score.

There are two possible reasons why we might have seen this difference. First, perhaps we saw this difference in the two groups we tested because northern students really are more intelligent than southern students – that would be nice and interesting and we'd probably want to tell people all about this finding. But there is another reason why we might have seen that difference between the two groups we tested: perhaps northern students and southern students are really the same, but we happened to see a difference in the people we tested just by accident – just like how a group of people and a group of their clones might get slightly different scores on a test by accident. The first explanation says that the two types of student really are different; the second explanation is the null hypothesis: it says that any difference we saw in the people we studied doesn't really mean anything.

Our task is to choose between these two explanations, and the t-test can help us do this. As with most statistical procedures, the t-test says 'Let's assume for a moment that the null hypothesis is true: let's assume northern students and southern students are really the same – they all come from the same population. If northern and southern students really are the same, what are the chances of taking two lots of students and getting a group with an average score of 46 and a group with an average score of 37?' This is exactly the same as saying 'If we gave this intelligence test to a group of people and a group of their clones, what are the chances that one lot would get 46 and one lot would get 37?'

If you work through the t-test by hand, as I have in Appendix B (which, remember, you should read next), you'll calculate the t statistic for the data you are analysing. In the worked example, I had a group of 26 northerners who got an average score of 46 on a test and a group of 26 southerners who got an average score of 37. When I analysed the data I got the result $t = 2.64$. Does this mean the two groups were different or not? To decide, just like with the chi-squared test in Chapter 10, we need to get a critical value which can tell us whether or not the statistic we have calculated is significant, given the number of people we have tested.

After calculating this result of $t = 2.64$ I looked up the critical value for the test, at the .05 level, and found that with 52 participants in the study, the critical value is 2.01 (this is also shown in Appendix B). The t-value I calculated was greater than this critical value, so we know that we have a significant result. Because the analysis is significant, it looks as though the null hypothesis is wrong: the two groups we are comparing probably *are* different from each other, as there is less than a .05 probability of seeing the data we collected if the null hypothesis is true.

When I ran the same analysis using statistical software, I got the following result (which I've written in the formal way that we usually report statistics, with the degrees of freedom in brackets):

$t(50) = 2.64, p = .006$

This again confirms that the chances of seeing that difference between the northerners and southerners, if both groups really are the same, is really low: the likelihood is .006, or 0.6%. As this is so low, it's much more likely that northerners and southerners are actually different on this test, and so that's what I'd conclude. *I saw a low p-value, and so I tell people that northerners and southerners seem to perform differently on this test.*

◉ The Mann-Whitney *U* test, and the idea of ranks

The *t*-test, for comparing two groups, is a powerful parametric procedure. If two groups really are different, a *t*-test is quite likely to find this, because of its power. The reason it is so powerful is because it can make various assumptions – it has *parameters*. For example, it assumes the scores you have collected more or less follow a normal distribution, that they are interval or ratio data, and that there aren't any outliers in the data. However, what do you do if those assumptions aren't met? What if your data have some serious outliers, or are ordinal measurements? In this case you have to use a less-powerful test which doesn't make all these assumptions. If you want to compare two groups and can't use a *t*-test, you'll often use a Mann-Whitney *U* test instead.

Again, the full details of how to calculate the *U* test are in Appendix B, to avoid breaking up this chapter too much. The main thing I want to highlight right now, as it is a new idea, is that the Mann-Whitney test works by using **ranks**. To show you what this means, consider these test scores from three dancers and three drummers:

	Dancers	Drummers
1	12	15
2	26	11
3	19	326

The numbers in the table are the actual test scores each person provided. If we were using a *t*-test we would do calculations on these scores, but with a non-parametric test we don't carry out our calculations on the scores. Instead, we put the scores into rank order and do our calculations on these new numbers.

You'll notice that the lowest score in the table came from the second drummer. If we wanted to rank the scores, then, we'd give this person a rank of 1, as their score was at the bottom. The next-highest score (from the first dancer) would get a rank of 2, and so on until the person with the highest score got a rank of 6. Here are the same people with their scores replaced by ranks:

	Dancers	Drummers
1	2	3
2	5	1
3	4	6

You'll notice that everybody is still in the same order as before – the person with the lowest score also has the lowest rank, for example – but some nice things have happened. In particular, the one score that really stood out from the rest in the original data (the third drummer's extreme score of 326) no longer looks like such an outlier. The Mann-Whitney U test would then be calculated from these new numbers, and would tell us whether one group tends to have higher ranks than the other. This is just the same as working out whether one group tends to have higher scores than the other, but the outlier has been dealt with.

Most non-parametric tests work with ranks in this way, and you'll see two examples of this when you read the details in Appendix B.

⊙ Comparing two groups of scores with repeated-measures data

I have now introduced two different tests for comparing two sets of scores. You have the independent-samples t-test for when you want to compare two groups and, if the t-test's assumptions are not met (for example when you have ordinal data, or big outliers), you have the Mann-Whitney U test.

Just as you have a parametric t-test and a non-parametric alternative for comparing two groups, there is also a t-test and a non-parametric alternative for when you have a repeated-measures design. Let's say you have taken a group of people and tested them twice, before and after giving them training. You would naturally want to know whether their scores on the second test differed from their scores on the first test. Normally, you would use a repeated-measures *t*-test, but if the assumptions for this were not met, you would use the *Wilcoxon matched-pairs signed-ranks test* instead, as this is the non-parametric equivalent.

Again, the full details of these two tests are in Appendix B, where you'll see they have a lot in common with the tests you already know – I've deliberately arranged that section of the book so that the concepts build into an overall picture as you read through it, and you should head over there now. But just before you do, let me finish this chapter with a useful table summarizing the four main tests that are available to you for when you need to compare two groups of scores to see whether or not they are, on average, the same.

	Parametric data	Non-parametric data
Independent samples	Independent-samples *t*-test	Mann-Whitney *U* test
Repeated measures	Repeated-measures *t*-test	Wilcoxon matched-pairs signed-ranks test

◁◉▷ Chapter summary

It is very common to have two sets of scores and to want to know whether or not they are, on average, different to each other. For example, you might test a group of men and a group of women and want to know if the two genders perform differently on that test. You have four main tests available for this, and the one you choose depends on whether you have parametric or non-parametric data, and on whether you are using an independent-samples or a repeated-measures design.

Chapter 14

Looking at relationships – measures of correlation

Each statistical test pretty much does one of two things: it either looks at differences or it looks at relationships. In the last chapter we looked at differences – we saw various tests that can take two sets of numbers and tell you whether, overall, those sets are different. In this chapter we're going to look at statistical tests that take two sets of numbers and tell you whether they show a relationship.

As an example of how we might use relationships, imagine a politician looking at children's education. Politicians are forever worrying about their budgets, so ours might look at the national school system and ask, 'Do schools really need all this money we give them? *Is there any relationship* between the amount of money we give to a school and how successful it is?' In this case, our politician wants to know whether schools that have more money, have more success.

When we have two measurements, and we want to know how strong is the relationship between them, we can often use a technique called **correlation**. What is the relationship between schools' budgets and their success? What is the relationship between a country's wealth and its crime level? What is the relationship between the amount of time people spend studying for exams and the scores they get? Correlation answers questions like these in a really simple way: it gives us a number between zero and one. When the number is close to one, the two measures have a strong relationship; when the number is close to zero, the two measures have a weak relationship. It really is that simple. If there is a strong relationship between study and exam scores, so that people who study a lot get better exam results, a correlation test will give a score close to one.

⊙ When relationships are strong, we can make predictions

To give you a feel for what I mean by 'a strong relationship', take a look at Figure 14.1. This shows the number of children attending my school over 50 years as it grew from being a small school to being ... well, a slightly larger small school. You can see there is a strong relationship between the number of boys and the number of girls: the numbers changed in a very similar way over the years such that the more boys there were at any time, the more girls there tended to be. The relationship is not perfect – sometimes the number of boys went up or down more than the number of girls – but it is close.

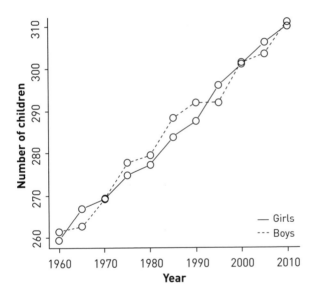

Figure 14.1 The number of boys and girls at my school over a period of 50 years

Because the relationship between the number of boys and the number of girls is close, we can do something useful with these numbers. If I told you how many girls were at the school in any year, you could make a fair guess at how many boys were there at the same time. Try it: look at the graph and guess how many boys were at the school when there were 301 girls. You can probably make a really accurate guess, and the reason you can do this is because the relationship between the number of boys and the number of girls is so close. If the relationship wasn't close, you wouldn't be able to make this guess.

👁 Away from the extremes

All correlation tests give us a number somewhere between zero and one. This number is called the **correlation coefficient**. A correlation test gives a result of zero – 0.00 – when there is no relationship at all between two measures, and it gives a result of one – 1.00 – when there is an extremely close relationship. Most relationships in the real world are somewhere between these extremes; we usually see correlations with values like .85 or .39. All you need to remember is that the higher this number is, the stronger the relationship between your two measures. The stronger the relationship, the more the measures tend to change at the same time. (The relationship between the girls and boys at my school has a value of .96. This is very close to 1.00, and so we know that as the number of girls changed, the number of boys tended to change in a very similar way.)

The best way really to get a feel for how correlation works is to look at examples. So here are a few examples of correlations from recent scientific studies. With each, I will explain how I am interpreting the correlation, and this should give you a feeling for how correlations are used to understand relationships.

- A study found that in married couples, the correlation between how recklessly a person drives a car and how recklessly their partner drives is .56. This correlation is well above zero, which tells me that if I meet someone who is dangerous behind the wheel, there is a fair chance their partner will be a bad driver too. Similarly, if I meet someone who drives cautiously, there is a fair chance their partner will also be a careful driver. However, because the correlation is below 1.00, I also know there must be many couples who will not fit this pattern. The relationship between a person's driving and their partner's driving exists, but it is not entirely clear. I see all this from the correlation of .56.[12]

---

12 Taubman-Ben-Ari, O. (2008). Couple similarity for driving style. *Transportation Research Part F, vol. 9*, pages 185–93.

- There is a correlation of .85 between how much testosterone a male camel has and how long it spends having sex. This correlation is quite close to 1.00, so I know this is a strong relationship: without too many exceptions, the more testosterone a camel has the longer it will spend ... well, *humping*.[13]
- There is a correlation of .87 between how long a potato crop stays in the soil and how much damage the potatoes suffer from insects. The longer the crop stays in the ground, the more damage it will suffer. This correlation is quite close to 1.00, so I know this should hold true for most crops, although there will be a few exceptions.[14]

Summary

Correlation gives you a number between zero and one. The closer it is to one, the stronger the relationship between your two measures.

◉ Getting a sense of direction with correlation

The other thing you need to know about correlation coefficients is that they can be positive or negative. When a correlation is positive, this means that as one measure goes up, the other tends to go up also; if a correlation is negative, this means that as one measure goes up the other tends to go down.

There is a positive relationship between the number of clothes you wear and how warm you feel: the *more* clothes you put on, the *more* you feel warm (notice I said 'more' = 'more'). There is a negative relationship between the air temperature and the number of clothes you wear: the *more* it is warm, the *less* you wear clothes (notice I said 'more' = 'less'). In other words as temperature goes up, number of clothes goes down: a negative relationship.

All the correlations I have described so far showed positive correlations: the *more* time potatoes spend in the ground, the *more* the insects eat them (more = more); the *more* recklessly a person drives, the *more*

13   Deen, A. (2008). Testosterone profiles and their correlation with sexual libido in male camels. *Research in Veterinary Science, vol. 85*, pages 220–6.

14   Kuhar, T.P. and Alvarez, J.M. (2008). Timing of injury and efficacy of soil-applied insecticides against wireworms on potato in Virginia. *Crop Protection, vol. 27*, pages 792–8.

recklessly their partner drives (more = more). But what about negative relationships? Here are a few more examples from recent research:

- A study in Turkey found a correlation of −.58 between a city's altitude and the number of tuberculosis cases in that city. The correlation is negative, so *more* altitude means *less* tuberculosis (more = less). The relationship is fairly strong, at −.58, but it is still some way from −1.00. This means altitude is a useful predictor of tuberculosis levels in a city, but it cannot tell me everything. (If you are curious, population density was also important.)[15]
- A study of prisoners found a correlation of −.17 between being psychopathic and being able to tell when other people look sad. The negative correlation means the *more* psychopathic a person is, the *less* they can tell when somebody looks sad (again: more = less). However, the correlation is quite close to zero. Indeed, it is much closer to zero than −1.00, showing this is only a weak relationship. With a correlation this weak we would expect to see a lot of people who do not fit the pattern.[16]
- A hospital-based study found a correlation of −.49 between a patient's age and how satisfied they were with their medical treatment. This is a negative correlation, which means older patients were less satisfied than younger patients (*more* age = *less* satisfaction). The strength of the relationship – almost halfway between 0.00 and −1.00 – tells us this is a relatively strong effect, but knowing a patient's age wouldn't let you predict their satisfaction perfectly.[17]

Summary

In a positive relationship, when one measure increases the other tends to increase also; in a negative relationship, when one measure increases the other measure tends to decrease.

15 Tanrikulu, A.C. and others (2008). Tuberculosis in Turkey: high altitude and other socio-economic risk factors. *Public Health, vol. 122*, pages 613–19.

16 Hastings, M.E., Tangney, J.P. and Stuewig, J. (2008). Psychopathy and identification of facial expressions of emotion. *Personality and Individual Differences, vol. 44*, pages 1474–83.

17 Silvestri, L. and others (2008). Is perception of nursing care among orthopaedic trauma patients influenced by age? *Journal of Orthopaedic Nursing, vol. 12*, pages 64–8.

👁 **Understanding the look of relationships**

When using correlation, it can be very useful to look at relationships on scatterplots. Seeing the relationship between two measures when it is plotted can tell you a lot. To give you a feel for this, I have graphed four different relationships in Figure 14.2. In these graphs, each dot represents one person, simultaneously showing their score on the two different measures.

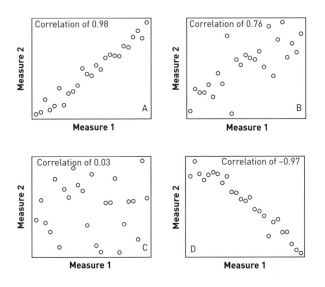

Figure 14.2 Examples of correlations showing different relationship strength and directions

Graph A shows a strong positive relationship. You can see the dots tend to slope upwards from left to right, and more or less all fall on a straight line. This means, in general, the higher an individual is on measure 1 the higher they are on measure 2. The relationship between measure 1 and measure 2 is close. We can see this by the high correlation statistic and also by the points on the graph almost all following the same straight-line pattern.

Now look at graph B, which shows a weaker positive correlation. Overall, the points still tend to slope upwards as we move from left to right – the points on the right-hand side tend to be higher than the points on the left-hand side – but the pattern is not so clear as it was in graph A. This is a weaker relationship, and the points look less as though they are trying to fall on a line.

Graph C takes this further, and shows a correlation of almost zero. You can see there is no slope to these points at all, and they look nothing at all like a line. Instead, they look like a shapeless cloud on the graph. This cloud-like shape is a really useful clue, which tells us the two measures are completely unrelated. An individual who gets a high score on measure 1 could get any sort of score on measure 2. This last point is really important: if an individual in graph C has a high score on measure 1, you have no way of knowing what their score was on measure 2. Try it: if I tell you I got a high score on measure 1, what do you think I scored on measure 2? You've no way of knowing, have you? This is really different to graph A, where there is a stronger relationship: with graph A, if I said I had a high score on measure 1 you could probably guess my score on measure 2. I'll say more about this in a 'going further' section later.

Finally, graph D shows a strong negative relationship. You can see the points almost fall on a straight line, like they did in graph A, but this time the slope runs *downwards* from left to right. This shows that as one measure increases, the other tends to decrease – a classic negative relationship.

Summary

When individuals are plotted as points on a graph, you can see the correlation between two measures by how the points lie. When the points tend to lie near a straight line, this shows there is a strong correlation. When the points tend to slope up from left to right, we see a positive relationship; when the points tend to slope down from left to right, we see a negative relationship. But when the points look like a shapeless cloud, there is very little or even zero relationship between the two measures.

◉ Correlation: some words of warning

Correlation is a really simple statistical procedure. You take two lots of numbers, run a correlation test, and this gives you a number between minus one and one, describing how close the relationship is. It is all very straightforward.

Do you remember right back at the start of this book, I described statistics as being our tools in psychology? Well teaching somebody about correlation always feels a lot like handing them a chainsaw: I want to take them by the shoulders, gaze into their eyes and earnestly say, 'This is a really useful tool if you use it properly – but for goodness' sake be careful!'

Because correlation is so easy to use – any spreadsheet program will do correlations for you – the technique is used all the time. But just because we *can* do a correlation test on any two sets of numbers, this doesn't necessarily mean we *should*. And just because two sets of numbers correlate, this doesn't necessarily mean we should tell anybody about it. There are a few things we need to be careful about, and I will briefly run through these now.

Cause and effect

This is a terribly important point: just because two measures correlate with each other, and so change at the same time, we can never say that one *caused* the other to change. Sadly, people make this mistake all the time.

As an example of how we have to be careful when looking at correlations, consider this: between the year 1930 and the year 2010 there was a big increase in the amount of air travel and a big decrease in the number of chimney sweeps. If we ran an analysis on these numbers, we would see a strong negative correlation between the amount of flying people did each year and the number of chimney sweeps who were in business. But this definitely does not mean people's flying habits somehow *caused* the chimney sweeps to lose their jobs! The amount of air travel and the number of chimney sweeps changed at the same time, but for completely different reasons. There was no cause and effect. The phrase people use here is 'correlation does not imply causation,' and you are sure to encounter this saying again.[18]

---

18 If you really want to show off, when people make the mistake of seeing cause and effect just because two measures change at the same time, you can say *cum hoc, ergo propter hoc*, which means 'it happened with this, therefore it happened because of this.' A very similar logical mistake is called *post hoc, ergo propter hoc*, which means 'it happened *after* this, therefore it happened because of this.'

The first version is what you say to people when they see two things change together and assume one change caused the other, like with air travel and chimney sweeps. The second version is what you say when one event happened after another and somebody assumes the first must have caused the second. For a very clever joke about this, have a look at http://xkcd.com/552/ – this cartoon is pinned up in pretty much every statistics lab.

Here is another example of the cause-and-effect problem: tall children perform much better in school than short children. In other words, there is a clear correlation between a child's height and their academic ability. So should concerned parents start stretching their kids on racks to help them get ahead in school? Of course not! Taller children do better at school not because they are tall, but because they are *older*. In statistics, this is known as the **third variable problem** or, more poetically, a **lurking variable**. We see a relationship between two measures – height and school performance, in this case – but the relationship is only there because of something else, a third variable lurking outside our study. In this example the third variable is age. Age is the lurking variable which affects both height and school performance.

Even when there is genuine cause and effect between two measures, it is easy to get them the wrong way round. For example, there is a clear relationship between the amount of crime in a city and the number of police officers: cities that have a lot of police officers have more crime. But this definitely doesn't mean the police officers are committing all the crimes!

In this example it is pretty clear that the cause and effect is the wrong way round, but it can also be much more subtle, so always be on your guard for this mistake – in your own work and in other people's.

Summary

Just because two measures correlate, this tells you nothing about why or how they are related.

Look for lines that are not straight

When I showed you correlations on graphs, I finished by saying, 'when the points tend to lie near a straight line, this shows there is a strong correlation.' The key phrase here is 'straight line'. The correlation test can only see straight lines, and is blind to any other pattern. If you have two measures that are closely related, but the relationship does not look like a straight line, correlation will simply not see it.

To show you what I mean, have a look at Figure 14.3. There is clearly a relationship between the two measures – the points all fall on a line – it's just that the line is S-shaped, instead of straight. This means correlation won't see this relationship. If you used a correlation test on the numbers in this graph you would get a result near zero, and might fail to notice that the two measures are actually very systematically related.

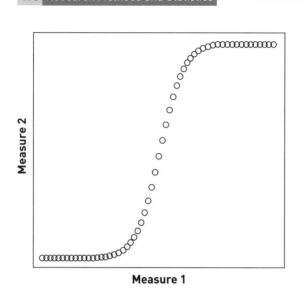

Figure 14.3 An example of a clear relationship between two measures which doesn't follow a straight line

There *are* ways of measuring bendy relationships like this one, and you might learn about this if you study statistics further. The main thing I want you to remember for now is that people make this mistake a lot. If somebody ever tells you there is no correlation between two measures, you should always ask 'Was there really no correlation? Or was there a relationship that didn't look like a straight line?' A careful researcher always looks at a graph to make sure they are not missing anything, and will be able to answer this question.

Summary

Correlation can only see straight lines. If two measures are related in a different way, correlation will miss this relationship.

There is always *some* correlation

The final warning I want to give you about correlation is this: you will probably never see a correlation of exactly zero. Whenever you take two lots of numbers and correlate them, you will always see *some* relationship. So when you see a relationship between two measures you should always ask yourself whether it really means something, or whether the correlation appeared just by accident – as happens sometimes.

To show you what I mean by an accidental correlation, I just created two sets of 30 random numbers and looked at whether these correlated with each other. Now let's be absolutely clear: I plucked these numbers out of the air. In fact, I got them from random.org, which produces really really random numbers – far more random than any normal computer can produce. So the numbers I correlated were utterly meaningless, and the two sets should show no relationship to each other at all.

However, when I did a correlation test on my two sets of numbers, I found a result of .41. The test was telling me there was a moderately strong relationship between these two sets of measurements, even though I had just invented them! This was crazy. I created two new sets of random numbers and tried again. This time I got a correlation of .18, which was closer to zero but still suggested some relationship. But how could there be a relationship between two lots of random numbers?

I carried on, inventing sets of numbers and looking at the correlation between them. The next ten times I generated random numbers and correlated them I got coefficients ranging from –.45 to .30.

What this demonstrates quite clearly, I hope, is that even when there is no real relationship between two measures, sometimes the numbers will vary together just by chance, making it look as though there is a relationship. So when you use a correlation test and see a relationship, how can you know whether this is showing you something interesting or not?

There are three answers to this. First, as we saw in Chapter 3, it is always better to test large samples rather than small samples, and this applies to correlation as well. To show you what I mean, I did my random number correlations again but now, instead of using two sets of 30 random numbers, I used two sets of 100 random numbers. This time, my correlations only ranged from –.05 to .10. With two lots of 100 random numbers, then, I only saw very small relationships; when I used two lots of 30 random numbers I saw correlations up to –.45. The larger sample prevented me from seeing bogus relationships.

The second way you can protect yourself from being misled by correlations is by looking at the p-value for the test. We have seen p-values quite a lot now (and I will show you how to get one for correlation soon). Remember that all statistical tests produce a number called p, which you can use to decide if what you saw in your sample is likely to generalize to other people. If your correlation has a high p-value – and by 'high', we usually mean anything over .05 – this suggests you should probably stick with your null hypothesis, and say that the relationship is probably not important. In this case, you know you should probably not get excited about your correlation.

The final way to protect yourself from being misled by correlations is quite simply to use your brain! Whenever you find a relationship between two sets of numbers, ask yourself whether it is really a sensible finding. Does it *matter* that the two measures correlate?

To show you what I mean, I have just looked up some statistics from around the European Union. Did you know there is a correlation of .57 between how many dairy farms a country has and the amount of sea-freight its ports handle? No, I didn't know that either. This is quite a strong relationship, but does it really tell us anything interesting? I doubt it. The fact the numbers correlate is almost certainly just a fluke, and the correlation is not telling me anything useful. I wouldn't bother to report this finding to anyone (except you, clearly, but I like to think of us as friends. You're looking good today, by the way).

Summary

Two sets of numbers will always correlate, at least a bit. When you see a correlation, you need to decide whether or not this is a real relationship. Using large samples, checking the *p*-value from the analysis and using common sense all help you avoid mistakes.

◉ Reporting correlations

Perhaps the most important thing when you report a correlation is the coefficient itself, known as *r*. You usually also report the degrees of freedom for the correlation (which are the number of measurement pairs, minus 2) and whether or not the correlation is significant (which you get from tables of critical values, which are easy to find online).

So, for example, let's say I have 20 pairs of measurements (which means I have 18 degrees of freedom), a correlation of $r = .76$, and I have found from a table of critical values that this is significant at the .05 level. I would simply report this as $r(18) = .76, p < .05$.

◉ Going further: measuring how much numbers vary – the coefficient of determination

On one day each week, I take my dog for a particularly long walk in the woods. I do this exactly once per week, and each week I pick the day at random: one week it might be Sunday, the next week it might be Wednesday, and so on. I would like you to guess which day I took my walk for each of the past five weeks. Go on: guess away.

Unless you are very lucky, you just guessed wrongly. This shouldn't surprise either of us: you have a one in seven chance of guessing which day I went out in the first week, a one in seven chance of guessing which day I went out in the second week, and so on. Multiplying these sevens together tells us there is only a one in 35 chance of guessing all five days correctly.

So here is a fact that will make your task easier: last week I took my walk on a Tuesday.

That should help you quite a bit. Instead of guessing which day I went out for five weeks you are now guessing for only four weeks. By telling you which day I went out last week, I have given you one-fifth – 20% – of the information you need to know what I did over the past five weeks.

If I then told you I went out on Saturday in the previous week, you would now have 40% of the information you want; if I told you what I did on all five weeks you would know 100% of the information you want, as surely as if you had been stalking me. The point I'm trying to make is this: *if there is a set of information, it is possible you will only know part of it.* So you might know 100% of my movements over the past five weeks, or you might know only 60%, for example.

Way back in Chapter 1, I started out by saying measurements always vary from one another. If I count the number of people in each house on my street, the number of people in each house will be different. If I measure the speed of each vehicle passing along a road, they will each be travelling at a different speed – at least slightly. If we collect a load of numbers from anywhere, they will not all be the same, they will vary. And here's where the dog-walking example comes in: sometimes you will understand all of the variation in a set of numbers and sometimes you will only understand some of it. Sometimes, when there is a definite pattern to the numbers you have collected, the variation in those numbers will make complete sense to you. Other times, when there is no pattern to the relationship, the variation will be a mystery. Look back at Figure 14.2: you 'understand' the variation in graph A because it follows a clear pattern; you don't understand the variation in graph C because there is no pattern.

With correlation we have a useful little trick to measure exactly how much we understand the variation in a set of numbers. If you take a correlation coefficient and square it, this tells you how much of the variation in your numbers you understand. Look back at Figure 14.1, which showed the number of boys and the number of girls attending my school over several decades. There was a correlation of .96 between the number of boys and the number of girls, showing the two sets of numbers were closely related.

Now here's the clever bit: if we take this correlation coefficient of .96 and square it, we get a value of .92. This means we understand 92% of all the variation in those numbers. If you know how many girls went to my school in any year, you have 92% of the information you need to know how many boys were there at the same time. Look at Figure 14.1 again: if I tell you the number of girls in a certain year was 301, you know the number of boys must also have been very close to 300. You can rule out a huge range of numbers – the number of boys clearly isn't less than 295, and it clearly isn't more than about 305: there is only a handful of numbers that could be correct. This works because the number of boys and the number of girls are so closely related: if you know number of girls, you have 92% of the information you need to know exactly how many boys attended the school at the same time.

This number, which we calculate by squaring the correlation coefficient, is called the **coefficient of determination**. It is a measure of how well one measure can predict another, and is a way of making correlations quite easy to understand. Let's look at one more example. As we saw earlier, there was a correlation of −.58 between a Turkish city's altitude and its level of tuberculosis infection. The negative correlation told us that more altitude meant less infection (it's a negative relationship, so more = less).

The correlation between the cities' altitudes and their infection levels was −.58, and if we square this number we get .34. This means that if we know how high a city is, we have 34% of the information we need to know exactly how much tuberculosis there was. Thirty-four per cent of the variation in cities' infection levels can be accounted for by variations in altitude. We would need more information if we wanted to explain the remaining 66% of the variation in infection levels.

So the coefficient of determination is closely related to the correlation coefficient – it's just that number squared – but has a slightly different meaning. Personally, I find it easier to understand than the basic correlation coefficient, as it more clearly relates to the real world. It is a measure of exactly how much we understand the variation in a set of numbers, and that's quite a concrete idea.

Summary

If you square a correlation coefficient, this tells you how much of the variation in your measurements you understand – the amount of variation in your numbers you can explain, or account for.

Parametric and non-parametric correlation coefficients

Just like in the last chapter, where we were comparing two sets of scores to see whether they differed, in correlation we have both parametric and non-parametric tests available to us. There are actually a whole load of different correlation tests out there, but by far the most common two are the **Pearson's product-moment correlation coefficient** and **Spearman's rho**. Pearson's test is a parametric procedure and so does its calculations on the original scores that were collected; Spearman's test, just like the Mann-Whitney test we saw in the last chapter, is calculated using ranks. It's easy to remember which way round these go, as 'Pearson' and 'parametric' both begin with the same letter.

The big issues

The main lessons I want you to take away from this chapter are all the things we have covered so far: what a correlation coefficient means, and when to be careful in interpreting one. As such, like when I covered tests for comparing two means, I've focused here on what the tests do, and how to understand them, and have put all the calculations for these correlations in Appendix C. You should go and read that appendix next, now that you have an idea of what correlation is all about.

One thing to notice, just before we end the chapter, is that in the Appendix C calculations, I analyse the same set of data using both Pearson's and Spearman's tests, but get different results. Pearson's test gave me a result of $r = .90$ and Spearman's test gave a result of rho = .80. Spearman's test, because it is a less-powerful, non-parametric test, underestimated the strength of the relationship between the two columns. This is a good illustration of why it's better to use the more powerful parametric tests whenever the data make this possible.

◉ Chapter summary

Correlation lets us measure how close the relationship is between two variables. However, when two variables are closely related, we have to be careful not to assume that one causes the other to change.

Chapter 15

Analysing and presenting qualitative data

With qualitative data, we are often interested in the themes that appear when people are free to say whatever they like. If people who are speaking freely mention a subject, especially if they mention it more than once, there is a good chance they feel that subject is important. We also tend to be interested in the exact words people use when they talk about those subjects. As such, many qualitative reports will include direct quotations from participants, supported by your own interpretation or analysis.

To give you an example of this, I once carried out a series of focus groups with bus drivers, to examine their experiences of work and of sharing the road with other vehicles. From a transcript of the interviews, several clear themes emerged. In reporting these, I would describe the theme and then give illustrations of how people talked about them:

> One of the key themes to emerge from the study of bus drivers was how vigilant the drivers needed to be, especially as they are handling such a large vehicle.
>
> 'Y've got this *vehicle* that you've got to *try* and drive round the city centre with (.) and... you... got to be looking *everywhere* [...] and obviously there might be things you miss or... cos you've got you're concentrating there you're concentrating here and your mirrors (.) and *everywhere*.'
>
> *Male driver, 33, Oxford*

👁 Finding themes in qualitative data

Finding themes in transcripts is often central to qualitative research, and there are various approaches to this task. For example, there are established methods called **grounded theory** and **interpretative phenomenological analysis**, which each describe a series of steps for processing interview transcripts to uncover the themes they contain. Both methods try to explore the data, and let themes emerge themselves, without the researcher imposing any theory or expectations.

I'm not going to go into detail about these two approaches, as they can get very involved, and there are various complexities which would just bog us down at this stage (for example, the two people who invented grounded theory fell out after writing their book, and each developed a different version of the method). Instead, I will describe a general approach to dealing with qualitative data which has a lot in common with these more technical approaches – especially grounded theory – and which reflects the process that many people go through when processing qualitative data to uncover themes. But I would encourage you to look into these more advanced methods if you seriously want to get into analysing qualitative data in the future.

👁 Coding your data

Let's assume you have recorded some interviews, have typed each interview up into a transcript and now want to analyse these to see what they tell you. First you'll probably want to read through the transcripts a couple of times, making notes on any themes that seem to emerge, or underlining any words that seem to be used a lot. You shouldn't really have much of a plan at this stage; instead, you'll be looking for topics that pop out from the text. You might also flag up any comments or statements from the interviewees that seem particularly good for illustrating these topics – you can use them in your write-up like I did with the example above.

Once you've got some idea of the sorts of themes that the text contains, you might start noting which sections of the transcript relate to each theme. And you might do this at various levels of detail. For example, you might first make fairly basic notes about what each section of the text is discussing, and then try to look at this at a deeper level, moving from simple comments on what the text says towards a more theoretical understanding.

To give you an example of this process, I happen to be doing some analysis at the moment on motorcyclists' conversations about safety. Here is a small extract from my transcript and notes – notice how the comments right next to the transcript are quite superficial, but the comments to their left, which I added later, become more theoretical. In this conversation, a relatively new motorcyclist ('Jon') is asking two more experienced riders for advice on how to put his knee to the ground when riding round corners. (In case you don't know, this is a fairly flashy thing to do, normally only done by racing motorcyclists.) The main thing we were interested in during this study was how motorcyclists view the issue of safety.

Higher-level notes	Basic notes	Text
	Mentions being new.	**Jon:** I'm new to biking and have got a [big bike]. Have you got any advice on getting your knee down? I really want to be able to say I've done it. What's the best way to get started?
Hostility. Because he's an outsider/ newcomer?	Immediate criticism. Consequences of accident.	**Dave:** Crash your bike. Keep riding like an idiot and you'll get your knee down soon enough. Just remember to carry a donor card.
	Defensive. Asks again.	**Jon:** I don't ride like an idiot. I only try it when it's safe, so have you got any tips?
Diffusing the discussion?	Suggests practising in a safe place.	**Bryan:** Find a bend with oil on it! Seriously, though, go on a track day and learn off the road where it's safe.
Group identity based around skill & responsibility?	"us" = Jon's not 'one of the group' yet. Control. Responsibility. Also, says "we". Discipline. Speaks for the group. Consequences of accident.	**Dave:** The thing is, Jon, your sort of attitude really annoys us. Going fast is easy but staying in control is hard. If you've got a big bike you have to be responsible. We use discipline – for our own safety and for other people's safety ... and for our parents' peace of mind.

From this sort of record, we can see the themes that emerge (thinking about the consequences of an accident was mentioned twice just in that short passage), and we can also look at what these themes say about our research question. This excerpt, for example, might suggest that one aspect of motorcyclists' views on safety is that 'proper' bikers aren't risk takers, and that if a newcomer wants to become one of the group they need to both gain experience and ride in a particular (safe) way.

◉ Presenting qualitative data

Once you have gone through the encoding process and got some ideas about the themes that appear in your data, you will want to show this information to people. Very often, this will involve the sort of presentation I showed back at the start of this chapter: a description of the theme that emerged, with some commentary from you, followed by a representative quotation from the original data. So, if I were writing up the motorcyclist study, I might include some text like this:

> It was common for riders to talk about themselves as a group. Words like 'us' and 'we' were frequently used, and many riders took it upon themselves to speak for all 'real' motorcyclists. To riders who saw themselves as part of this group, important traits included self-control and discipline, and an awareness of the consequences of risky behaviour.
>
>> 'The thing is, Jon, your sort of attitude really annoys us. Going fast is easy but staying in control is hard. If you've got a big bike you have to be responsible. We use discipline – for our own safety and for other people's safety ... and for our parents' peace of mind.'
>>
>> *Male rider, 27*

You might also want to give some numbers to show how often different themes were mentioned, and a graph can be useful for this. For example, my motorcycle study might end up with something like Figure 15.1 to show how often riders mentioned different sources of danger.[19] From this graph it is immediately obvious that the riders who were interviewed seem to see other road users as the main source of danger on the road.

---

19   Just to be clear, all the data I've included here aren't real – they're modified versions of the real data which I've created for illustration.

This finding might then be explored in more detail, perhaps using quantitative methods.

This general pattern is common in research: qualitative methods are used to explore a new area, and to discover what it is that needs to be studied, and then quantitative methods are used to probe these subjects in more depth. Without this qualitative work, though, I might never have known that other road users were seen as the biggest danger, and would not have known to investigate this further.

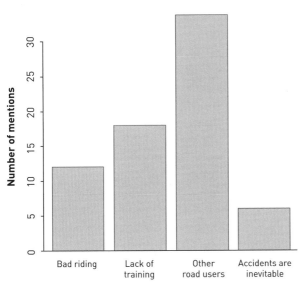

How often different sources of danger were mentioned

Figure 15.1 An example of a graph showing how often various themes emerged in some qualitative data

◉ Chapter summary

Processing qualitative data often involves seeing what themes emerge from people's words. Usually, we try to do this in a way that develops new insights and theories, and so we try to let the themes emerge, rather than try to confirm a theory.

Reports, and some thoughts

Chapter 16

Writing research reports

Carrying out a study and analysing its results are, in many ways, just part of the research process. It's not much use carrying out a wonderfully designed and executed study if you then don't tell anybody about it! Almost all research projects end with a report, describing what the research involved, how it was conducted and what was found. Although (as with everything in life) there are exceptions, the vast majority of research reports follow a similar format, organized under similar headings, and so I'll follow these headings in this chapter to give you an idea of what to think about as you write each section.

👁 Title and abstract

The title of a study should be informative, telling people as much as possible about what the study involved. Let's say we have carried out a survey on people's attitudes to elephants, and in particular we have looked at whether people have a preference for African elephants or Indian elephants. In this case, a really bad title might be:

A study on elephants

This title would probably suggest to people that the elephants were the participants! It certainly says nothing about what was measured. A much better title might be something like:

Do people's attitudes reveal a preference for African or Indian elephants?

which more clearly describes what the study was about. In this case I've phrased the title as a question, which is quite a common approach, given that research is all about asking questions. Another way I might have phrased this title is:

> An investigation into whether people's attitudes towards elephants reveal a preference for African or Indian elephants

Following the title, a report should have an *abstract*: a short (usually one paragraph) but detailed description of the study and its findings. In the case of our elephant study, the abstract might read like this:

> Gammon and Oddfish (2010) found that people are attracted to partners with large ears, and went on to speculate that people might also prefer African elephants to Indian elephants thanks to their larger pinnae.[20] This prediction was tested on a sample of 100 people. Participants were shown photographs of both types of elephant and asked to rate each on several properties such as attractiveness, and the extent to which the participants would like to own the animal as a pet. Participants were also assessed on their familiarity with each type of elephant. Contrary to Gammon and Oddfish's prediction, the data showed that Indian elephants were rated significantly higher than African elephants on all the measures. Moreover, this could not be explained simply by one type of elephant being more familiar than the other. These data suggest that the ear-size theory might not apply to other species.

A good abstract should be written so that a person can get a really good idea of what the study involved, and what it found, just from reading the summary. Obviously the rest of the report is going to be important for more detail, but it should be possible to read an abstract and know all the key facts about the study.

Introduction

This section will cover the background to the study, show why it was needed, and, in a quantitative project, discuss the predictions that were tested. A good introduction has a beginning, a middle and an end. It will

---

20   *Pinnae* – the plural of 'pinna', which is the name for the fleshy flap stuck to each side of your head. You probably call this flap your ear, but technically you'd be wrong, as most of your ear is inside your head.

usually start by discussing the work that has gone before: what have other people said about this subject? It might go on to discuss any gaps in our knowledge, or problems with previous work that need to be addressed, before ending with a clear summary of what the current study tried to do. In short, the introduction should show where your study came from and why you did it.

A good tip for writing an introduction is that, when the reader gets to the end and sees what your study was about, they should feel 'Ah yes, of course!' Your study should feel like it's the logical thing to do given what we knew before. So, for example ...

> **Beginning:** Some researchers recently found that people are attracted to other people with large ears. They suggested that this might also be true for how we feel about non-human animals, and specifically mentioned African and Indian elephants, which are extremely similar except for the size of their ears, as the ideal way to test this.
>
> **Middle:** However, so far this prediction has never been tested. I have also thought of a possible complication: if we see any preference then this could be because one type of elephant is more familiar than the other.
>
> **End:** *As such* this study will measure people's feelings towards the two types of elephant and also assess how familiar each type is. We predict that people will prefer African elephants over Indian elephants.

As you get to the end of this introduction, you should get that feeling of 'Ah yes, of course!' – given what the first two parts of the introduction said, what else could the study possibly involve?

Method

Here you describe exactly what the study involved, and your main aim is to give people enough detail about what you did so that they could, if they wanted, **replicate** your study exactly. The method section is usually divided into subsections.

Participants

Who was tested? How many? How old? What gender mix? Where did they come from? Were they paid for taking part? Were there any criteria for including or excluding people?

In our elephant example, a simple Participants section might read something like this:

> One hundred participants (50 male, 50 female) were recruited using an opportunity sample. Their mean age was 38 years (standard deviation 6.3 years). None were paid for taking part.

That is short, but might be sufficient for this study. In other studies it might be important to mention other information. If I were carrying out a study on car drivers, for example, I would need to report how much driving experience the participants had.

Materials

What equipment was used in the study? Be as specific as possible: if you used Version 11.6 of some software, say so. Why? It might later turn out that Version 11.6 had a bug in it ...

In this case, our Materials section would be quite simple, and might look something like this:

> The materials for this study were two printed sheets. The top of each sheet showed a photograph of an elephant – either African or Indian – and the bottom of each sheet had a series of four questions: 'To what extent do you like the look of this animal?', 'To what extent would you like to own this animal as a pet?', 'How angry does this animal look?' and 'How cuddly does this animal look?' Participants marked their answers on the sheet using 7-point Likert scales, with ends labelled '1 – Not at all' and '7 – A great deal'.

Design

Did you test people more than once, or compare groups? Or did you use a correlational or observational design? What were the independent and dependent variables? If you used a repeated-measures design, did you counterbalance the study? (With the elephant study, we certainly should counterbalance, so that half the participants judge the African elephant first and half judge the Indian first).

To continue our example write-up, the Design section might look like this:

> In this Experiment, participants were tested in a counterbalanced repeated-measures design. Half rated the African elephant then the Indian elephant, and half performed the ratings in the reverse order.

The independent variable was the type of elephant (African or Indian) and the dependent variables were the ratings on the four questions.

Procedure

This final subsection of the Method describes exactly how the study took place. Again, it is important that you give enough detail that somebody can picture what it was like to take part in your study, and could replicate what you did. By giving people enough information to imagine exactly what your procedure looked like, they can see whether there might be any problems with what you did. For example, imagine you read a study which said 'Participants had their hearing tested in the middle of the steel factory where they worked' In this case, you'd say 'Hold on a moment! How can you test somebody's hearing in a noisy factory? That's stupid.' But if the report had just said 'Participants had their hearing tested', and didn't mention this detail, you'd never be able to spot the problem with the study. So, while avoiding obviously trivial points, do give plenty of detail.

A good tip for writing the Procedure section is to describe your study by focusing on what each participant experienced. So, for our elephant study, the Procedure might look something like this:

Each participant was tested individually in the same quiet room. First, each participant signed a consent form and provided background information about their gender, age, and their familiarity with elephants. Then each participant was presented with the first rating sheet, showing either the African or the Indian elephant. They were allowed as much time as they wanted to answer the questions. When they had finished with the first sheet the researcher took this away before presenting the participant with the second sheet, showing the remaining elephant. The participant was again given as long as necessary to answer the questions for the second elephant. After they finished the second rating sheet, participants were debriefed and given an opportunity to ask questions before the study ended.

Results

Start the Results section with descriptive statistics to show what, overall, you found. Use tables or graphs if you think they will make the results easier to understand (but try to avoid presenting the same data more than once). In our elephant study, we would be particularly interested in the average rating for the two types of elephant, and some measure of how much people varied around these averages. Means and standard deviations for all the measures, in other words.

Then, once you have described the overall effect – in this case, once you have shown that people rated the Indian elephants higher on average – you go on to present your inferential statistics. These tell us how reliable is the effect you have just described. In this case, they help us judge whether the preference for Indian elephants is likely to generalize beyond the specific people who were tested.

◉ Discussion

This is probably the place where you have most freedom to say what you want about your study – and so it's usually the part people find most difficult to write! It's a good idea to begin with a paragraph summarizing the study and its findings. 'This study set out to see whether a preference for people with large ears was also seen when people judged elephants. The results showed ...' From here, you will usually go on to talk about how your findings relate to other people's work and what they tell us about psychological theory. Always try to look to the big picture here: how has our understanding of the world changed as a result of your study?

Towards the end of your Discussion section, it is usually good practice to be reflective, and discuss the strengths and weaknesses of your own study. Every study involves making design decisions – in this case, we chose to show photographs of elephants rather than video, or real elephants. What else could have been done differently, and how might this have changed the findings? Try not to fall into the common trap of tearing your own study to shreds, leaving the reader wondering why you ever bothered with such an awful study (this is something I see a lot in students' work). By all means be critical, and genuinely explore what might have happened if your design decisions had been different, but look also at what was good about your study.

◉ Conclusions

End the main part of your report with a short, simple summary of what you found. It is also appropriate here to mention any concerns from the

Discussion which were so major that they might affect the validity of the conclusions. For example, let's say that after you completed the elephant study you found that you had accidentally recruited all your participants from St Julian's Hospital for Trampled African Elephant Handlers. This fact would seriously weaken your conclusion that people prefer Indian elephants, even if your statistical tests were significant. As such, it is vital that a person looking at your conclusions also has this information.

👁 Chapter summary

A research report tends to use a common series of sections. These introduce the project being reported, describe how the research was carried out and what it found, and then summarize the findings and discuss their wider implications.

Chapter 17

A few short warnings about statistics

Whenever you carry out statistical analysis, your tests can only ever be as good as the numbers you give them. If you do an analysis with some faulty numbers, your findings will be faulty. After all, a statistical test is just a set of calculations: it doesn't know where your numbers come from or what they mean. If you take the average of seven cows and nine lettuces, you've only yourself to blame when you end up with a weird beef-vegetable hybrid that is an affront to nature.

Many of the problems you might encounter with your numbers can be spotted early on, when you are summarizing them before analysis. So here are a few common issues to watch out for when you are looking over the numbers you have collected. These issues could make your statistics unreliable if you don't notice them; knowing about these issues will also make you a better judge of other people's research – even experts make mistakes sometimes, and it's good to be able to spot them.

Floor and ceiling effects

Let's say I had a group of six-year-old children and wanted to assess their hand–eye coordination. And let's say I decided to do this by getting them to drive a powerful sports car around an obstacle course. Clearly, the children would all crash the car more or less immediately, and each would get a score of zero. When all the measurements in a set are right down at the bottom end of the range like this we call it a floor effect: all the scores are as low down as they can get, as if lying on the floor. It is a sign that the test we used was too difficult.

Similarly, if I took a group of really clever people – the Nobel Prize committee, say – and gave them 20 simple mathematical problems designed for 8-year-olds, they would all score 20 out of 20. We call this a ceiling effect, as all the scores are as high as they can be (imagine helium-filled balloons that have been released in a room, all sitting up against the ceiling at exactly the same height).

Floor and ceiling effects, where all the scores in a group are at the bottom or the top of the range, are a problem for two reasons. First, many statistical tests only work if the numbers you are analysing are different from one another: if all the numbers you are dealing with are exactly the same, or only vary from each other a tiny amount, your tests will often not work properly (technically, if all your numbers are more or less the same, there is no **variance**).

The other reason to look for floor and ceiling effects is because they tell you that you did something wrong when collecting your data. If all your data are down on the floor, or up on the ceiling, the tests or measures you used were badly chosen, or the individuals you tested were. Sometimes it will be obvious you made this sort of mistake as soon as see your numbers ('I can't believe I expected 6-year-olds to drive a car! It was far too difficult for them.') but other times the effect of a floor or ceiling can be quite subtle.

To show you what I mean, let's say I wanted to test a new sports coaching technique, to see whether it helps people to run faster. And let's say I wanted to know whether the technique works on world-class professional athletes as well as a bunch of my drinking buddies. Can you see what will go wrong if I coach both these groups? It will look as though the coaching technique only works for my friends and not the professional runners. My friends, who are unfit slobs, can show a huge improvement in their running abilities. But the professional runners are pretty much as fast as they are ever going to get – they are at the ceiling – and so cannot show very much change at all.

⊙ Regression to the mean

One other problem to watch for when you have collected information from a group more than once is a phenomenon called **regression to the mean**. To show you how this works, let's think about a long-term illness. Rheumatoid arthritis is a condition where the body's immune system attacks its own joints, often the fingers and wrists. It is a painful problem and causes a lot of unhappiness to sufferers. I have developed a new cure: whenever a joint starts to ache badly, people should just put on a hat backwards, dip the joint in honey and then let a horse lick the honey off while singing a song. Within a few days, the joint will start to feel better.

Now here's the scary thing: if somebody with arthritis followed my advice they would probably find it worked, even though I just invented this 'cure' off the top of my head. The reason it would 'work' is that conditions like arthritis naturally swing between bad periods and good periods. If someone with arthritis – or any other long-term condition – is ever feeling particularly bad, they just need to wait a few days and they will start to swing back towards their normal level anyway. In other words, when they are at their lowest point, there is nowhere to go but up. (Similarly, when they are feeling good this means they are soon going to feel worse.)

Because, in a long-term illness, bad periods are always followed by an improvement, *anything* you do to somebody during a bad period – waving crystals at them, giving them homoeopathy – will appear to have helped, even though it really had no influence.

The name for this effect, where extremes are naturally followed by less-extreme periods, is regression to the mean ('regression' means 'going back', so the name means 'going back towards the average'). It can fool us into thinking we have seen a change when in fact we have not.

To see how regression to the mean might affect our research, let's say I give all the students in my statistics class an unexpected multiple-choice test. Once they have stopped high-fiving each other and have completed the test, I choose the top ten students to compete in a national statistics contest – where they all perform badly and get soundly beaten. The reason my best students perform worse in the competition than during the first test is because of regression to the mean.

Here's how it works: a multiple-choice test isn't a 100% accurate measure of someone's knowledge: it isn't like weighing somebody, where I would get a definite measurement. Instead, a multiple-choice test involves a certain amount of random variation: all the students in my class would have a bit of luck one way or the other when they took the first test: some would have been lucky and guessed some answers correctly, others would have been unlucky with the questions that came up. The ten students in my class who got the very best scores were almost certainly lucky on the day of the test; their good luck boosted their scores above what they really should have been. Then, during the competition, regression to the mean kicks in: these students, who had good luck the first time, will mostly be less lucky the second time, because once they've been really lucky there's nowhere to go except to be less lucky.

If that doesn't make much sense, imagine you are one of the people taking the tests. And imagine on the first day you were really really lucky with the questions you were asked – you opened the paper and couldn't believe your eyes: everything you had studied was right there on the test. Woo! But what is more likely to happen during the second test: you go from being really lucky to being really-really-really-really-super-extra lucky, or you have worse luck? There is much more scope for your luck to get worse than there is for it get better, so this is what's likely to happen.

What I should have done when choosing my championship statistics team is give several tests and choose the ten people with the top average score. This would balance out any good and bad luck over several tests to get an accurate picture of each person's ability.

(The situation I have described here is famously seen a lot in sport, where promising young athletes often don't live up to early expectations, or where players or teams suddenly get worse after having an exceptional year. An athlete who stood out as the best junior in the country was probably experiencing some good luck, which nudged them ahead of all the other promising young things. This naturally regresses back down shortly after they are signed to an expensive contract, much to the annoyance of their new boss. Similarly, whoever stands out as the nation's best player in a sport this year, or whichever is the 'best' team, almost certainly has luck on their side; they will probably go downhill next year – just as the person who can't do anything right this year will probably improve.)

You need to look out for regression effects whenever you are comparing scores in a 'before-and-after' situation. This is really common when you are testing a drug, a teaching method, a therapy or whatever: you test a group of people before the treatment and you test them again afterwards and look at how they change. If the measurements you are taking can in any way be affected by random factors, including errors in your measurements, then any difference you see could be caused by regression to the mean rather than your treatment: a group of sick people might improve because they had nowhere to go but up, not because you did anything to them; a group of runners might get faster because they had a bad day the first time and a good day the second time, not because of your coaching.

And the place you *really* need to watch out for this issue is when you test people twice, and use the first test to choose the best or worst participants. That's what my statistics test example was showing you: if you use a test to pick the most extreme members of a group for further testing, they're probably going to be less extreme when you test them again, just through natural variation.

◉ Outright lies

I have described two issues to be aware of when describing your own data, or looking at other people's descriptive statistics. There is also something else you need to be alert for when looking at other people's numbers: outright lies. I was inspired to write this section by an advertising leaflet I just found pushed through my front door, and which now sits proudly next to my desk. 'In a recent survey,' it announces, '99.98% of our customers said that they would recommend us to their family and friends.' Then, in much smaller letters, it adds 'Based on a survey of 60 customers.' Oh really? In what possible way can 60 people produce a statistic of 99.98%? If all 60 customers said they would recommend the company, this is 100% of the customers; if just one person disagreed this gives 98.33%. Where on earth did the 0.02% come from? Was somebody mostly in favour of the company, but one of their elbows disagreed?

One of the other great statistical lies I have seen for myself was on a performance report from an ambulance service (which I won't name: it was many years ago and I'll assume they've cleaned up their act since then). This included a graph, showing how often they arrived at incidents within 10 minutes, which looked a lot like the example in Figure 17.1.

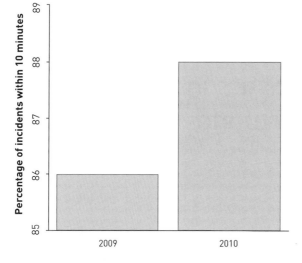

Figure 17.1 An example of a graph with a dubious *y*-axis

Looking at the graph, my first reaction was of course, 'Wow! They really improved last year.' But, as I'm sure you've spotted, the ambulance service was just being naughty, vastly exaggerating the change by starting the axis from a high number rather than zero.

What I am saying, then, is sometimes people do try to deceive with their numbers. They are particularly likely to do this where money is involved. It never hurts to have a slightly cynical viewpoint when looking at other people's statistics.

Chapter 18

Statistics in the real world

In this book I have tried to teach you statistics 'properly': I have shown you that it's all about starting out cautiously, with the idea that there is nothing happening, and sticking with that idea unless you find good evidence that it's wrong. This approach is important, and you should definitely get used to thinking that way.

However.

The reality is that when people carry out research for real, they usually prefer to find an effect rather than find no effect – they are happier if they can reject their null hypothesis and say they have discovered something new. Researchers prefer to say 'Look! There's a relationship between a person's diet and how well their memory works' rather than 'Wow! Knowing what people eat tells us nothing at all about how well they can remember things!'

There are various reasons for this. It is just human nature to find a positive discovery more interesting and exciting than a negative discovery. And there are fewer positive effects out there in the world for us to find, so finding one is a big deal. Let's say, for the sake of argument, that there are just 20 factors which affect how well memory works – practice, age, and so on. Since there are so few influences on memory, discovering a new one is exciting. But, in contrast to this small number of positive factors, there will be *billions* of things which don't affect your memory: the sleep patterns of somebody you've never met, the economy of Zimbabwe, the number of books for sale in Washington, and so on. If I announce 'Look! I've studied the relationship between the economy of Zimbabwe and how well people can remember things and found there's no link!' then who'd going to be interested? Nobody, that's who.

Given that people are more interested in new discoveries than in new non-discoveries, it's handy to be able to glance at statistics – in your own work, or in other people's reports – and know whether or not there is an effect there. And so here is a useful table that might help you do that, and that might help you put all the statistics we've covered into context:

If you have found an effect, such as a difference between some groups or a relationship between some measurements ...

These statistics will be large	These statistics will be small
chi-squared	p
t (t-test)	U (Mann-Whitney statistic)
r (Pearson correlation)	W, or T (Wilcoxon statistic)
rho (Spearman correlation)	
Z (position on the normal distribution)	
Pretty much any other statistic you might meet in the future, especially F	

You can see at a glance that statistics tend to be large when you have found an effect with just three exceptions: the Mann-Whitney U statistic, the Wilcoxon statistic and, most importantly of all, the p-value that you get at the end of every test. So what I am saying is that if you want to know whether there is a difference between some groups, or a relationship between some measures, the main question you need to ask is whether the p-value is low. If it is low (and usually, as you have seen, 'low' means less than .05), then you have probably found an effect. In many ways, using statistics for real can be as simple as that.

Appendix A
Normal distribution table

This table lets you go between points on the normal distribution and percentages. You can use this table in two ways. You can start with a point, some distance away from the mean (we call this number Z, and measure it in standard deviations), and see what percentage of the normal distribution falls below this point; or you can look up a percentage of the distribution to find the Z value. The mean is defined as zero.

For example, if you look at $Z = 1$, which represents one standard deviation above the mean, you will see that 84.13% of the normal distribution falls below this point (in other words, if you find the point which is 1 standard deviation above the mean, for any normally distributed set of numbers, 84.13% of the numbers fall below this point and 15.87% fall above this point). Or you can look up a percentage. For example, if you look up 2.28% you get the result $Z = -2.0$. This means that if you find the point 2 standard deviations below the mean, 2.28% of the distribution will be below this point.

As the mean in this table is zero, zero is the middle of the distribution, and sure enough, you can easily see that 50% of the distribution is below the point $Z = 0$. Giving the distribution a mean of zero also means that negative Z-values refer to standard deviations below the mean and positive Z-values refer to standard deviation above the mean, which makes things simple.

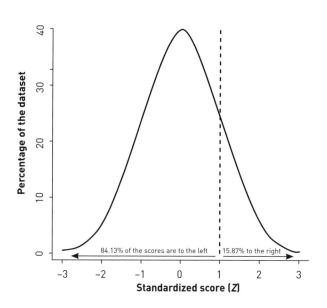

Z	percentage	Z	percentage	Z	percentage
−3.0	0.13	−1.0	15.87	**1.0**	**84.13**
−2.9	0.19	−0.9	18.41	1.1	86.43
−2.8	0.26	−0.8	21.19	1.2	88.49
−2.7	0.35	−0.7	24.20	1.3	90.32
−2.6	0.47	−0.6	27.43	1.4	91.92
−2.5	0.62	−0.5	30.85	1.5	93.32
−2.4	0.82	−0.4	34.46	1.6	94.52
−2.3	1.07	−0.3	38.21	1.7	95.54
−2.2	1.39	−0.2	42.07	1.8	96.41
−2.1	1.79	−0.1	46.02	1.9	97.13
−2.0	2.28	0	50.00	2.0	97.72
−1.9	2.87	0.1	53.98	2.1	98.21
−1.8	3.59	0.2	57.93	2.2	98.61
−1.7	4.46	0.3	61.79	2.3	98.93
−1.6	5.48	0.4	65.54	2.4	99.18
−1.5	6.68	0.5	69.15	2.5	99.38
−1.4	8.08	0.6	72.57	2.6	99.53
−1.3	9.68	0.7	75.80	2.7	99.65
−1.2	11.51	0.8	78.81	2.8	99.74
−1.1	13.57	0.9	81.59	2.9	99.81
				3.0	99.87

◉ Examples of using this table

Using statistical tables like this is one of those tasks that can seem daunting when you first do it, but which makes complete sense after a bit of practice. To help you get started, here are a couple of examples which will show you how this table can be used. Follow these examples through and try to work out what I did.

- *I have devised a test that measures how good people are at taking photographs. When a lot of people take this test, the mean score is 40 points and the standard deviation is 12 points. How can I quickly find the top 10% of people?* If you want the top 10% of people, you are looking for the point on the distribution where 90% of the distribution falls to the left and 10% falls to the right. If you look down the table, you can see that the nearest score to 90% is 90.32%, which is next to $Z = 1.3$. With this test, then, the mean score, plus 1.3 standard deviations, is $40 + (1.3 \times 12) = 55.6$. This means 9.68% of your people scored 55.6 or more on the test. Everybody else – the remaining 90.32% – scored less than this. A score of 55.6 is close to being the cut-off for the top 10%. You would need a more detailed table – or some statistical software – if you wanted to find the score which cuts off *exactly* the top 10%.

- *I have a group of people. Their mean height is 170 cm and the standard deviation of their heights is 10 cm. How tall are the people in the bottom third of my group?* You are interested in the bottom third of the people, so you want to find the point where 33.33% of the distribution is to the left and 66.67% is to the right. The nearest percentage in this table is 34.46%, which has a Z-score of –0.4. This means that if you subtract 0.4 standard deviations from the mean height, you more or less have the height which cuts off the bottom third of your people. In this case, the mean height minus 0.4 standard deviations gives 166 cm $(170 - [10 \times 0.4])$. The shortest 34.46% of the sample are 166 cm tall or less, which is close to the answer we were looking for. Again, you'd need a more detailed table, or some statistical software, if you wanted a more exact answer.

- *I have given some people an intelligence test. What percentage of the people are within two standard deviations of the mean?* This is slightly more tricky. You are after the people in the middle of the distribution, so need to cut off some people at the top of the distribution and some people at the bottom. We start by looking up $Z = 2.0$ (two standard deviations above the mean), which tells us that 97.72% of the sample fall below this point. But that's not quite the answer we want, because we don't want to include the very low-scoring people on the left of the distribution. So we look up $Z = -2.0$, which gives 2.28%. We subtract one from the other: 97.72% – 2.28% = 95.44%. This is the percentage of people who are within 2 standard deviations of the mean. The people right down at the bottom, below 2 standard deviations from the mean, and the people right up at the top, above two standard deviations from the mean, have been cut off.

Appendix B
Worked examples of tests for comparing two means: t-tests, the Mann-Whitney U test and the Wilcoxon matched-pairs signed-ranks test

Here I will work through the steps needed to compare two sets of scores. First I will do an independent-samples t-test by hand, then I'll do the same with a repeated-measures t-test. Finally, I'll calculate non-parametric versions of these two tests using the Mann-Whitney and Wilcoxon procedures. I'll also give you examples of the sort of output you get if you use a computer to do the same calculations.

Remember that when you want to compare two sets of scores, the process for choosing a test is as follows. First, ask yourself if you have parametric or non-parametric data. If your data are parametric, you can use one of the t-tests: the independent-samples test if you have compared two different groups of people or the repeated-measures t-test if you have tested a single group twice. If your data are non-parametric then you'll use the Mann-Whitney test if you have independent samples, and the Wilcoxon test if you have repeated measures.

👁 Independent-samples t-test

The independent-samples t-test takes two sets of scores and asks whether or not they are, on average, different from each other. The null hypothesis for this test is that the two groups we're comparing are the same, and that any differences we see don't really mean anything. We'll stick with this idea unless the two groups prove to be really different. If this happens, and the analysis tells us that our findings are really unlikely to have happened if the null hypothesis is true, then we'll abandon the null hypothesis and say that the groups probably are different.

The version of the t-test I am using here only works when the two groups you are comparing have similar standard deviations. If the groups you want to test have very different standard deviations, you have to use a slightly different formula – or better still, use statistical software which will deal with this complication automatically.

To get us started, here are some data. Let's say we take a group of 26 people from the north of the country and 26 people from the south, and we give them a test, finding these data:

	Northerners	Southerners
Number of people (n)	26	26
Mean score	46	37
Standard deviation	12.4	12.2

It certainly looks as though the 26 northerners, on average, got a higher score than the 26 southerners. But are the two groups really different, or is this difference that we've seen too small to get excited about? A t-test will help us decide.

For a situation like this, where the groups have similar standard deviations, we can use this formula:

$$t = \frac{\bar{x}_1 - \bar{x}_2}{\sqrt{\frac{s_1^2}{n_1} + \frac{s_2^2}{n_2}}}$$

$\bar{x}_1$ is the mean score for group 1 and $\bar{x}_2$ is the mean score for group 2

s_1 is the standard deviation for group 1 and s_2 is the standard deviation for group 2

n_1 is the number of people in group 1 and n_2 is the number of people in group 2.

Following this formula, we can produce a 'recipe' for calculating the t statistic:

1 Start with the bottom part of the equation, below the line. This tells us to square group 1's standard deviation and divide this by the number of people in group 1. We then do the same for group 2. This gives us $\frac{s_1^2}{n_1}$ and $\frac{s_2^2}{n_2}$

2 Add these two numbers together.

3   Take the square root of the number you have just calculated. You have now done everything below the line in the equation.

4   Take the mean score for group 1 and subtract the mean score for group 2. This gives you everything above the line in the equation.

5   Now you have calculated everything below the line (in step 3) and everything above the line (in step 4), you just divide one number by the other to get t.

I'll now follow these steps for the two groups being used here.

1   For group 1, $\dfrac{s_1^2}{n_1} = \dfrac{12.4^2}{26} = \dfrac{153.76}{26} = 5.91$

    For group 2, $\dfrac{s_2^2}{n_2} = \dfrac{12.2^2}{26} = \dfrac{148.84}{26} = 5.72$

2   Adding these two numbers together, we get $5.91 + 5.72 = 11.63$.

3   Taking the square root of this, we get $\sqrt{11.63} = 3.41$.

4   We subtract group 2's mean score from group 1's mean score. This gives us $46 - 37 = 9$.

5   We now divide the top part of the equation by the bottom part. $9 \div 3.41 = 2.64$. So this is the answer to our analysis: $t = 2.64$.

We then need to look up a critical value of t. Like with the chi-squared test we saw in Chapter 10, to do this we need to know how many degrees of freedom our test had, and this is related to how many people we tested. In this case, we had two groups of 26 people, so 52 people in total. And we have already taken two statistics from the data: the average for each group (because it's the two groups' average scores that we are comparing here). As such, the degrees of freedom for this test are $52 - 2 = 50$. *For an independent-samples t-test, the degrees of freedom are the number of people, minus 2.*

Using the table further down in this chapter, I've just looked up the critical value for a two-tailed t-test with 50 degrees of freedom and an alpha cut-off of .05, and I found that it is 2.01. Here's a little snippet of the t-table to show you where this number came from ...

df	Significance level (alpha), two-tailed		
	.10	.05	.01
...	...	...	...
40	1.68	2.02	2.70
50	1.68	**2.01**	2.67
60	1.67	2.00	2.66
...	...	...	...

Remember that we calculated t for our data as 2.64. This is greater than the critical value of 2.01, so we know that the p-value for these data must be less than .05, and that therefore we have a significant result. We can reject the null hypothesis and conclude that our northerners very likely did get higher test scores, on average, than our southerners.

Finally, I took the original data (the original set of 52 scores which are summarized in the first table) and ran the same t-test using computer software. This gave me the following result:

```
t(50) = 2.64, p = .006
```

You can see how the computer analysis has given us a bit more detail. When we worked by hand, we calculated a value of t and compared that to a critical value. Because the t statistic that we calculated was larger than the critical value, we knew that p must be less than .05, but that's all we knew. The computer analysis has let us go further, by giving us the exact p-value. Now we can see that not only is p less than .05, it is well below this cut-off: there is only a .006 probability – a 0.6% chance – that we'd see a difference like this between 26 northerners and 26 southerners if the two groups were really the same. This chance is so low, we can happily say that northerners and southerners almost certainly *aren't* the same.

(In case you come from the south of the country and are feeling victimized at this point, you should note that on many tests, low scores mean better performance. I'm not saying which way round this test works!)

◉ Repeated-measures *t*-test

This version of the t-test is used when you measure the same set of people on two occasions and want to know whether their measurements, on average, changed. You can also use this test for comparing two **matched-pairs samples**, and so it is sometimes also known as the 'matched-samples t-test'.

This test is actually pretty simple, so let's take some data and have a look at how it works. Here are the scores from eight people who took a cognitive test twice, once before they had training in super-secret mental powers and once after they had been trained. We are interested in whether or not the scores changed after the training.

Person	First score	Second score
1	36	45
2	41	39
3	19	24
4	27	36
5	33	41
6	24	29
7	46	37
8	31	39
Mean	32.0	36.3
Standard deviation	8.9	6.7

You can see from this table that six people got a higher score the second time and two people got a lower score. To analyse these data, we start out, as usual, by deciding what we would expect to see if the null hypothesis is correct. Remember that the null hypothesis always predicts that there will be nothing going on. So in this case, our null hypothesis would be that there is no difference between the first set of scores and the second. In other words – and this is the key to understanding this test – we start out by predicting that the mean score for time 1, minus the mean score for time 2, equals zero. So let's add the differences to the table to help us see any changes:

Person	First score	Second score	Difference
1	36	45	9
2	41	39	–2
3	19	24	5
4	27	36	9
5	33	41	8
6	24	29	5
7	46	37	–9
8	31	39	8
Mean	32.0	36.3	4.1
Standard deviation	8.9	6.7	6.4

The average difference is an increase of 4.1 points. This certainly isn't zero difference, as our null hypothesis predicted, but is it far enough from zero that we can reject the null hypothesis, and conclude instead that people tended to get better after the training? The repeated-measures *t*-test will tell us. The formula for this is much simpler than the independent-samples version:

$$t = \frac{\bar{x}_D}{s_D/\sqrt{n}}$$

$\bar{x}_D$ is the average difference (4.1 in these data)

s_D is the standard deviation of the differences (6.4 in this case)

n is the number of differences (8 in this case).

The really important thing to notice – I mean, *really* important – is that all the calculations here are done using the 'differences' column in the table, not the original scores. For example, although there are 16 scores, there are only 8 differences, and so the number 8 is the one we use in our calculations.

To calculate *t*, we simply drop these three values into the equation:

$$t = \frac{\bar{x}_D}{s_D/\sqrt{n}} = \frac{4.1}{6.4/\sqrt{8}} = \frac{4.1}{6.4/2.83} = 1.81$$

So *t* = 1.81 for these data. Now we just need to see whether or not this exceeds the critical value. If it does, we know we have seen a statistically significant change between the first set of scores and the second.

To look up the critical value, we need to know the degrees of freedom for this analysis, and once again this is based on the data table's 'differences' column. In this example, there are 8 differences, and we have taken one statistic from them – their mean. So *the degrees of freedom for the repeated-measures t-test are the number of differences, minus one*. In this case, then, the degrees of freedom are $8 - 1 = 7$.

Below is another extract from a table showing the critical values of *t*. You can see that with 7 degrees of freedom, at the usual .05 alpha level, the critical value for *t* is 2.36. In this case, our *t*-value was lower than 2.36. This tells us that *p* is greater than .05, and that therefore we have not seen a significant difference. We would conclude that the super-secret brain training most probably made no difference to people's test scores, and that the small difference we saw was probably just a coincidence.

df	Significance level (alpha), two-tailed		
	.10	.05	.01
...	...	...	...
6	1.94	2.45	3.71
7	1.89	**2.36**	3.50
8	1.86	2.31	3.36
...	...	...	...

When I ran this same test on a computer, I got this output:

$t(7) = 1.8162$, $p = .1122$

This confirms that p is greater than the usual .05 cut-off, and gives us slightly more information, showing us the exact probability of seeing a difference at least as large as the one we saw in our data if the null hypothesis is correct.

👁 Reference table: critical values of t

Here, for your reference, are tables of critical t-values for one- and two-tailed tests. To avoid the table being ridiculously large, I haven't given every possible degree of freedom. If your test has a degrees of freedom value that isn't on this table, just use the next-lowest value. So, for example, if your test has 42 degrees of freedom, you should use the 40 degrees of freedom row as that's the next-lowest. Note that in the first table I've highlighted the two critical values that I used in the examples above, so that you can see exactly where they came from.

1 Critical values of t for two-tailed tests

df	Significance level (alpha), two-tailed		
	0.10	0.05	0.01
1	6.31	12.71	63.66
2	2.92	4.30	9.92
3	2.35	3.18	5.84
4	2.13	2.78	4.60
5	2.02	2.57	4.03
6	1.94	2.45	3.71
7	1.89	**2.36**	3.50

	Significance level (alpha), two-tailed		
df	0.10	0.05	0.01
8	1.86	2.31	3.36
9	1.83	2.26	3.25
10	1.81	2.23	3.17
12	1.78	2.18	3.05
14	1.76	2.14	2.98
16	1.75	2.12	2.92
18	1.73	2.10	2.88
20	1.72	2.09	2.85
25	1.71	2.06	2.79
30	1.70	2.04	2.75
40	1.68	2.02	2.70
50	1.68	**2.01**	2.68
60	1.67	2.00	2.66
70	1.67	1.99	2.65
80	1.66	1.99	2.64
90	1.66	1.99	2.63
100	1.66	1.98	2.63
Infinity	1.64	1.96	2.58

2 Critical values of t for one-tailed tests

	Significance level (alpha), two-tailed		
df	0.10	0.05	0.01
1	3.08	6.31	31.82
2	1.89	2.92	6.96
3	1.64	2.35	4.54
4	1.53	2.13	3.75
5	1.48	2.02	3.36
6	1.44	1.94	3.14
7	1.41	1.89	3.00
8	1.40	1.86	2.90
9	1.38	1.83	2.82
10	1.37	1.81	2.76
12	1.36	1.78	2.68
14	1.35	1.76	2.62
16	1.34	1.75	2.58
18	1.33	1.73	2.55

	Significance level (alpha), two-tailed		
df	0.10	0.05	0.01
20	1.33	1.72	2.53
25	1.32	1.71	2.49
30	1.31	1.70	2.46
40	1.30	1.68	2.42
50	1.30	1.68	2.40
60	1.30	1.67	2.39
70	1.29	1.67	2.38
80	1.29	1.66	2.37
90	1.29	1.66	2.37
100	1.29	1.66	2.36
Infinity	1.28	1.64	2.33

The Mann-Whitney U test

This test is a non-parametric alternative to the independent-samples t-test. You can use this when you want to compare two separate groups, but for some reason a t-test is not possible (perhaps your data are not normally distributed, for example).

Let's say we test two groups of people and get some scores. I've used groups called Architects and Builders, as that way it's really easy to see which group we are calling group A and which we are calling group B.

Architects	Builders
14	6
6	4
9	12
12	3
10	2

To calculate U, we first line up all the scores from the lowest to the highest, like this, being careful to keep a note of which group each score belongs to:

Score	2	3	4	6	6	9	10	12	12	14
Group	B	B	B	A	B	A	A	A	B	A

Once we have done this we give each score a **rank**. This means that the lowest score gets a rank of 1, the next score gets a rank of 2, and so on. So I start doing this, working from the lowest score to the highest:

Score	2	3	4	6	6	9	10	12	12	14
Group	B	B	B	A	B	A	A	A	B	A
Rank	1	2	3							

At this point I hit a snag: the next two people in the table are tied, with the same score of 6. I can see there are also two people further along the table who are tied with the same score of 12. But the solution is simple: we just average out the ranks. I know that the next two people in the list need to get ranks of 4 and 5, because they are the fourth and fifth people in the row, so I just take the mean of these: $(4 + 5) \div 2 = 4.5$, which means each person gets a rank of 4.5. The same happens for the two people who tied with a score of 12. This now gives me ranks for everybody in the table:

Score	2	3	4	6	6	9	10	12	12	14
Group	B	B	B	A	B	A	A	A	B	A
Rank	1	2	3	4.5	4.5	6	7	8.5	8.5	10

We are now ready to calculate the Mann-Whitney U statistic, and we actually need to do this twice, once for each group. Whichever group gets the lowest result will give us our final U-value. Here are the formulae for doing this for the two groups:

$$U_A = \sum R_A - \frac{n_A(n_A+1)}{2}$$

$$U_B = \sum R_B - \frac{n_B(n_B+1)}{2}$$

If those equations scare you, just take a moment to look at each part on its own. n_A is the number of people in group A, n_B is the number of people in group B, $\sum R_A$ is the total of the ranks for group A, and $\sum R_B$ is the total of the ranks for group B. So using these equations is just a question of dropping in the right numbers and doing a little bit of multiplying and dividing. Simple!

We know that the number of people in each group here is 5, so this means that $n_A = n_B = 5$. We also know that the ranks for group A are 4.5, 6, 7, 8.5 and 10. Adding these together, we get a total of $\sum R_A = 36$. We also know that the ranks for group B are 1, 2, 3, 4.5 and 8.5, and if we add these together we find $\sum R_B = 19$.

Dropping these numbers (5, 5, 36 and 19) into the equations, we can calculate the U statistic for each group like this:

$$U_A = \sum R_A - \frac{n_A(n_A+1)}{2} = 36 - \frac{5(5+1)}{2} = 36 - \frac{30}{2} = 21$$

$$U_B = \sum R_B - \frac{n_B(n_B+1)}{2} = 19 - \frac{5(5+1)}{2} = 19 - \frac{30}{2} = 4$$

The lowest of these two values is 4, so this is the U-value we will use as the result of our test. To see whether this is statistically significant, you can compare it to a table of critical values. For example, there is a really useful table online, at http://math.usask.ca/~laverty/S245/Tables/wmw.pdf. If you look at that table, where the row labelled 5 and the column labelled 5 both meet (as there were 5 people in each group), you'll find a critical value of 2. *The Mann-Whitney test is one of only two tests where the result needs to be lower than the critical value to be significant.* In this case, our result of 4 was not lower than the critical value of 2, so we know the difference between the architects and the builders was not significant.

When I ran this test on my computer, I got these results:

```
U = 4, n(A) = 5, n(B) = 5, p = .0927
```

which gives us just a little bit more information. Not only can we see that the p-value was greater than .05, and so not significant, but we can see exactly what the p-value was.

Checking the significance of U with large samples

Something you need to know if you are doing your calculations by hand is that you can only use significance tables for U when you have quite small samples (20 people in each group or fewer). If you have larger samples then you need to calculate a Z score and look this up in Appendix A. To calculate a Z score for a Mann-Whitney statistic you need to use this formula:

$$Z = \frac{U - \frac{n_A n_B}{2}}{\sqrt{\frac{n_A n_B (n_A + n_B + 1)}{12}}}$$

Although it might look quite complex at first glance, this formula is not actually that bad, as it only involves three variables. You simply need to use n_A (the number of people in group A), n_B (the number of people in group B), and U, which you have calculated using the method above. You plug those numbers into the formula and then it's just simple arithmetic. Honestly!

So, for example, let's say I have two groups of 30 people, which means n_A and n_B both equal 30, and let's say we've used the procedure described above to find that U equals 389. We simply pop these numbers into the equation like this:

$$Z = \frac{389 - \frac{30 \times 30}{2}}{\sqrt{\frac{30 \times 30 (30 + 30 + 1)}{12}}} = \frac{389 - 450}{\sqrt{4575}} = \frac{-61}{67.64} = -0.90$$

Now that we've found a result of $Z = -0.90$, we just need to look this up in Appendix A. When we do so, we see that 18.41% of the normal curve lies to the left of $Z = -0.90$. Because this value of 18.41% is greater than the usual cut-off, of 5%, we know that this result is not statistically significant.

👁 The Wilcoxon matched-pairs signed-ranks test

This is a non-parametric test for analysing paired data, and so it is an alternative to the repeated-measures t-test. If you have read the rest of this appendix, then the way this test works should make a lot of sense. Like with the repeated-measures t-test, we are interested in the differences between each pair of scores, rather than the scores themselves; and like with the Mann-Whitney test, we do our calculations on ranks instead of the raw data.

Let's take the data we used earlier for the repeated-measures t-test and give each of the differences a rank. The only catch is that while we do the ranking, we will ignore any minus signs. So, as you'll see from the table, I gave the person with a difference of –2 the lowest rank because if we ignore any minus signs then 2 is the lowest number in the difference column. Just like with the Mann-Whitney test, you can see that I have averaged the ranks where people were tied. And if there had been anybody with a difference of zero, then I would ignore them in my analysis. That's not an issue here, as everybody had some sort of difference between their first and second score, but look out for this in your own data.

Person	First score	Second score	Difference	Rank of the difference
1	36	45	9	7
2	41	39	–2	(–) 1
3	19	24	5	2.5
4	27	36	9	7
5	33	41	8	4.5
6	24	29	5	2.5
7	46	37	–9	(–) 7
8	31	39	8	4.5
Mean	32.0	36.3	4.1	
Standard deviation	8.9	6.7	6.4	

Although we ignored any minus signs when we did our ranking, at this stage we pay attention to them again. Remember, if the null hypothesis is correct, and the two sets of scores are the same overall, then there should be the same amount of upwards change in the scores as there is downwards change. So, if the null hypothesis is correct, the ranks that came from positive numbers should add up to more or less the same total as the ranks that came from negative numbers.

Look again at the data we have here. You can see that six of the ranks came from positive differences, and if we add these ranks together we get $7 + 2.5 + 7 + 4.5 + 2.5 + 4.5 = 28$. Only two of the ranks came from negative differences, and if we add these ranks together we get $1 + 7 = 8$. These numbers are quite different, so it looks as if there was more upwards change in the scores than there was downwards change.

The Wilcoxon statistic is simply whichever of these two numbers we have just calculated is the smallest. In this case, the ranks from the negative set gave the smallest total, adding to just 8. This means 8 is the Wilcoxon statistic for the data we've used here. Make sure you can see exactly how I got this Wilcoxon statistic of 8 – look back at the table if necessary.

Now, there's one little point here that might cause you confusion if you go further with learning and using statistics. In his original paper, Frank Wilcoxon[21] used the symbol T (for 'total') to describe this statistic. However, presumably because people often confused this with t (from the t-test), most people today instead use the symbol W to describe the Wilcoxon statistic. It doesn't matter too much which symbol you use, as long as you're totally clear in your writing. I'll use W for now.

We got a result of $W = 8$ for these data, and to see whether or not this indicates a significant difference we need to look up a critical value in the table below. The test's results are significant if the Wilcoxon statistic we have calculated is less than, or equal to, the appropriate critical value. In this case, where we tested 8 people, the critical value at the .05 level is 4. We calculated $W = 8$, and as this is larger than the critical value, we do not have a significant result. *Remember: the Wilcoxon and Mann-Whitney tests are the only tests where a statistic is significant when it is below the critical value; in all other tests, your statistic needs to be above the critical value to be significant.*

	Two-tailed significance level		
Participants	0.10	0.05	0.01
6	2	–	–
7	3	2	–
8	5	4	–
9	8	6	2
10	10	8	4
11	14	11	6
12	17	14	8
13	21	17	11
14	26	21	14
15	30	25	17
16	36	30	21
17	41	35	26
18	47	41	30

▶

---

21 Wilcoxon, F. (1945). Individual comparisons by ranking methods. *Biometrics Bulletin, 1,* 80–3.

19	54	47	35
20	61	53	36
21	68	59	41
22	76	66	47
23	84	74	53
24	92	81	60
25	101	90	67
26	111	98	74
27	121	107	82
28	131	117	90
29	141	127	98
30	153	137	107
40	288	264	218
50	467	434	371
75	1114	1054	937
100	2047	1955	1776

NB For a one-tailed test, just halve the significance levels at the top of each column. So, for example, if you're doing a one-tailed test, the second column gives you critical values at the .025 level and the third column gives you critical values at the .005 level.

◉ Test yourself: some exercises

If you want to make sure you've understood the procedures in this appendix, here are two data sets. The first can be analysed using either an independent-samples *t*-test or a Mann-Whitney *U* test; the second can be analysed using either a repeated-measures *t*-test or a Wilcoxon test. I've given you the answers below, so this is the ideal chance to make sure you understand these tests before trying to analyse data of your own.

Independent-samples data

I took a group of 10 journalists and a group of 10 computer programmers, and gave everybody a test of their typing speed, measured in words per minute. Here are the raw data and some descriptive statistics. Use a *t*-test and a Mann-Whitney test to see whether the journalists and the programmers, overall, type at different speeds. You'll be testing the null hypothesis that, overall, the two groups are the same, and that any differences you might see are not meaningful.

	Journalists	Programmers
	46	40
	21	58
	34	64
	37	33
	34	49
	65	58
	47	62
	42	28
	51	44
	36	39
Mean	41.3	47.5
SD	11.1	12.6

With a t-test, you should have found no significant difference. t, with 18 degrees of freedom, equals -1.17 (or thereabouts, allowing for rounding off), $p > .05$ (critical value for t is 2.10, two-tailed. Note that the sign on a t-test isn't very important – if you swapped the two groups around the sign would flip from negative to positive. Many people just ignore it). Reporting this in the usual style I would write $t(18) = -1.17$, $p > .05$.

A Mann-Whitney test should also have told you that the difference is non-significant. You should have found that $U = 38$, and that the critical value is 23. Remember, with this test the statistic needs to be lower than the critical value to be significant. Reporting this formally, I might write $U = 38$, $n(A) = 10$, $n(B) = 10$, $p > .05$.

Repeated-measures data

I took a group of 10 students and got them to take part in the *unipodus* test, which involves timing how long each person can stand on one leg. Then, as each of these students had been caught plagiarizing their coursework, I connected them to the mains supply and violently electrocuted them for five minutes before testing them again. Use a repeated-measures t-test and a Wilcoxon test to see whether their scores changed significantly as a result of their electrocution.

Person	Time 1 (seconds)	Time 2 (seconds)
1	48	4
2	24	2
3	87	6
4	19	1
5	26	0
6	38	2
7	41	0
8	18	4
9	61	9
10	26	7
Mean	38.8	3.5
SD	21.8	3.1

A t-test should have shown you a clear change in the students' scores: t, with 9 degrees of freedom, equals -5.50, and this is statistically significant, since the value is more extreme than the critical value of 2.26, two-tailed. Reporting this formally, I might write $t(9) = -5.50$, $p < .05$.

A Wilcoxon test should also have shown you a significant change, with a statistic of zero which is less than the critical value of 8. Formally, I might write $W = 0$, $N = 10$, $p < .05$.

Appendix C
Calculating correlations

👁 Pearson's correlation

The formula for Pearson's test comes in various forms. Here I've used
one of the simplest: this version can be used when you have two equally
long columns of numbers and it will tell you the correlation between
those two columns (you need a slightly different formula when the two
columns aren't the same length). You can use the test to check the null
hypothesis that the two columns are not related.

To show you the test in action, here are two columns of numbers. I'm
just going to call the first column x and the second column y.

	x	y
	12	14
	25	17
	41	36
	21	24
	16	10
Mean	23.00	20.20
SD	11.20	10.21

Now we need the formula for calculating the correlation between the
two sets of numbers. Brace yourself, because here it comes:

$$r_{xy} = \frac{\sum_{i=1}^{n}(x_i-\bar{x})(y_i-\bar{y})}{(n-1)s_x s_y}$$

Don't panic! Here is what all the bits of that formula mean:

r_{xy} is the correlation between measure x and measure y – this is what you are calculating

$x_i - \bar{x}$ tells you to subtract the mean of the x scores from each of the x scores and $y_i - \bar{y}$ tells you to subtract the mean of the y scores from each of the y scores

$\sum_{i=1}^{n}$ tells you to start at row 1 and work up until you reach the last row. In this example, there are 5 rows in the data, so $n = 5$. This bit of the equation, then, is saying 'add together everything else on this line of the equation, and do this for each row of data from 1 to 5'

s_x is the standard deviation for the first column and s_y is the standard deviation for the second column

That's all pretty nasty, but I think that it'll make a lot more sense when you see me work through it now. I'll convert the formula to a 'recipe' which we need to follow to calculate the result:

1 The bottom of the equation, which reads $(n-1)s_x s_y$, tells us to take n and subtract 1, then multiply this by the standard deviation for the x column, and then multiply this result by the standard deviation for the y column.

2 Now on to the top part of the equation. The first step in calculating $\sum_{i=1}^{n}(x_i - \bar{x})(y_i - \bar{y})$ is, for each row in the data table, to take the x score and subtract the mean of the x column to get a number, then take the y score and subtract the mean of the y column to get a second number, then multiply these two numbers together to get a result for that row.

3 Then, to complete the top part of the equation, add together the results you have just calculated.

4 Divide this number you have just calculated by the number you calculated in step 1. This finishes the whole process and gives you the correlation cofficient, r_{xy}.

So now I'll follow these steps for the data in my table.

1 I start with the bottom part of the equation. Remember that there are 5 rows in my table here, so $n = 5$. Multiplying together $n - 1$ and the two standard deviations gives me $(5 - 1) \times 11.20 \times 10.21 = 457.41$.

2   I then, for each row in the table calculate $(x_i - \bar{x})(y_i - \bar{y})$. I know the mean of column x ($\bar{x}$) is 23, and the mean of column y ($\bar{y}$) is 20.2. So here we go:

x	y	$(x_i - \bar{x})$	$(y_i - \bar{y})$	$(x_i - \bar{x})(y_i - \bar{y})$
12	14	$12 - 23 = -11$	$14 - 20.2 = -6.2$	$-11 \times -6.2 = 68.2$
25	17	$25 - 23 = 2$	$17 - 20.2 = -3.2$	$2 \times -3.2 = -6.4$
41	36	$41 - 23 = 18$	$36 - 20.2 = 15.8$	$18 \times 15.8 = 284.4$
21	24	$21 - 23 = -2$	$24 - 20.2 = 3.8$	$-2 \times 3.8 = -7.6$
16	10	$16 - 23 = -7$	$10 - 20.2 = -10.2$	$-7 \times -10.2 = 71.4$

3   Now I add together the results in the last column. This gives me $68.2 - 6.4 + 284.4 - 7.6 + 71.4 = 410$.

4   To finish, I divide this value by the number I calculated in step 1. This gives me $410 \div 457.41 = .90$.

So there's the result – the Pearson correlation between those two columns of numbers is $r = .90$: a strong positive correlation.

As with most tests, you can then look up a critical value for r to test your null hypothesis – just check online (search for 'critical values of r'). The degrees of freedom for a correlation test are the number of pairs you tested, minus 2. So in this case, where there were 5 pairs of numbers, the degrees of freedom were 3.

Looking up the critical value for this test online, I find that for three degrees of freedom at the .05 level, the critical value is .88. Our correlation of $r = .90$ is higher than this, and so is statistically significant – we know there must be less than a .05 chance of seeing this relationship if the null hypothesis is correct (In reality, mind you, I wouldn't get too excited about a correlation with just five pairs of numbers, no matter what the p-value says). I could report this is $r(3) = .90$, $p < .05$.

Spearman's rho

Good news! This is simplicity itself. You can calculate Spearman's rho just by replacing all your original scores with ranks and then following the exact same procedure as Pearson's test. If I took the data I used in the last section and put them into rank order, replacing the lowest score with a rank of 1, the next-lowest score with a rank or 2, and so on, they would look like this:

	x (ranked)	y (ranked)
	2	3
	8	5
	10	9
	6	7
	4	1
Mean rank	6	5
SD	3.16	3.16

When I carried out a Pearson correlation on these numbers, I got the result rho = .80. I use the term rho, instead of r, to show that this is a non-parametric result from ranked data.

Glossary

aim what you hope to achieve with a piece of research.

alpha the cut-off criterion against which we judge **p-values** when deciding whether or not to accept a **null hypothesis**. When a p-value is less than alpha, which is usually .05, we tend to reject the null hypothesis and say we have found an effect in our data. Alpha can also be thought of as the maximum probability of a **Type I error** that we will tolerate.

alternative hypothesis the idea that there is a positive answer to your research question; the idea that there is an effect in your study. You accept this idea when the evidence against your **null hypothesis** is strong.

baseline measurement a measurement which you can use to judge whether another measurement has changed. For example, you might take a baseline measurement from a group of people before doing something to them. If a later measurement is different from the baseline, you know that your manipulation has had an effect.

beta the probability of making a **Type II error** in a study.

bias anything which changes a study's findings from what they really should be, e.g. choosing inappropriate participants for a study could bias the results.

bimodal distribution a set of numbers which has two most-common numbers in it.

binomial test a statistical test for deciding whether two groups are equally sized.

categorical variable any measure, such as gender or nationality, which can only take a limited set of values. cf. **continuous variable**.

central tendency a measure of the midpoint in a set of numbers. An average.

cluster sample a way of choosing a **sample** which uses existing groups of people to make the task easier. For example, choosing schools at random as a way of getting a sample of children – the schools are clusters of children.

coefficient of determination in **correlation**, a measure of how much one set of numbers can predict changes in another set. It is the **correlation coefficient** squared.

confidentiality respecting the privacy of the participants in a study, which means not identifying them in reports without their permission, as well as storing their data securely so nobody else can see it.

confound occurs when something you are not interested in affects the results of a study.

continuous variable any measure, such as time, which can change by small amounts. cf. **categorical variable**.

control the process of keeping conditions as stable as possible in an experiment, so that if you see any effects after your experimental **manipulation**, you can be confident that the manipulation caused them rather than any other possible causes which might have changed during the study.

control group in an experiment, a group of people who do not experience any **manipulation**. This provides a **baseline measure** against which the experimental group can be compared.

correlation a technique for seeing how closely two sets of numbers are related.

correlation coefficient a number, somewhere between −1.00 and +1.00, which describes the strength of the relationship between two sets of numbers.

counterbalancing involves mixing up the order in which people are tested in **repeated-measures** designs, as a way of avoiding **order effects**.

critical value is obtained from a table, or from software, and used to judge whether a test statistic is significant. If a test statistic, such as *t* or chi-squared, passes the critical value, you know your data show a statistically significant effect.

data a set of measurements. Note that the word data is plural.

debrief a conversation, or document given to the participant, at the end of a study which explains the background to the research and seeks to ensure the participant has come to no ill effects as a result of taking part.

dependent variable in an **experiment**, this is the **variable** you measure, to see whether it changes as a result of your **manipulation**.

dispersion a measure of how much a set of numbers varies around its midpoint.

distribution the way a set of numbers is spread out – refers to how often each number is seen in that set.

ecological validity the extent to which a study's findings describe behaviour in the real world.

ethics the principles of what is, and what is not, acceptable behaviour when carrying out research.

ethnography another name for **participant observation**.

experiment a method of study whereby everything is held constant except one **manipulation**. If there is a change in your measure of interest whenever the manipulation takes place, you can be confident the manipulation caused the change.

experimenter effect occurs when the person collecting data affects those measurements somehow, e.g. by treating some participants differently to others.

extraneous variable something that you are not interested in which might affect the results of an **experiment**.

fatigue effect in a **repeated-measures** design, the effect of being more tired during a second test than the first.

field experiment an experiment carried out in the real world, rather than a laboratory, in the hope of achieving greater **ecological validity**.

generalizing in research, this refers to the process of judging a **population** after studying a **sample** taken from it.

grounded theory a method for finding ideas and themes in text. In grounded theory, the researcher allows the themes to emerge by themselves, without looking for any particular findings.

homogeneity of variance a situation where two or more sets of numbers are spread out in a similar way.

hypothesis a prediction about what you will see in a piece of research.

independent samples testing more than one group of people as part of a study, cf. **repeated measures**.

independent variable in an **experiment**, this is the **variable** you **manipulate**.

informed consent the process whereby a participant agrees to take part in research knowing exactly what it is they are agreeing to.

interpretative phenomenological analysis a method for analysing qualitative data.

inter-rater reliability a measure of how much two independent raters agreed on what they were observing. Often done using a measure of **correlation** between their ratings.

investigator effect see **experimenter effect**.

laboratory study is carried out in a controlled environment.

longitudinal study a study where the same people are tested at various points in time to investigate their development.

lurking variable see **third variable problem**.

manipulation the change or test that is carried out in an **experiment**.

matched-pairs design a study design where each participant in one group is matched to a similar person in another group.

mean a measure of **central tendency** where some numbers are summed then divided by the number of numbers. What most people mean when they say 'average'.

median a measure of **central tendency** which describes the middle number in a set when that set is arranged from lowest to highest.

mixed methods using both **quantitative methods** and **qualitative methods** in a single study.

mode the most common number in a set.

naturalistic experiment an experiment where you study the effects of a naturally occurring **manipulation**.

negative relationship in **correlation**, a situation whereby as one measure tends to get higher, the other tends to get lower.

noise changes in scores or measurements caused by things you are not interested in.

non-parametric tests tests which make few assumptions about the data being processed. These tend to have less **power** – but be more flexible – than **parametric tests**.

normal distribution a particular pattern in a set of numbers where the average number is seen most often, and the further a number is from the average, the less often it is seen. A true normal distribution follows a very particular 'bell-shaped' curve.

null hypothesis the starting point for every study, which says there is nothing going on: there is *no difference* between the groups you are comparing or *no relationship* between the measures you have taken. Research usually involves looking for evidence to decide whether or not to stick with this idea.

objective capable of being clearly and definitely measured. cf. **subjective**.

Occam's Razor the idea that when given two equally good ideas, you should choose the simplest.

one-tailed hypothesis a prediction which states both that there will be an effect *and* what that effect will look like. cf. **two-tailed hypothesis**.

operationalizing means deciding exactly how you will study particular measures. For example, if you were studying intelligence, you would need to decide exactly what you mean by 'intelligence' and how you will measure it.

opportunity sample a **sample** chosen because the people happen to be convenient.

order effects in a **repeated-measures** design, effects seen in the study caused by the order in which people were tested. For example, when people are tested twice on a task, the first test might give them **practice** on the task, which affects their second measure.

outlier a measurement which looks very different from the rest of the measurements in a set.

paradigm in Kuhn's philosophy, a paradigm is an established set of ideas and beliefs about a given subject. It can also refer to a method for studying a particular topic, e.g., a perception researcher might refer to the 'two-alternative forced-choice paradigm'.

parametric tests statistical tests which make assumptions about the data being processed. These tests usually have more **power** than **non-parametric tests**.

participant observation a type of study where the researcher embeds themselves in a place, or in a group, to observe what goes on there. Also known as **ethnography**.

Pearson's product-moment a common **parametric** measure of **correlation**.

placebo effect the tendency for people to show responses in a study when they falsely believe they have experienced the study's **manipulation**.

population the group of people about which you hope to reach a conclusion in a study.

positive relationship in correlation, a situation where as one measure tends to get higher, the other tends also to get higher.

power in statistics, the ability a procedure has to find an effect if it really exists.

power analysis a technique for calculating how much **power** a study has, or for calculating how many participants you would need to study to see a particular effect.

practice effect in a **repeated-measures** design, a person might improve in their second test because the first gave them practice on the task.

qualitative research involves analysis of text and words in order to answer questions. Usually does not involve using numbers. cf. **quantitative research**.

quantitative research involves measuring people in order to answer questions. cf. **qualitative research**.

quasi-experiment an 'experiment' where people are not randomly allocated to different groups.

quota sample very similar to a **stratified sample**.

regression to the mean the tendency for measures that have any element of chance in them to get more average over time – extreme measurements tend to be followed by less-extreme measurements.

random sample a **sample** of people chosen randomly, as a way of trying to eliminate **sample bias**.

rank the position of a score in a set of scores which has been put into order.

reliability the extent to which a test measures something consistently.

repeated measures testing a group of people more than once.

replication repeating a study to see if the same results emerge, as a way of checking whether a study's findings were correct.

research question a specific question which you wish to answer when carrying out a study. Usually takes the form of a proper question such as 'Do people get better at solving puzzles after drinking coffee?'

sample the group of people you test in a study. The sample is intended to be the **population** in miniature.

sample bias occurs when your sample does not look or behave like the **population** it is supposed to represent.

sampling error see **sample bias**.

skew distortion in a **distribution** of numbers which means it is not symmetrical.

Spearman's rho a common **non-parametric** measure of **correlation**.

standard deviation a measure of **dispersion** that suggests the typical amount by which the numbers in a set are different from the **mean**.

standard error of the mean a measure of how uncertain you are about the mean of a group of scores. If you have tested a **sample** then the mean of its scores is an estimate of the whole **population**'s mean; the standard error gives you an idea how likely this estimate is to be accurate.

stratified sample a **sample** chosen so that its demographics – age, gender, etc. – look just like the demographics of the **population** that the sample is to represent.

subjective not capable of being rigorously measured. Defined according to people's feelings. cf. **objective**.

third-variable problem a situation where two measures appear to be **correlated** but the link between the measures is caused by a third variable you might not have examined.

triangulation studying a question in more than one way in an attempt fully to understand it.

twin study a **matched-pairs** study where each twin takes part in a different condition.

two-tailed hypothesis a prediction which states there will be an effect but does not say what this will look like. cf. **one-tailed hypothesis**.

Type I error where you claim to have seen an effect when really there wasn't one. More strictly, where you incorrectly reject the null hypothesis at the end of a study.

Type II error where you claim there is no effect when really there is one. More strictly, when you incorrectly retain the null hypothesis at the end of a study.

validity the extent to which a test measures what it claims to measure.

variable anything which is measured or manipulated in a study.

variance a measure of **dispersion** which describes how spread out a set of numbers is. The square of the **standard deviation**.

Index

Reading guide

This table identifies where in the book you'll find relevant information for those of you studying or teaching A-level. You should also, of course, refer to the Index and the Glossary, but navigating a book for a particular set of items can be awkward and we found this table a useful tool when editing the book and so include it here for your convenience.

Topic	AQA (A)	OCR	Edexcel	WJEC	AQA (B)	Page
Aims	x				x	12
Bias	x				x	24, 43
Case studies	x	x	x	x	x	29
Categories	x					50
Chi-squared	x		x	x	x	116–31
Confounding variables	x	x	x	x	x	35
Control	x		x			17, 34, 36
Correlation coefficient	x	x	x		x	183–4
Correlational analysis, data	x	x	x	x	x	181–96
Counterbalancing	x	x	x		x	39
Critical value	x	x	x			122, 125
Dependent variable	x	x	x	x	x	36
Directional	x					168–71
Ethics	x	x	x	x	x	54–61
Experimental design	x	x	x		x	36–8
Experimental method	x	x	x		x	29–44
Experimenter effects			x			35
Extraneous variables	x	x			x	35
Field experiment	x	x	x	x	x	247
Generalizing	x				x	25
Graphs	x				x	86–95
Homogeneity of variance					x	174–5
Hypothesis	x	x	x	x		14
Hypothesis – alternate		x	x		x	99
Hypothesis – null	x	x		x	x	99
Hypothesis – one-tailed	x	x	x	x	x	168–71
Hypothesis – two-tailed	x	x	x	x	x	168–71
Hypothesis testing	x		x			98–102
Independent groups	x	x			x	36–7
Independent variable	x	x	x	x	x	36
Inferential analysis	x					65, 97
Interval	x	x	x	x	x	151–3
Interviews	x		x	x	x	48